STICKY-BLUE!

Cover pictures:
HMS *Howe* (Imperial War Museum) and
(inset) the author aged sixteen

Boy Seaman/Bugler Jim Lipscomb and the author, on the
quarterdeck of HMS *Howe*. (*Author's collection*)

ROBIN ROWE

STICKY-BLUE!
A Boy and a Battleship

1995

Published by
Devonshire House
Christow
Devon EX6 7LU

© Copyright Robin Rowe 1995

ISBN 0-9524513-0-1

British Library Cataloguing in Publication Data
A catalogue record for this book
is available from the British Library

Typeset in Times 11/12pt by Scriptmate Editions
Manufacture coordinated in UK by Book-in-Hand Ltd
20 Shepherds Hill, London N6 5AH

Contents

Illustrations

To the Royal Marine Boy Bugler

Being drummers as well, Royal Marine Buglers have the nick-name 'Sticks'. But the *Boy* Bugler (now long gone) with his blue uniform and a vague resemblance to 'Little Boy Blue' of nursery rhyme fame, was more often than not called

'Sticky-Blue'

With acknowledgements to the following for the use of photographs as indicated: The Royal Marines Museum, the Imperial War Museum and Reg Goldsmith of the HMS Howe Association.

I would also like to thank the Royal Naval Submarine Museum, Gosport, and Gus Britton, a walking encyclopedia of underwater affairs, for their kind help and information on the 'Charioteers' and the 'Turtle'.

The Reason Why

'Tell us how you joined, old soldier?' was a joking demand often heard in the Royal Marines. 'How' was easy to answer but when asked why, the old soldier was not nearly so sure of his ground. In my case I don't believe I ever really knew the answer either at the time of joining or during my fifteen years service. But now I think my reason was something like this:

School was a pretty irregular pastime for me, partly because my parents moved about a good deal and partly because if it was not a boarding school I often played truant. With one particular school in Kensington which I disliked, and whose masters not surprisingly didn't seem to like me, I used to spend my days in the South Kensington Natural History and Science Museums. In that time I learnt a lot about animals and Stone Age man, lightning and steam engines, and how Bleriot flew the channel. Another thing I learnt when I happened to attend one or two music lessons was a song about Admiral Benbow:

'Bill Benbow the tanner at Shrewsbury did dwell
He taught his son Johnny and thrashed him as well
He 'prenticed him early a butcher to be
But John loved adventure and ran off to sea'

Other verses described him living merrily, surviving battles and tempest and being made 'a Captain and Admiral too!' It was also claimed 'And ne'er a battle he fought and he lost!'

He was mentioned in my favourite book 'Treasure Island'. Jim Hawkins was born in the Admiral Benbow Inn and set out from there on his adventures.

Both John Benbow and Jim Hawkins were my heroes. I was at Benbow's side when:

'A cannon ball knocked off his leg with a bump
He merely said "Hmpf" and fought on with a stump!'

And I became Jim Hawkins, with Israel Hands the mutineer, dirk between his teeth, pursuing me up the mizzen shrouds:

'Something sang like an arrow through the air: I felt a blow and then a sharp pang, and there I was pinned by the shoulder to the mast. In the horrid pain and surprise of the moment—I scarce can say by my own volition, and I am sure it was without a conscious aim—both pistols went off, and both escaped my hands. They did not fall alone; with a choked cry, the coxswain loosed his grasp upon the shrouds, and plunged head first into the water.'

In those terms going to sea was exciting and one day I decided to set out as well. There was after all the example of my elder brother Stanley who, at sixteen had put his age on to seventeen and a half and joined the Royal Marines. Having finished his training he was on the battle-cruiser *Hood*.

We lived in Weston-Super-Mare at the time and I was thirteen and 'between schools'. So one morning after having a good breakfast, I made a sandwich and with threepence—all the pocket money I had left for that week—I slipped out of the house and headed south towards Plymouth, whence embarked all the great English seafarers.

By the time I passed Brent Knoll some five miles out, I had eaten my sandwich but I pressed on. Near Burnham I sat down for a rest. I had walked about ten miles and my legs were beginning to ache. There seemed to be an awful lot of Somerset and Plymouth was as far away as ever. Perhaps it wasn't such a good idea after all. Reluctantly I got to my feet and walked back home.

When my mother asked me where I'd been and I told her that I had run away from home but had come back, she was very upset; though whether at the going or the coming back I wasn't quite sure. When father came home from work, he didn't punish me but assumed an air of hurt silence and would not speak to me for days.

My chance for adventure came in unfortunate circumstances about a month later. It was 1941 and on 24 May the *Hood* was sunk by the *Bismarck*. There were only three survivors and my brother was not one of them.

Stanley had thoroughly enjoyed being in the Royal Marines, the life suited him and he was doing particularly well. At the time he was killed he had been put forward as a candidate for a commission.

Rightly or wrongly my parents thought that such a life might do me some good and so my father—having got around to communicating again—asked, 'Would you like join the Royal Marines too?'

With the brashness of my thirteen and a half years I thought about it for at least thirty seconds. There was a war on and I could be part of it at sea. Not everyone got killed and the Royal Marine uniform looked great.

The ghosts of Admiral Benbow and Jim Hawkins beckoned.

'Yes!' I said.

R.R.
Christow, Devon 1995

CHAPTER 1

The King's Shilling

After a long cold train journey from Bristol to Portsmouth I was feeling tired and damp, like the October day that was just drawing to an end. The back of the 15 cwt lorry was draughty but I shivered as much with lack of food as cold, as we made our way from Fratton Station to Eastney Barracks on the last leg of, what was for me, a fateful journey.

It had been a long day—Monday the thirteenth of October 1941—and I had travelled from Weston-Super-Mare via Bristol to Portsmouth by war-time train, with little to eat and drink since I had left my parents. I still had my three shillings subsistence allowance that the Recruiting Sergeant had given me. There had been precious little to spend it on during the journey. Not that I was hungry; I felt too lost and numb after the day's events. Joining up at the age of thirteen years, eleven months and two days felt like going to a new boarding school. There was the same cold lump in the pit of my stomach.

When my parents and I had arrived that morning at the recruiting office in Bristol, I found that I was not the only one joining up that day. Four other boys eager to serve His Majesty in the Royal Navy were due to take a medical with me.

The examination was carried out in a separate room behind the front office; but to all intents and purposes it need not have been separate because throughout the proceedings, the office staff came in to consult filing cabinets that were in the room.

Although we were going into different services, the examination was the same and the doctor had got it down to a slick operation when dealing with numbers, running through the tests as if we were on a production line. There were the usual eye charts on the wall which we had to read first with one eye shut then the other, a proceeding which immediately cut short the naval career of one of our number when he failed to get past the fourth line.

A colour blindness test followed which eliminated another of us. Feeling rather like a rapidly depleting Ten Little Nigger Boys we were then told to undress.

Stripped of our clothes and our dignity, we learnt that modesty plays no part in service life and there we were with our puberty on display, while the whole world seemed to walk in and out of the room.

As we stood in line, the doctor listened to our hearts one by one, thumped our chests, then going round the end of the row he thumped on the line of backs.

'I'm sorry but I can't pass you!' the doctor said to the middle boy. 'You can go and get dressed.'

The two of us who were left looked at each other speculatively, wondering which one was next.

The doctor continued his task, rapidly checking four ears, two mouths, four feet, eight limbs in rapid succession without finding fault with any of them.

'Now I want you to jump up and hang on to that bar over there.' He pointed to a horizontal bar suspended some six feet off the ground.

We both leapt at the bar, my fellow examinee getting a firm grip first time, but in my nervousness I missed with one hand and fell off.

'Come along lad!'

The recruiting sergeant had just wandered in. I looked at him dumbly thinking I had failed the test.

'Get up on the bar!' he added, to my relief. His remark had been one of encouragement not an intimation of failure.

I succeeded on the second attempt and there we were, two pink carcases hanging from the beam like pigs in a slaughterhouse

'Now touch the bar with your chins and stay there!'

With an immense effort I pulled myself up and rested my chin on the bar but the next moment nearly fell off in surprise as the doctor got hold of my testicles and said 'Cough!'

I gave something between a grunt and a snort which obviously wasn't good enough, for he repeated the order. This time he seemed satisfied for he passed on to the other boy and went through the same performance.

My arms started to ache and I began to wonder how long we had to hold on in order to pass the test. Just as I was slowly descending to the ground, he told us to get down and I dropped to the floor with relief.

Other tests followed in front of varying sized audiences from the other room, involving a variety of postures, acrobatics and indignities until finally the doctor said, 'Right you can get dressed now,' adding to the recruiting sergeant 'Two fit specimens for you!'

It took us both a few seconds to realise we had actually passed and were the only two out of the original five to be pronounced fit.

Our grins at each other were cut short by the Recruiting Sergeant and the Chief Petty Officer telling us to hurry up and get dressed.

In the office again, my full particulars and description were minutely recorded, rather like a young offender. It was as if they thought I might escape but the truth was quite simple. They had to have physical details of the body they now owned for identification purposes alive or dead. Ever meticulous, the services like to know it is the right person they are paying, housing, feeding or burying.

Then followed the ceremony of swearing in, signing on and in general becoming a member of His Majesty's forces. Swearing on the Bible to serve

His Majesty and appending my name to a document stating that I would serve for a period of twelve years after the age of eighteen, was not quite the end of it all.

The colour sergeant took a cash box from his desk and from it gave me a shilling.

'That's the King's Shilling, lad,' he informed me, 'Which means that His Majesty King George has paid you for your allegiance and you are now in the Royal Marines!'

I had heard of the King's Shilling. In the old days a recruiting sergeant, in full regimental dress with a red, white and' blue cockade in his hat, would often try to slip the King's Shilling to a recruit. As he sat in an inn, regaling all with tales of glory and honour, he would be most generous to a likely lad, treating him to a pint of ale into which he had dropped a coin. Once the lad had accepted the spiked drink he was a soldier.

The colour sergeant, dressed in Blues with a red sash across his chest and a red, white and blue cockade in his hat, didn't offer me a drink. Instead he gave me three more shillings subsistence allowance for the day, a railway warrant and the time of a train for Portsmouth.

In the afternoon I said my goodbyes to my parents and departed from Temple Meads station for my new life. As I settled down in the compartment I felt a bit down; but then I supposed I was luckier than the olden day recruit. He would have had to walk.

The truck lurched as we turned a sharp corner and came to a halt. The truck driver let the tail gate down with a bang.

'Here we are. Out you get!'

We had arrived at Eastney Barracks and as I got out of the truck there came the sound of the main gates slamming shut behind us. I looked back. Just discernible in the blacked out night were the big gates with their spikes along the top and enormous trench mortars crouching menacingly on either side.

I followed the driver through the door of the building next to the gate, past a blackout screen and into the guardroom.

'Wait here!'

Nervously I stood by the door and glanced around. The room was large, with whitewashed walls and a big fireplace in which a small coal fire tried its best to look cheerful. In the centre stood a couple of trestle tables with long wooden benches on either side. Against the walls were ranged beds about two feet apart, with racks and pegs above them on which were various bits of equipment, belonging to the beds' temporary occupiers. Lying on the beds or seated at the table the off-duty guard relaxed; reading, playing cards or writing letters.

They eyed me curiously, a welcome diversion from the boredom of their twenty-four hour duty.

'You joining up?' demanded a voice from the table.

The card game stopped and all around the room expectant faces turned towards me.

'Yes.'

'What, for twelve years?'

'Yes.'

'You stupid little sod!' exclaimed a marine sitting on one of the beds.

'Go on, piss off out of it while you've got the chance!'

'Twelve bloody years in this fucking lot!' said another, pen poised above a writing pad.

'You'll regret it!'

'Go on, bugger off home while you've got the—'

The advice tailed off as the sergeant of the guard came out from a little office adjoining the guardroom.

'Come in here, son.'

Heads buried themselves back in books, cards were reshuffled and letters continued, as he glared around the room.

'Don't take any notice of them, they're HOs.'

'Hostilities only,' he explained, seeing my bewilderment. 'In for the duration of the war.'

I nodded, not feeling any more reassured by knowing what they were, still less by what they had said.

'The duty bugle corporal will come to fetch you shortly.'

I just had enough time to look around the cubicle and notice the various standing orders for guard duties, which were stuck onto pieces of plywood, when in came the duty bugle corporal.

I was surprised to see how small he was. I had imagined that all Royal Marine NCOs would be big men of commanding presence; but Corporal Chapman—for so he introduced himself, was about an inch short of my own five foot three. He also looked incredibly old.

'What's your name, son?' he asked.

'Rowe, Corporal,' I replied.

'Boy Bugler Rowe,' he corrected. 'That's what you'll say from now on. What's your name?'

'Boy Bugler Rowe, Corporal.'

'That's better. Come on then. We'll get you turned in for the night and start making a soldier of you in the morning.'

With his words some confidence began to return after my guardroom reception.

As we walked out into the night, the still air was shattered by a blast from six or eight bugles not twenty yards from where we walked.

'First Post!' shouted Corporal Chapman by way of explanation.

We continued our way across a small parade ground and into the first barrack block, looming large and solid in the dark. Silhouetted against the sky to the right was the clock tower, from which the quarter hours chimed day and night.

The barrack room was a longer replica of the guard room, with beds all down each side and at the end. Each bed had its shelf and pegs behind it on the wall. With a sort of military perversity equipment, bugles, drumsticks and other bits of equipment were hung on the pegs, whilst clothes, which I had normally hung on pegs (although my parents would dispute that I ever did anything of the sort), were folded neatly on the shelves.

The floor was scrubbed white, as were the tables and stools in the centre of the room. By the fireplace was a sort of trophy built up of buckets, brooms and squeegees, whilst the overall pervading smell was of bar soap, boot and metal polish.

From every bed a face turned towards the door as we entered, staring curiously at the new arrival. The corporal in charge of the room asked me my name and I replied in the correct manner, bringing a nod of approval from Corporal Chapman, who seemed to have taken on a proprietorial air, like someone who has just taught his dog a new trick.

Corporal Collins, for such was the room corporal's name, now took charge.

'Right! Now let's find you a bed. Old Soldier!'

He turned to an older boy who was sitting by the fire. 'Show him how to make his bed down. He can have that one in the corner.'

The old soldier, who was all of sixteen and a half, led me down to the end of the room; with all eyes following our progress.

The bed was an iron truckle bed, with the bottom end that pushed under the top half. Strapped to the iron headboard was a mattress, on top of which balanced four blankets and two sheets neatly folded, sheets between blankets, like a layer cake.

Having completed the bed-making to his satisfaction, the old soldier turned to me.

'OK dump your gear on the bed and I'll show you where the wash house and heads are.'

'Heads?' I queried.

'Shithouse!' said the owner of the bed next to mine.

'Shit in it, Hornsey!' the old soldier commanded, much to my astonishment. 'Get your head down!'

It was all part of the language of this new world into which I had entered. The first told Hornsey to keep quiet and the second to lie down and go to sleep.

Having gathered my soap and towel I followed the older boy out of the barrack block, where once again I was blasted by another bugle call from close range, only this time by a single bugler.

'Defaulters,' I was informed cryptically.

My guide, a quiet spoken boy, asked me my name told me his name was Jim Wilson and that he was the senior bugler in my room.

The wash house was some hundred yards away through the drill shed and, like everything else in the barracks on a large scale, with rows of basins and along one side about twelve bathrooms.

Having washed in cold water and cleaned my teeth we walked back as the clock struck ten and I was once again deafened by the buglers sounding Last Post.

As I undressed, the boy in the bed next to me asked who I was where I came from and why had I joined? The first two questions were easy enough to answer but the third was becoming a little more difficult, and as I got into bed, the feel of the hard straw palliasse and pillow brought home to me the vast difference between what I had left behind and what was before me.

The clock chimed quarter past ten and another bugle call demanded the immediate switching-off of the lights.

I sat up in the dark, thinking of the day's events. Perhaps the men in the guard room were right. Maybe I should have 'pissed off'. Then again I couldn't because I had already cooked my goose by taking the oath of allegiance to His Majesty King George VI, his Heirs and Successors, and to have gone as advised would have made me a wartime deserter.

But I was probably more used to being away from home than many other boys, having been to boarding schools. The first time was when I was seven at a convent school for girls that took boys up to the age of eleven. I sobbed and cried, until a large and frightening nun told me severely to 'stop that noise at once, because tears would not alter anything!'

Recognising the truth in her words and the menace in her tone I ceased immediately.

Thereafter home and school became two distinct lives. I learnt to live one and simply banish the other as if it never existed. Homesickness became a brief experience between leaving home and arriving at the gates of school, sometimes forced to the fore when compelled to write a weekly letter to my parents. 'Goodnight!' said the boy in the bed next to mine.

With that friendly voice the other existence vanished, homesickness was over. Hopefully letter-writing was not compulsory.

'Goodnight!' I replied.

I sank down into the rustling bed and got my head down.

CHAPTER 2

Buttons, Boots and Bugles

'Rise and shine! Wakey! Wakey! Wakey! Show a leg! Show a leg! Show a leg! Come on my sons, the sun's burning your eyeballs out!'

I was awakened from a fitful sleep, disturbed the whole night through by the barrack clock, by the lights being switched on and a loud voice accompanied by banging on buckets.

It was Corporal Collins rousing out his charges to another day. It was also a very dark morning, thus belying his warnings about the sun.

As he walked down the room, one or two sleeping forms that showed no signs of stirring were given a rap on the legs, which effectively evoked some signs of life.

Surprised that I had not heard Reveille I got out of bed whilst everyone hurriedly dressed, folded their blankets and rolled up the mattress. Meanwhile two boys took buckets outside and came back with water, scrubbers and soap for scrubbing out. First all the beds on one side were pulled out to the centre and that side was scrubbed down. Then the other side in turn received attention and finally the middle of the room.

As the buckets were taken to be emptied, Reveille sounded—6.30. No wonder I hadn't heard it before. In between pushing beds back into place, Hornsey, the boy with the bed next to mine, found time to tell me that the boy buglers room was always the cleanest in the barracks. Hardly surprising with the head start we were given.

Only after the room was deemed spick and span were we allowed to go off to the wash house to perform our morning ablutions. The next call was Defaulters so Hornsey informed me. 'Yes, I know,' I replied.

'How do you know that?' he asked.

'I heard it last night and Wilson told me.'

The morning had begun like every other from now on. From Reveille until Lights Out all day and every day, my life was to be regulated by the bugle, what I was to wear, when to parade, eat, stand easy, turn on lights, turn them off again, be punished, go to church, turn in, turn out etc.

The next call came just as we got back to our room from the wash house and was easily recognisable.

'What's that one?' asked the persistent Hornsey.

'Cookhouse.'

'It's called Men's First Meal Call, not Cookhouse,' said Hornsey, triumphantly putting me in my place.

Ten minutes later another call.

'That's Men's Second Meal Call,' said another boy. 'Breakfast!'

Under the general supervision of Wilson, all the boys took it upon themselves to tell or show me what to do, it just depended on who was nearest at the time.[1] One boy had already shown me how to fold my blankets and make the bed up that morning. Now another rustled up a spare mug, another found a knife, fork and spoon—eating irons he called them—then as a bunch they escorted me over to the dining hall where I was pushed into the queue to get porridge, rissole and tomatoes and a slice of bread and margarine. Another boy then saw that I got my mug filled with the strongest tea I had ever had, after which we all sat down to eat.

In between mouthfuls shovelled down at a fearsome rate, questions were fired at me about name age where was I from why did I join (always the eternal question) had I got any relations in the Corps. I told them about my brother in the *Hood*. That seemed to satisfy their curiosity for a bit.

The whole meal was over in about 15 minutes and we were off again, piling our plates in one place washing our eating irons in a huge sink of hot, greasy water.

Back in the barrack room, everyone started getting ready for the eight o'clock parade and as they were all busy I had time to look at my new comrades. Titch Hornsey was as his nickname suggested, smaller than the others. He was also the most junior, which was one reason why he was pleased that I had arrived on the scene to take over the mantle of newest recruit or sprog. Not only that, I was over a year younger than him. The others looked the same as any crowd of boys of my own age, except for a look in their faces that said, despite their tender years, they would survive.

One boy got dressed in blues with a broad red stripe down his trousers and the legend Royal Yacht on his shoulder. He was a Musician and as a boy he had to live in barracks, unlike the rest of the band who lived out with their families. He was in fact the only boy in the band at that time.

Apart from the Old Soldier, these were the only recognisable faces for me that morning, the others I would get to know as the week went by—Kennedy, Farmer, Haynes, Taylor, Jackson, Minnel, Blakely, Pendered; some from local families others from different parts of the country. Together with Hornsey these were the class that I was to join.

During the course of all this preparation, other NCOs started arriving, ready for the day's work. Last of all came the Bugle Major.

He was an elderly man, with his rank displayed on the right sleeve of his uniform; four inverted chevrons with a buglehorn above. The other NCOs wished him good morning with due deference, while the rest of the room bent their heads over their cleaning. As he walked around the room talking to one or two of the boys he spotted me sitting on the edge of my bed.

'What's your name, lad?'

I stood up and said 'Boy Bugler Rowe, Bugle-Major!'

He gave me a piercing stare with one eye half closed.

'Right, boy,' He eyed my hair, only three days previously cut to what I had thought was very short indeed.

He turned to Corporal Gorman.

'First thing, take him down to the barbers and get some of that hair off. Then down to the stores.'

Bugle-Major Dick Newman was one of the longest serving bugle-majors in the Corps. He had a glass eye, which was why he squinted as he looked at you, but the remaining eye missed very little.

Now, as the boys donned their equipment for parade, he stood in the middle of the room surveying us all, like a military Fagin about to send his proteges out to work. I sat on my bed like Oliver Twist, waiting to learn all the tricks of the trade.

When all the boys had departed to go on parade, Corporal Gorman took me over to the barber's shop. There were three chairs and I was placed in one and shorn of all the hair around the back and sides of my head, to about an inch above my ears. This was of course the proverbial short back and sides so beloved of the services. Not content with that, the barber cut the hair on the top of my head to about an inch in length.

'Don't want it flopping into our eyes, do we?' he said jovially.

As I rose from the chair, my eye caught the piles of hair on the floor. I looked into the mirror and saw the counterpart of the boys in the barrack-room, ears made prominent by the lack of hair. But the face staring back at me had more the look of a shorn sheep than a world survivor.

I was next taken to the main stores from whence I drew my kit. Most things like underclothes were put up against me for fit. They were in about three sizes, and I was given the smallest which was still too large. The thick flannel vests were enormous and came down past my knees and the 'short' sleeves past my elbows. In their itchiness they would have been excellent hair shirts for olden day monks. The long john underpants were equally coarse and, as I found out subsequently, not worn by anybody. My battledress and greatcoat were tried on and fitted surprisingly well.

Great care was taken in the fitting of my boots. I was made to walk up and down in them and told to make sure they were comfortable, neither too tight nor too loose.

The very last thing I had to do was to take my identity discs and my knife, fork and spoon down to the markers shop to get my name and number stamped onto them. Here also was ordered my type, which is a piece of beechwood with name and number carved on the edges in reverse and used to mark one's kit.

When finally I staggered back to the room with all my kit Corporal Gorman told me to change into my uniform. Eagerly I put on vest, pants, shirt, socks, battledress and boots and reported ready for inspection. I was approved of and shown how to put my cap badge in and also how to wear it.

The field service cap, sometimes mistakenly called the forage cap, is some thing that thankfully has passed into history. Balanced precariously on the side of one's head, it was certainly the most awkward thing to wear, being liable to fall off with any sudden movement. Parade grounds could be littered with them, particularly on a windy day.

As I gathered up my old clothes, another Lance Corporal, who had been watching the proceedings came up to me.

'What are you going to do with them?' he asked, pointing to my clothes.

'I suppose I'll send them home.'

'It'll cost you 'arf-a-crown to send them,' he said, 'And anyway, you're not allowed to wear civvies from now on, so they won't be much good to you.'

'Tell you what I'll do,' he continued. 'I'll take 'em off you and give you fifteen bob into the bargain. There's a lot of poor kids around here as needs 'em and will be pleased to have 'em!'

So I donated my clothing to the impoverished young of Southsea.

Five and a half years were to pass before I would put on civilian clothes again. During the war 'other ranks' were not allowed to wear anything but uniform, and to be caught out of it would be tantamount to desertion. But I really could not have cared what happened to my civvies as I stood proudly for the first time in my uniform. With Royal Marines written on my shoulder-flashes and a brass drum on my right arm proclaiming I was now PO/X5136 Boy/Bugler Robin Rowe.

As with all Drummers and ex-Drummers my nickname would be 'Sticks'; but most Marines had a special name for us boys, more a term of endearment—'Sticky-Blue'.

Having been taken down to the Dry Canteen (as opposed to the 'Wet' where they sold beer) to buy cleaning gear, for the rest of the forenoon I was given a thorough course of instruction on cleaning my buttons, boots and bugle, and also how to stow my kit in my kit bag and on the shelves behind my bed.

Corporal Gorman showed me how to insert the button stick behind the buttons on my greatcoat, not all at once but every other one, to prevent creasing and strain on the button stitching. An old toothbrush was then used to put the metal polish on, and when it was dry the buttons polished with the button brush.

'Only use Bluebell, son. That stuff you got from Pussers and things like Brasso and Soldiers Friend are no good. The shine don't last no time at all. Silvo's no good on brass neither, we just use that on the silver bugles. Just use Bluebell and you won't go far wrong.'

'Always take your cap badge and numerals out to clean, then you won't dirty the cloth. Anyway you must clean the backs as well.'

Kiwi Boot Polish was the best for boots. Cherry Blossom or Wren's left a sort of blue bloom on the boot and the difference could be seen by any eagle-eyed RSM.

When the boys came in to the room at lunchtime, I was greeted with a howl of envy.

'You jammy bastard!' one boy said, pointing out the Royal Marines flashes on my shoulders to the others. 'Look at this! He's got the new flashes!'

The others came over to examine my shoulders and join in the chorus. It appeared that I was the first bugler to have shoulder-flashes rather than the brass RM on the epaulettes as the others had.

'Has Charlie Nelson bought your civvies?' asked another.

'Yes, he gave me fifteen bob,' I replied.

'You could have got a quid for them.'

'Well, at least they have gone to someone who needs them,' I said.

'The only one who gets anything out of that, besides Charlie, will be the bloody pawnshop and the wet canteen. He flogs them to a place round the corner for double what you got!'

Charlie Nelson, he went on, was the Bugle Major's nephew and always had something going on in the money-making line. If there was a deal going he would be at the back of it. Charlie always had deals going, not necessarily illegal, buying and selling or doing a favour of whatever which usually ended up to his financial advantage.

The class of boys which I was joining had been in training for three months and, in order to catch up with them, some intensive work was done on me by the various NCOs during the next couple of days.

I was given individual instruction on simple drill movements, such as turning left, right and about. The positions of attention, at ease, the quick and slow march and the position of the bugle, standing, marching and at the ready.

Fortunately, as the son of a soldier I already knew a bit about it. When I was six we were in India and my elder brother and I used to drill, with him shouting the orders and me going through all the movements that we had copied from the soldiers. With my Diana air gun, I sloped and ordered arms, marched and turned about with great enthusiasm. The parade grounds and roads were usually very dry and as, the troops marched and turned, they would create clouds of dust. Thus for me, one of the main objects of drill was to stamp about and make as much dust as possible, to the detriment of shoes and clothes. The success of our parades could be measured by the ticking off we got for getting ourselves dirty.

As basic drill came fairly easily to me, I was soon on parade with the other boys each morning.

Bugle practice was carried out every morning and afternoon on the sea front outside the barracks, from whence there was a gateway leading past the boat house and slipway and on to the beach. Through this gateway we were marched and, with as great a distance as possible separating us from the rest of mankind, the Bugle Major and the NCOs put us through our scales and calls to the accompaniment of the screaming seagulls.

With a German invasion imminent, Southsea front was covered with barbed wire and other beach defences and civilians were banished from the foreshore. The place had an unkempt and neglected air and scattered amongst the sand and seaweed blown onto the road were pieces of rusty metal from the size of a pea to lumps weighing an ounce or more. They were bomb and shell fragments; litter from a different kind of visitor to those in days of peace.

We were segregated into groups consisting of the latest classes to join and then the intermediates including those about to pass out. The creme de la creme were those who had passed out and the old soldiers who had returned from sea service. They were distinguishable from the learners by having tassles on the end of their bugle cords; and they usually went further along the beach, there to practise in a slightly more relaxed manner than the rest.

As I had to catch up on my class I was put in the charge of one of the men buglers for individual tuition, until my lips and 'embouchure' could cope with the scales and other technicalities of bugling.

My tutor was 'Curly' Regan, a thickset boy about eighteen years old from Lichfield, with curly hair and acne. He was one of a number of men in for the duration, who were training as buglers and usually destined for shore based units, such as the Marine Battalions or Commandos. By some curious twist of reasoning, such postings were regarded as more dangerous assignments suitable for men. Royal Naval ships, at that time being dispatched to the bottom of the sea at an alarming rate, were considered safer for boys.

Curly was not all that pleased to be assigned as a wet nurse to a little kid and his manner of imparting knowledge was basic and to the point.

He took me along to a secluded part of the front.

'There are five notes on the fookin' bugle, C,G,C,E,G!' he announced in his Staffordshire accent. 'Like this.'

He put his bugle to his lips and blew the scale about a foot from my ear.

'When you blow you must tongue the notes, like this!'

He proceeded to spit rapidly in my general direction. 'You know when you smoke a cigarette and you get a bit of tobacco on your tongue?'

'I don't smoke,' I replied.

'Well if you did you'd fookin' well spit it out like this!' A further demonstration filled the air with fine spray.

'Now try it yourself!'

I duly spat as he had shown me, thereby getting some of my own back on him.

'Right now try and blow bottom G.'

As I blew into the bugle only a sound of rushing air came out.

'Use your tongue and blow a raspberry into it, like this!' Another blast in my ear.

This I did and made a sound rather like a disgruntled sea lion.

'Oh, come on! Harder than that!' Curly waved a large fist under my nose.

After much huffing and puffing on my part and counter demonstration on his, I managed a reasonable note.

'Now try the scale,' he said.

With a great effort I managed two notes.

'Go on! Yer bleedin' pig's orphan, you can do it!'

But try as I might I could not get the next note. The muscles in my cheeks ached and my mouth just blew out at the sides.

'OK, have a rest,' he relented.

Not for long however, because I was made to have go after go at trying to get a scale out of the wretched instrument. By way of encouragement Curly would wave his ham-like fist in my face—making sure he was not being observed by the Bugle-Major—and amid dire threats and oaths, order me up and down a scale of which I could just about get three notes. At the end of the first session my lips were sore and my cheeks just one aching mass.

'How's he getting on?' asked Cpl Collins.

'Well he's a bit weak but he'll do better tomorrow.'

Curly glared at me menacingly.

My heart sank as I thought of days of tutelage in the shadow of his fist. The sooner I could manage the scale, the better it would be for me.

There was nevertheless something in his method because I became so determined that it was only a week before I could just about blow all the scale and get a grudging acknowledgement from him that I was getting somewhere.

Having taught me one or two easy calls and enriched my vocabulary with some choice phrases, Curly at last pronounced me proficient enough to join the others of my class.

At the time of my joining a Bugler's training lasted about seven or eight months because, as one of our number put it in later years, we were turned out as quickly as possible as 'cannon-fodder' for the never-ending demand of an expanding (and often submerging) Royal Navy. During those few months we had to learn about sixty or seventy basic calls and their different meanings and variations. Together with two fanfares and two bugle marches they were the minimum requirement for passing-out on the bugle.

Time did not allow us to learn to read music and we were taught more by repetition than anything else. There were the time-honoured *aides memoires* that all buglers knew to the tunes of most calls. Some were relevant to the meaning, like Men's Second Meal Call:

'Oh, Pick 'em up, Pick 'em up!'

'Hot potatoes, Hot potatoes'

'Pick 'em up, Pick 'em up!'

'Hot potatoes, Oh!'
Some irrelevant, like Cable Parties:
'Oh, you chuckle-headed bounder!' (The Bugle-Major's polite version)
But the best remembered were the ones such as Rum Call:
'Oh Lucy, Lucy don't say no!'
'For under the table you must go!'
'Up with your petticoat, down with your drawers.'
'My little winkle just fits yours!'

As well as being our classroom, the beach also provided an excellent means of punishment for any misdemeanour. One morning we were going through various calls that were very much alike and could also have different meanings. In order to get the differences firmly into our heads, the Bugle Major was going down the line asking us questions and making us blow the calls alternately.

'Now the 'Incline'. What's its sea-service name?—Farmer!'

'Paravane Parties, Bugle Major!' Farmer replied at the other end of the line from me.

'Right! Next boy blow the Close!'

Haynes next in line, blew the Close.

At that moment something smacked onto the pebbles not far from where I was standing, followed by a seagull that swooped down and ate the mussel that it had just dropped and cracked open.

I had never seen them do this before and was fascinated by it. Then I noticed that the beach was littered with shellfish, cast up by a storm the night before. Was it only the one gull, or had they all learnt the same trick? No, other gulls were picking up mussels and dropping them. I watched another one climb up to about thirty feet and let go of its meal.

'—which will now be demonstrated by Rowe if he cares to join us!'

With the gull's mussel my thoughts came crashing to earth, as I tried desperately to drag from my sub-conscious what had been going on. I sprang to attention and brought my bugle to the ready, making a rapid calculation of the number of boys between me and Haynes and the various calls that had a resemblance to the Close.

I blew the 'Extend', to be greeted by a grinning silence from the others. Aware of a mistake, I stood rigidly to attention, my eyes fixed straight to my front. Dick Newman walked slowly towards me and interposed his face between mine and the horizon, so that I could only stare into his one cold blue eye.

'You insipid little boy!' he said, using his favourite expression 'Since you are so fond of watching what's happening on the beach you can go and get better acquainted with it.'

I was sent off to double up and down the shingle, with my bugle held over my head, until 'Stand Easy', when we were fallen out for a break.

As I stood there panting, Kennedy, ever the realist remarked, 'Just as well it was it wasn't drum practice, you'd have had to hold your drum over your head!'.

'Ha! Ha! You shouldn't have joined!' laughed Titch Hornsey. Sympathy was the last thing one got.

Drum beatings were learnt on trestle tables in the barrack room, usually in the afternoons and evenings. Standing along the length of the table we practised our rolls, flams, drags, paradiddles, mess beatings and drum solos, with the NCO in charge beating time with an entrenching tool helve; a sort of short pick handle. The same implement maintained discipline, being used to administer sharp raps on the knuckles to show we were 'not there for a skylark'.

It was one thing to learn around a table but quite another to play on a drum whilst marching, so for this we again resorted to the sea front. The first thing I had to master was keeping the drum in a playable position. With the drum carriage or sling over the right shoulder and the drum against the left thigh, it was more or less easy when standing still. On the march a totally new dimension was added, when the drum took on a perverse life of its own. At the slightest provocation, it would swing round to the side and any breeze, or change of direction on the part of the drummer, would have it straying around the back of his leg. My first attempt at countermarching, which is a one hundred and eighty degree wheel by each column, reduced what was a reasonably disciplined military formation to a chaotic shambles. I wheeled round successfully but the drum decided to continue on the old course. One minute I seemed to be playing quite well and the next there was no drum to hit, it having gone around to my rear. It then had second thoughts and decided to join me by swinging round to the front, in the process hitting the drum of the boy in the next rank. Caught off balance, he collided with the next rank and the whole class came to a tangled, giggling halt. Giggling that is except for the Corporal in charge who, in order to restore 'Good order and Military Discipline' had us doubling up and down the promenade for the next ten minutes.

Like all other drummers before or since, I gradually acquired the art of keeping the drum in place by adopting a sort of swinging motion of the left leg as I marched. As a result of this habit, many marines swore they could always tell an ex-drummer by his gait.

As time went on and proficiency in using our instruments progressed, we were required to go with the band on the morning parades, to march the training squads down to the sea service batteries for gunnery practice. This was a mixed blessing because we had to parade with our full equipment of drums and bugles, entailing hours of cleaning and preparation every night. Yet it was a stage in our training that meant we were no longer just 'Makey-learn' buglers (a favourite phrase of the bugle-major's) but were actually fit enough to go with the Divisional Band. Not however in the public eye as we had not yet got our blue uniforms.

So one morning, at the age of fourteen and two months, I found myself proudly standing in the third rank of drummers with the Royal Marines Band Portsmouth Division, resplendent in their 'blues' with the insignia 'Royal Yacht' on their shoulders.

The third rank was obviously not where the best drummers were placed and it was also made hazardous by the bass drummer about whom I had been warned. Corporal Gosbee, impressive in his tiger skin apron with head and paws hanging down his back, obtained great pleasure in trying to knock the hat off the drummer next to him with the bass drumsticks. A pleasure not shared by the de-hatted boy, who more often than not got a (literally) staggering blow on the head.

However I was willing to risk this just to be there. Nor could the occasion be marred by my being given an extra parade for having a dirty drum. The previous evening had been spent taking it apart, cleaning the shell and blancoing all the buffs, ropes, sling and leg guard, as well as cleaning all the rest of my equipment. As we waited ready to fall in and march out on parade, somebody started 'skylarking' and in playing around my drum came off the sling and rolled its way through the dirtiest bit of ground it could find. Horrified I picked it up to find that my beautiful whitened buffs and drummer's plaits were smeared with mud. No amount of scraping and cleaning with my shirt sleeve (the only thing I could think of that did not show) would return its hitherto pristine condition. So I resigned myself to getting a 'blast' at least on inspection but fortunately Cpl Collins, who had been on duty in our room the previous night and had seen my drum then, was the NCO accompanying the adjutant on his inspection. So I was let off with having to report to him that evening with the offending item re-cleaned; and, as I had to have it clean for the following morning, it did not really matter.

But nothing could detract from the moment as we played 'South Australia' (the same tune as 'I Know a Lady Sweet and Kind') whilst the inspection was carried out, finally marching off the parade playing the Regimental March, 'Life on the Ocean Wave' followed by 'Viscount Nelson'. It reminded me of the time when, at the age of eleven, I had been taken to the Royal Tournament at Olympia and I had watched with envy boy drummers in a military band, all resplendent in dress uniforms. Now I was one of them.

CHAPTER 3

Ninepence a Day

Apart from bugle calls that regulated barrack life, parades also dominated our lives. There were the formal morning and afternoon parades and inspections every day from Monday to Friday, with compulsory Church Parade on Sunday.

The Adjutant, Captain Peter Norcock, was also Officer Commanding the Band and Drums Company and as such was responsible for the boys. On every morning parade he would inspect us from head to toe, starting with the cap badge and continuing right down, sometimes to the soles of our boots, where the instep was also expected to be highly polished. Bugles were inspected to see that they had been polished right down into the bell as far as one could see. Sometimes equipment had to be removed so that the backs could be looked at. The slightest bit of dust would be the subject of a reprimand and if repeated on a subsequent occasion, earned an extra parade to be carried out in our own time in the evening with one of our NCOs doing the inspection.

On Fridays there was an extra and welcome parade for pay. For this the Band and Drums Company was distributed around the four other companies A, E, I and N. As they were quite large these units were split into Right and Left half-companies, the right half consisting of the continuous service or regular marines whilst the left half were the HOs. My pay company was 'I' under the command of a Captain Carter whose favourite saying when in argumentative mood was, 'I don't give a fish's tit!'.

At about 12 o'clock, after being mustered on the parade ground, the companies were marched one by one to the pay office. As our names were called out we had to step up to the table, repeat our pay number and salute, after which we were handed our money in cash. Strictly speaking my pay was ninepence a day, which made a weekly sum of five shillings and threepence. But as we were paid to the nearest sixpence it meant that we were paid only five shillings a week. The other threepence was kept back and either paid three monthly on what was known as a quarterly settlement, or when we went on leave. Quarterly settlements could be a very good thing if one was in pocket as we usually were. Sometimes due to overpayment or because of having pay deducted, some hapless marine would go up to the table only to be told, 'Not Entitled!'. Known as a 'Nor' Easter', it was just about as welcome as the wind from that direction.

Out of our five shillings we had to buy cleaning gear for all our equipment, which amounted to quite a considerable sum. There was metal polish for our bugles, drums, buttons and brass work on our webbing equipment, white blanco for our drums and drum slings and green blanco for the webbing equipment and of course, boot polish. There were also other items like tooth-paste, bootlaces, toilet and washing soap. Probably a little over half our pay was spent on these necessaries and the rest we had to ourselves.

At first one of the things on which I did not have to spend money was razor blades. Much to my chagrin, my kit issue had not included a razor because both the sergeant in the stores and my first day mentor Cpl Gorman saw that my face still had the bloom of childish fair hair they termed bumfluff. I disagreed, having on very close examination found that there was a definite darkening on my upper lip and sideboard regions. But had I asked for a razor I would have been told to put some milk on my face and let the cat lick it off, or to stand on the parade ground in a high wind.

So I held my peace and remained unshaven for nearly three months until I found an unexpected ally on parade in the shape of RSM Gilliam.

A Regimental Sergeant Major is the most senior non-commissioned officer in any regiment and, as such is responsible through the adjutant to the commanding officer for the discipline, cleanliness and general administration of the other ranks. He is also the only non-commissioned rank in the Royal Marines that is entitled to be addressed as 'Sir'.

Always a strict disciplinarian and much respected—or feared in the case of small buglers—RSM Gilliam had cap badge and buttons worn away by the constant application of Bluebell, the leatherwork of his Sam Browne belt and boots shone as if wet and the crease in his trousers could have cut through cheese. He expected this perfection from everyone on any parade of which he had charge.

This particular morning parade started like any other that I had attended. Along with about twenty other buglers, I had marched out to the flagstaff on the edge of the parade and at five minutes to eight precisely, under the orders of the Bugle Major we sounded off 'Markers'; a signal for the right hand marker of each company to fall in in single line under the orders of a drill instructor.

'Markers, NUMBER!'

The markers shouted their numbers rapidly from the right. 'One, Two, Three,—'

'At twelve paces interval from number one, outward TURN!'

Number one turned right and the remainder left.

'Quick MARCH!'

As the file marched away from the first marker each man chanted his number and the number of paces, halting and turning about as he reached the correct interval; the count then being taken up by the next.

'Number Two! Three, Four, Five, Six, Seven, Eight, Nine, Ten, Eleven, HALT!'

'Number Three, Three, Four, Five, Six, Seven, Eight, Nine, Ten, Eleven, HALT!'—and so on to the final marker.

RSM Gilliam had meanwhile taken up his position about ten yards in front of the buglers, whilst from between the air raid shelters that lined the further edge of the parade, the marines issued forth to form up in their respective units opposite their markers.

'Stand properly at ease!'

Movement ceased on the parade's edge

'Bugles READY!'

At the Bugle-Major's command, our bugles flashed out at arm's length and up to our lips in two movements.

All was still on the parade as we waited for eight o'clock to strike, the silence broken by the occasional seagull and the RSM himself. His keen eye missed very little as he surveyed the three or four hundred marines.

'Number 3, rear rank, 405 Squad. That's a rifle you've got not a pitchfork!' His words reached the offender some 75 yards away, echoing back off the barrack blocks beyond. 'Butt in line with the right foot! Straighten that right arm in front of you.'

As I stood to attention I could hear the Union Flag behind us fluttering in the breeze.

Again the silence was broken, this time by the barrack clock striking eight.

'Divisional Call, Sound Off!'

As twenty buglers blasted out the first note, the whole parade came to attention.

'Parade Call, Sound Off!'

The call, so familiar to many, rang around the barracks:

'Fall in A, Fall in B,'

'Fall in other companies!'

'Fall in A, Fall in B,'

'Fall in other companies!'

At the last note the spell was broken and the whole parade stepped off and marched on to the markers.

'Buglers, Stand at EASE!'

We stood at ease as the roll was called in each unit by the NCO in charge who, as he completed this task, took his place in front of his men.

During this time various officers had arrived on the scene. But instead of the adjutant, who usually took over the parade, Captain Carter (he of the fish's tit) walked on and placed himself behind the RSM.

When all the hubbub of calling the rolls died down, the RSM commanded, 'NCOs Report!'

'A Company, Right Half Company, present and accounted for, Sir!'

'A Company, Left Half Company, present and accounted for, Sir!'

Down through 'A', 'E', 'I' and 'N' the parade announced its presence, ending up with the motley crew consisting of all those rounded up from off-duty cooks, sweepers, storemen and so on.

'Compo-sight Squad pres-sent and accounted for, Sah!'. The colour sergeant in charge had his own way with pronunciation.

There was a further moment's silence as the parade stood to attention, whilst RSM Gilliam surveyed the scene, assuring himself that all was to his satisfaction. He then turned about to Captain Carter who was standing a matter of six feet behind him, saluted and reported in a voice that could have been heard well out to sea beyond the parade and seafront.

'Parade all present and accounted for, Sir!'

At this juncture the officers joined the parade to take charge and inspect their units and, as often happened, there were one or two officerless units, one of which the RSM would choose to inspect. But as he turned away from making his report, his gaze alighted on the buglers standing behind Captain Carter and we could all see that, in the absence of the adjutant, we were to have his undivided attention.

Starting from number one of the front rank he worked his way along. Few got off without some fault being found. If it was not cleanliness of equipment, it could be cap not on straight or not standing to attention properly.

Then he was in front of me, scrutinising every detail from the top of my head—not a difficult feat considering his advantage in height—down to my boots. As these were fairly new there had not been a great deal of time to 'bone' and polish them to the expected mirror shine.

'You want to work a bit harder on those boots!' he informed me and Spithead; and was just about to pass on to the next boy when he paused, gazed intently at my face and asked:

'Did you shave this morning?'

'N-no, Sir!'

'And why not?'

'I haven't got a razor, Sir! N-not issued, Sir!'

'Then you will go and draw a razor and have a shave! And in future you will shave every morning before breakfast!'

'Very good, Sir!' My wits returned enough to give the correct and age-old reply.

'It's not very good at all!'

'No, Sir!

He eyed me keenly, probably wondering if I was trying to be cheeky, which was the last thing in the world I had in mind as I tried to keep my eyes steady and unblinking to the front. Then turning towards the parade in general and the Bugle Major in particular he shouted:

'Take this drummer down to the stores now and see that he shaves immediately!'

And so it was announced to the whole of the Portsmouth Division of Royal Marines that I had officially reached one of the great moments in a boy's life and was now old enough to shave. With the eyes of the whole parade on me and feeling as if I had just been awarded a medal, I was marched off to draw a razor and have my first shave.

With about half our pay spent on cleaning materials, some of the rest was spent in the canteen on cups of tea and, on pay days when we felt flush with our weekly shillings, cakes and doughnuts.

There was an attraction for us in trying to get served by what we thought was the most beautiful creature in the universe. Rosie, for such was her name, had rich auburn hair, a peaches and cream complexion, and big green eyes. If you were lucky enough to be served by her, those eyes would look straight into yours and she would say, 'Yes, dear?' Or when she got to know your face, 'Hallo, love!' Words that, spoken by any other girl in that canteen, just did not have the hidden depth of meaning that Rosie could put into them. NAAFI tea was always a mockery of the real thing but, even if it were the very last dregs in the urn, when served by Rosie it became champagne and the cracked cup, her crystal slipper.

The other girls were old—at least twenty, some like grandmothers; but Rosie was eighteen or nineteen and we were teenagers too and so she was in the same age bracket. In reality Rosie was a very attractive and kindly girl whose motherly instincts were aroused by our extreme youth. She may have been aware of our adulation and whilst not consciously encouraging it, made a special effort to be nice to us. But far from being a mother figure in our eyes, Rosie was our pin-up from whom one glance and a smile would light up the whole week. We became a sort of collective suitor for her attentions. Each of us would recount our experiences to the others and any contact by one was an experience enjoyed by us all.

One evening we sat on the end of our beds, blanket on the floor in front of us, on which we were cleaning our drums. This was a lengthy chore which meant undoing the drummer's plait, loosening the rope all round and removing the brass shell and the pigskin heads. The shells having been cleaned and duly inspected by Corporal Mayne, we were busy re-assembling our drums, prior to blancoing the cords and buffs, when talk came around to who had got money and did we have enough between us to go to the canteen. Having mustered enough for most of us to buy a cup of tea—with the odd borrowing till pay day by some—talk came around to the possibility of seeing Rosie.

'She won't be there tonight it's her night off!' said Jackson, nodding his head.

The nod had nothing to do with approval of Rosie's absence. 'Jacko' happened to have a nervous tic that caused his nod in moments of stress.

'I expect she's got a date with some marine,' he added gloomily.

'She wouldn't go ashore with a bloody bootneck!' Farmer chipped in 'She's far too posh for that!'

'She wouldn't go ashore with you anyway,' said Kennedy.

'Nor you neither!'

'I bet she would!'

'Oh fuck off, Kennedy!' Farmer exclaimed.

'That's enough of that language!'

The reprimand came from Corporal Mayne sitting by the fire. 'Have you finished your drums, yet?'

'Nearly, Corporal,' said Kennedy.

With the drum on its side held with stockinged feet on the rim, he tightened the drum rope, turning the drum as he hauled away.

'Well anyway,' he returned to the subject between heaves, 'I bet she'd go out with me if I asked her.'

'You wouldn't even ask her! Bet you five bob!' replied Farmer 'Well two bob anyway,' he amended hurriedly as he realised that risking a whole week's wages was a bit rash. 'I don't want to take all your money.'

'Right, you're on!'

The next question was when, to which Kennedy said he would do it in his own good time.

Days went by however, with no move on Kennedy's part. When challenged he told us that he had to pick the time.

'You can't just ask her at any time. There's always too many people in a hurry around you in the canteen.'

'She was there yesterday evening, you could have asked her then,' said Jacko.

'How can I ask her out when I'm broke. I'll have to wait till next week.'

'When next week?' Titch Hornsey asked mischievously.

'Yes, when?' We all echoed, eager for our vicarious date with Rosie.

Poor Kennedy realised that he was in a corner and yet had to go through with it, or lose considerable face as our unofficial leader.

'Tuesday. Then I can take her out on Wednesday.'

But on the Sunday night before the fateful day came, a bombshell was thrown in our midst.

Apart from those on duty, we had all been ashore, some who had money to the pictures and others who lived locally to their homes. Most with neither money nor nearby home had been down to Milton Park, where there were parties (girls) of our own age to be chatted up as they giggled and promenaded arm in arm; some willing enough to be taken to some secluded corner behind the pavilion for the first clumsy attempts at more intimate relationships.

Except for those with mothers nearby to provide food, most of us had drifted back early to get something to eat in the dining hall. At weekends there was no set suppertime but bread, cheese and pickles, or else red cabbage and pig's head brawn—sometimes complete with the odd eyeball staring out of the jelly and chunks of whiskered skin—were set out on the serving tables for people to help themselves. As growing boys we were forever hungry and by eight o'clock even the attractions of Milton Park would be forsaken for the urgent summons of brawn and red cabbage.

That evening as we congregated in the barrack room, one of the last to come in was Jacko, obviously bursting with some bit of information he wanted to impart.

'Guess who I've seen tonight!' he shouted, his eyes wide and his nervous head nod going at full belt.

'Father Christmas!' somebody suggested

'No, seriously, you'll never guess!'

'Well, who then?'

'Rosie!' he exclaimed triumphantly 'and she was with Bluto!'

He had every one's attention now.

'Garn! You're kiddin!'

'Oh no!'

'Piss off, Jacko!'

'Honest I'm not kidding. They were just going into the cinema!'

The whole room was bereft of speech as the implications sunk in. It was bad enough to learn that our beautiful and hitherto unsullied Rosie was going out with anyone; but with Bluto!

Bluto was a physical training instructor who took us for PT. He had a small head with a swarthy face perched on enormous shoulders with great muscular arms and a barrel of a chest. His waist in comparison was minute and overall he was the very image of Popeye's longtime competitor for the attentions of Olive Oyl. Like many PTIs he had a Narcissus-like regard for his body and his strength, which he was fond of demonstrating to us. Once, when doing rope work we were required to climb right up to the top, a matter of some twenty feet, hand over hand without using our feet at all. Having watched us straining with our puny undeveloped arms to get about six feet up, he then twinkled up to the top and down saying as he went: 'There! If I can do it so can you!'

Earning the remark (sotto voce) from one of us, 'He's so musclebound he's got them between his ears as well!'

So we learned of Rosie's faithlessness and after some argument and suggestions that he ought to try spinach, Kennedy got Farmer to call off their bet about asking Rosie out and on the whole everyone agreed. We had all had the rug of romance pulled from beneath our feet.

For a while Rosie still looked at us with the same green eyes and called us 'Dear' or 'Love'. But there seemed to be something missing, the unacknowledged link between her and her admirers was gone. The beverage that she handed us was no longer nectar but took on the taste of stewed tea and the crystal slipper reverted to a thick cup, with NAAFI emblazoned on the side.

But worse was to follow.

One day she was no longer behind the counter. Enquiries of her fellows were met with purse-lipped evasions and from other sources came rumours of a falling by the wayside. In the gym we went through our daily exercises at the wall bars, vaulted over the horses and shinned up ropes, furtively looking into the beady eyes of Bluto as if we might see a hint of guilt or remorse perhaps to show that he was responsible for the downfall of our idol. However nothing showed to indicate that he was involved or that being so he had done the right thing by Rosie and married her. We however were convinced it was him and were deeply sorry for Rosie, for even if he married her, he could not have loved anyone but himself.

CHAPTER 4

Draft Chit

Most of the more important duties carried out by the buglers were performed by those who had passed out and awaited a draft to a ship, or those who had come into barracks from sea service. The latter were the more privileged ones who, apart from being allowed to smoke, not only performed guard duties but as drummers they played with the band on all ceremonial occasions and carried out such details as the Armistice Day ceremonies at the Cenotaph in London.

There was a steady trickle of older boys returning to barracks from all around the world, having completed their two and a half year commissions at sea, or else about to turn over to the ranks. Such people as Wally Waltham from the cruiser *Hawkins,* back from the South Atlantic, Cochran from the monitor *Erebus,* George off the cruiser *Enterprise* and Chester from the *Iron Duke.* So long had they been away that their webb equipment was the old style issued in 1939 that had not changed since the Great War. Len Chester who had been away longest, distinguished himself by appearing on parade in Khaki Service Dress, forage cap and puttees instead of battledress, like a time-warped Tommy from the Somme.

Commandeering the best beds in the far corner of the barrack room, the seventeen year olds formed a superior clique that regarded us youngsters with tolerant disdain. We in our turn looked up at them with envy, occasionally addressing them as 'Old Soldier' and listening to their lamp-swinging tales of far off oceans and places.

They were allowed ashore later than us juniors and we would watch them return in the late evenings breathing beer over everyone. They sang bawdy sea-songs, often to well known hymn tunes, whose lyrics we committed to memory against the time when we too would return as old soldiers.

On one occasion they all rolled back in a jovial and beery frame of mind, announcing to the startled and disbelieving room that they had been to Aggie Weston's.

'Aggie Weston's' was not as might be supposed a pub or other dubious place of entertainment but the Royal Sailor's Rest in Portsmouth. The nickname derived from the founder Agnes Weston, a tireless crusader at the turn of the century for temperance among the seagoing fraternity of Portsmouth. Her Temperance Union was well known and she set up a home where seafarers could get a meal and a bed for the night for their physical comfort, with bible readings and talks on the evils of alcohol for their spiritual welfare.

In time her Sailor's Rest earned the title Royal and she, Dame of the British Empire.

Hence the disbelief that this inebriated quartet could possibly have been to Aggie's. But on being pressed for further details Wally Waltham explained.

It had all started with a run ashore from Barracks in 1939 by the then fifteen year old George and a fellow bugler (the name escaped Wally's and George's fuddled minds for the moment). As was common to boy buglers much of the time, they had no money and were desperately hungry. Walking despondently around the town, they were just about to pass the Royal Sailor's Rest when a bright idea came to his friend's head.

'You can get a wet of tea and sandwiches or cakes free in here!' he said.

'Oh yeah, what's the catch?' asked George suspiciously.

'Well, you have to go to a prayer meeting or something first.'

'Fuck that for a skylark!'

'Well, at least we'd get some eats and a cuppa tea!'

George hesitated, balancing the cons of having to withstand the evangelistic ardour of bible-punchers against the pros of getting something to eat.

'We-ell, I suppose it won't do us much harm,' he said doubtfully as he followed his companion into the Sailor's Rest.

Once inside they were ushered into a room in which a Bible discussion was going on and for an hour, with rumbling tummies, they listened whilst various members of the group expounded on different aspects of the New Testament. Eventually and inevitably the talk came around to the evils of drink and seeing new faces, the discussion leader buttonholed the two boys and asked them to sign the Pledge. Feeling that to refuse would not only be rude but would also jeopardise their chances of the long awaited food, they put their names to a document foreswearing strong drink and for which, if they kept it up for two years, they would get a temperance medal.

George was duly drafted to the light cruiser *Enterprise* and for two and a half years, forgetful of having sold his birthright for a sandwich, sampled the sailor's delights of foreign travel in all the places they visited.

On this day the four old soldiers had nothing particular in mind as they went ashore but history repeated itself and being in the vicinity before the pubs opened—and hungry, George, forgetful of the pledge he had signed said, 'Let's go to Aggie's for a skylark and get a free tea and wad.'

So they went in and as they were ushered into the meeting room, who should be there but the very same discussion leader of three years before.

'I know you!' he said to the startled George 'You signed the Pledge, let's see about two years ago!'

'Oh, er, yes—'

The leader turned to the group.

'Meet one of our converts who signed the pledge in 1939!' Then turning to George. 'And you've kept off the demon drink all this time?'

'Er, um—' George muttered.

'Splendid! You must have your medal this afternoon!'

With the afternoon's discussion gone by the board, a special tea was brought in and with a short speech about how proud they all were of him, George was presented with his temperance medal.

After the presentation and a large tea; and having somehow dodged further pledge signing, George and his supporters made good their escape to the nearest pub for a celebratory beer.

We all sat spellbound by Wally's narration.

'Don't know how you had the nerve!' someone remarked.

'Well, I hadn't had a drink for two years,' George protested over our hoots of derisive laughter, 'Well, nearly true. I only drank when I was ashore.

After five months training buglers were usually deemed fit to take on some of the normal barrack duties and when my class reached that stage, I found that I was included despite the fact that I was three months behind. Although I could hit the top notes on the bugle it was another thing to sustain them for any length of time and my renderings of some of the calls were apt to be a little short on Es and top Gs. However this was not deemed to be a serious obstacle and I was delighted to find that I could now 'volunteer' for First and Last Post at nights, as well as take my turn on other duties which were welcome changes from the normal routine. One such was the sea service gun battery where the recruits learned gun drill under ship's routine and, in order to make it more realistic, a bugler was required to blow the normal calls used at sea. There were other duties such as guard bugler for the hutment camp where the Engineers were housed. Another duty was to supplement the main guard bugler because many calls had to be repeated in various parts of the barracks at the same time.

Naturally the sound was not confined to the barracks and the local population was continually reminded of their garrison status. Starting with Reveille at 6.30 in the morning—sounded off four times around the barracks and twice by the hutment camp duty bugler—to the crescendo of ten or so bugles rendering Last Post at 10.00pm and the final diminuendo of Lights Out at 1015, the citizens of Eastney regulated their day. Also living within bugle blast were our NCOs, including the bugle major, so no mistake or deviation from the strict tempo of any call went unremarked. For the same reason we had to be very careful to be on time with the calls, not only because of service personnel living within the area. There were quite a few civilians who would have no hesitation in complaining if we were late with a call.

The juniors, myself included, longed for the day when we would pass out, for not only would we gain the coveted tassles on our bugle cords and be indistinguishable from the old soldiers but our pay would go up an extra threepence a day.

It was a further two months before we were deemed fit to appear before the Adjutant to be tested on both bugle and drum. Then for days beforehand we all concentrated hard on trying to remember all the calls and their different meanings and names. We still had to know such bugled commands as the Quick, Double, Halt, Lie Down, Extend, Close, Charge (mounted or dismounted), Advance and Retire. Such calls had manoeuvred whole regiments on battlefields such as Inkerman and Omdurman and in far off places as Afghanistan, South Africa and New Zealand. But by the time of the Great War radio had overtaken the bugle as a means of transmitting orders, rendering these calls obsolescent on land although still used at sea with different meanings.

On the drum we practised our open and close rolls, solos, the Regimental March and Officer's Mess Beatings which we knew we would have to perform as tests of our stick movements and marching abilities.

On the dreaded day, we were mustered on the lawn not far from our barrack room in parade order with drums and bugles gleaming, awaiting Captain Norcock's appearance to test our marching, playing, and knowledge and skills on our instruments. As we stood easy, there were last minute panics as someone tried to remember how particular calls went.

'What's Special Sea Dutymen, for Christ's sake?'

'I gotta no balls, I lost them all!'

A whispered voice mouthed the words.

'What about Paravane Parties?'

'Same as Incline!'

'How does that go?'

'My head, my head, my wooden head!

My head, my head, my wooden head! Oh!'

However nerves settled down as soon as the examination started and in a matter of an hour or so, during which we were separately and together required to perform on bugle and drum, it was all over. We were now entitled to seven shillings a week and, as soon as the tassels were issued, we strutted around conscious of our newly adorned bugles.

The next step was to be drafted to a ship and we all eagerly scanned Drafting Orders on the notice board every day to see if our names appeared. But while all the others of my class gradually disappeared I seemed to be the unlucky one. The fact that I was only fourteen and two months held me back but there was also another reason. Nine months previously Captain Norcock, as Adjutant of Portsmouth Division, had penned a letter of condolence to my parents when *Hood* was sunk and my elder brother Stanley was killed. Doubtless he did not want to repeat the job on my behalf and was therefore looking for somewhere comparatively safe to post me. So it was not until four months later in May, when I was fourteen and a half, that my name, coupled with that of Wally Waltham, came up to join the detachment for Job No. J1669

Despite wartime secrecy and warnings of 'Careless talk Costs Lives', everyone knew that J1669 was HMS *Howe* the latest battleship to be commissioned and the last of the five King George V class ships. The Japanese had already reduced the number to four. On 10th December 1941, the *Prince of Wales* together with the battle-cruiser *Repulse* had been sunk in the Far East, thus incidently belying the idea of capital ships being safe havens for small buglers[1].

We were to commission her on the 1st of June, one hundred and forty eight years after the Glorious First of June, Lord Howe's great victory over the French off Ushant.

There were many things to go through before we were due to join the ship. For my part, embarkation training was a gradual process of being weaned away from the Band and Drums company to be an integral part of a ship's detachment. There were parades and inspections with the detachment and of course the inevitable kit inspections by the NCOs and officers.

The whole detachment mustered at the Sick Bay for medical examinations and a top up of various inoculations. The examination consisted of a perfunctory lookover as well as what was called a FFI. In a crowded community such as a ship, some infections could become rife and so we had to be found Free From Infection. We stood in long queues, awaiting our turn to drop our trousers and be examined by a Sick Berth Attendant with a torch, who searched for crabs and other lice, as well as eczema and impetigo.

I was most looking forward to getting my blues, so I was pleased that one of the first things to be done was to draw my sea service kit. Drawing anything from service stores is quite an experience. Everything is listed and described in back to front jargon. My blue uniforms were described as Tunics serge blue No. 2; Trousers tweed blue No.1 prs 2; cap, forage, blue 2. The white cap covers were Covers, white, caps forage for, 2. The list went on through sea service boots (with plain leather soles), tropical shirts and shorts, khaki drill uniforms and thick woollen Arctic long johns. By the time I had got down to Tops, hose, khaki, woollen, prs 2, I had an immense pile of kit suitable for service in any part of the world. It then only required my signature for me to stagger back to the barrack room carrying my Bag, kit, brown, large (full).

As time went on Wally and I gradually got to know the marines we were going to live with. Some of them had been with Wally in *Hawkins,* others were survivors from the aircraft carriers *Ark Royal* and *Eagle,* sunk in the Mediterranean. Yet others were going to their first ship, like me.

I was very lucky to have Wally with me and he became my mentor in everything we did. He took his responsibilities seriously and looked after me like an older brother. Maybe he remembered his own lack of knowledge when he first went to sea and was probably determined that I should not make the same mistakes like calling the senior NCO of the detachment by his rank of colour sergeant instead of by his appointment 'Sergeant-major'.

Finally when all was settled, the whole detachment was sent on two weeks embarkation leave. My parents had moved to Birmingham by this time, which was Wally's home town as well as some of the others, so that when my father met me at New Street Station he was surprised to find me escorted by four or five large marines.

It was good to be with my parents and small brother and sister again. My father proudly took me to his local to show me off to his friends. Like him they were mostly ex-service who had served in 'the last lot' and were either retired or engaged on some work relevant to the war. Unkindly called armchair warriors, they vicariously fought the war with maps and coloured pins on their sitting room walls. Each evening they foregathered in the saloon bar to discuss the latest situation in North Africa and what this man Rommel was about. If the entire Imperial General Staff had been wiped out by a chance bomb they could almost have taken over.

Because I was only fourteen my father was torn between announcing my tender years or pretending I was older so that he could buy me a beer. The problem was solved by the publican who turned a blind eye, saying that if I was old enough to go to war in a battleship, I was old enough to drink.

Leave was not the same as coming home for school holidays. For a start Birmingham was not my home, the house was strange to me and, apart from the family, I did not know anyone. The biggest difference was a change in my attitude. Whereas school had been a transient aspect of life as opposed to the permanence of home, my new life had become the stable aspect and home a temporary haven. I was a separate unit from what had been my family and no longer relied on them or felt an integral part of them. They were where I had come from but not where I now belonged.

When it came to say goodbye on New Street Station I was parting from people of whom I was fond but there was no great wrench as I settled back in my seat in the carriage. My thoughts were on my next train journey; north to the Glasgow shipyard and Job No. J1669.

CHAPTER 5

Joining Ship

Early in the morning on Monday 1st June, Wally and I staggered over to the drill shed with our kit bags, where marines from the *Howe* detachment were converging on a steadily growing pile of baggage. When packed my kit consisted of a large brown kit bag, about nine inches shorter than me and a smaller white bag about half my size. Even Wally, who was much bigger than me, could not carry both at once so we had to make two journeys. After seeing that all was properly marked with 'Job No. J1669' we went to the galley to be issued with a 'bag ration' consisting of huge doorstep sandwiches, of corned beef and cheese for our journey. Back in the barrack room we said our goodbyes to the others, the 'sprogs' who had just joined looking at me with envy as I had looked in my turn at others going off to sea.

'You lucky bastard!'

'Get some sea-time in!' said one of the old soldiers. As I went out of the room for the last time and walked towards the parade in my blues with my bugle by my side and carrying my drum in its ticking bag, a marine I knew came out of the next block and watched me swagger past.

'Where are you off to then?'

'I'm on draft to a ship.'

'Christ, the Jerries had better watch out!'

As I turned the corner on to the parade he shouted.

'Sticky-Blue!'

At Portsmouth Town Station we joined the train which had come from the Dockyard and already nearly full with some of our ship's company from RN Barracks. Fortunately there were carriages reserved for the two hundred marines and as Wally and I were one of the first to get on, we got corner seats in one of the compartments.

Finally, when all the baggage had been stowed in the guard's vans and various matelots, who had got off to buy papers and magazines, were chivvied back on board, we set off on our journey.

Most wartime train journeys seemed to be neverending, stopping at every station and at times in between; and this one was no exception.

Due to the importance of the industrial effort, goods trains had priority over passengers and even though as a troop train we were regarded as a special, we were quite often halted or sidetracked to give way to freight.

At one or two stations en route we were issued with a mug of tea, organised by whom I never knew; but it was always welcome. The problem on these occasions was to ensure that all were back aboard the train before it left. Even so one or two individuals were left behind in toilets in this way; to be sent on by the next train and charged with being absent without leave. Most of the time we halted away from platforms, to prevent people getting out and wandering off.

As soon as the darkness of wartime blackout descended, our progress became even slower. There were the usual hold-ups for goods trains and once for an air raid on some town ahead. Sometimes the train would halt in the middle of nowhere for a quarter of an hour, then very slowly start off—not necessarily in the same direction as before—to stop again after only another hundred yards.

One of the longest delays occurred in the small hours as we came to a jerking halt in what sounded like a large station. In our compartment, lit only by a single dim blue bulb, Wally was asleep opposite me, as were the others, slumped in neck-aching postures, each held upright only by his neighbours.

As I let the window blind up a fraction the marine next to me stirred and opened his eyes.

'Do you know where we are?' I asked.

He leant over and tried to peer out of the window from which we could see precious little. All names had been removed from stations to confuse would-be parachutists; a precaution that, together with the blackout, did not help the travelling public much either.

'Crewe, I reckon,' he shifted his cramped legs. 'We'll be here for bloody hours.'

Anxious for some fresh air after the dank, fag-smelling atmosphere of the carriage I opened the door and got out on to the platform. The change was marginally better with the typical railway odour of steam, coal smoke and hot engine grease. I sensed rather than saw the proximity of trains standing at other platforms, or in the associated sidings. Their engines emitted steamy sighs as they waited for some Fat Controller to send them on their way. From the marshalling yards came the sound of shunted goods trains; the clink-clank-clink of couplings echoing up and down the line as they moved.

As my eyes became accustomed to the dark I made out figures standing or sitting forlornly, with others wandering around vainly seeking someone who could tell them where their train was likely to be. Occasionally a whistle would blow in some other part of the station and a train would huff off into the night, whilst others arrived to serve their allotted time.

We must have waited about for two hours before there came a sudden activity on our platform. A porter started shouting something quite unintelligible, probably telling everyone to get on board—which I did. Then from the back end of the train a guard's whistle blew, a dim green light waved and, accompanied by some late door-slamming, we slowly moved out into the night.

As an important junction, Crewe came to feature in many of my wartime journeys. Oddly, no matter where I started from I never arrived during daylight hours and Crewe remained in my memory a town of eternal night. A sort of limbo where trains and people's lives came to a halt, whilst decisions were made on their future.

It was with a feeling of great relief that we arrived in Glasgow in the early morning, eager to get away from the atmosphere of the compartments in which we had been for what seemed years.

Glasgow and the Clydeside shipyards were working to full capacity and Fairfield's yard at Govan was no exception. When we arrived at the yard, we were marched to the ship through a mass of stores, machine shops, cranes, blacksmiths, all surrounded by huge sheets of steel and girders, drums with miles of cable, even gun barrels and complete turrets.

From a distance my first impression of the ship was that she was smaller than I imagined a battleship should be, probably due to my having only seen liners before, whose cliff-like sides were in direct contrast to the low profile of a warship. She was also dwarfed by two enormous cranes, one of which was at that moment lifting a complete twin-gunned turret high into the air destined, as I found out later, for the destroyer that was being fitted out alongside *Howe* and not visible from the jetty.

As I stepped over the brow on to the forecastle, the size and latent power became more apparent. With her length of 745 feet, a beam of over one and a half cricket pitches and, forward of the bridge superstructure, the great guns of A and B turrets, she was huge.

Like her sister ships, *Howe* conformed (more or less) to the maxima allowed by the Washington Agreement, with a standard displacement of 38,000 tons whilst her deep load, that is all up displacement with oil and water, was 45,000 tons.[1]

The ship was named after Richard, Earl Howe who, like me went to sea at the age of fourteen. But there the similarity of our careers ends because unlike me he left Eton to do it, fought many battles against the French, including the 'Glorious First of June' in 1794 and ended up as Admiral of the Fleet and General of Marines. Known as Black Dick in the navy, his nickname apparently had nothing to do with swarthiness but he had something of a forbidding look about him that could be intimidating. He was actually a generous man, fair and red-faced, the latter doubtless due to a life at sea and perhaps a liking for alcohol.

As we went below, passing along passageways, through watertight doors to our allotted messdeck, the first thing that struck me was the number of pipes, fanshafts and electric cable ducts running overhead everywhere. There was a great deal of noise with the rivetting and hammering of the dockyard 'maties', whilst in the background there was a continuous hum of machinery and fans supplying the lower decks with air.

Wally and I were on the band mess which was one of three in a messdeck on the port side midships on the main deck; that is, the deck immediately below the upper deck. The messdeck measured about twenty two feet by twenty seven at its longest, which is about the size of a largish sitting room. Much of the space was occupied by the three mess tables and benches as well as the cupboards for crockery etc, leaving—in stark contrast to the suite of cabins reserved for an admiral down aft—very little room for the fifty four souls whose living quarters it was to be.

Above the messes were bars on which to sling hammocks but, even with about two feet width per man there were not enough spaces on the messdeck for all its occupants, many having to find a billet in the passageways or flats as they were called. Hammock spaces were not allocated and it was one of the first things we had to procure as soon as we found our mess. This everyone did by tying something to the bar to show that that billet was taken.

From that moment on, having an experienced hand like Wally Waltham with me was invaluable and without him I would have been lost.

When we had drawn our bedding and hammocks from the store, he showed me how to attach the clews and lanyards, stow the palliasse and blankets inside, lash the hammock—correctly with seven turns—and stow it in the nearby hammock nettings. He then took me to find a piece of wood and make a stretcher to put across the clews at the head end. This is an old sailor's device to keep the hammock open when lying in it. Later when it came to turning in, he showed me how to sling my hammock tricing it up and making fast with a sheet bend.

Perhaps, as the young Howe joined his first ship, he had had the same mixed feelings as I did settling down into a greatly different life to anything either had experienced hitherto; and I had a lot to learn.

As the weeks went by Wally taught me all the unwritten rules and customs that governed conduct on the messdeck, that made living in a crowded area bearable and did much to avoid the minor irritations that can so easily developed into argument and even come to blows. For example, on marine's messes one never sat or lay on the table, although seamen did for some reason. To someone living in a house, with separate rooms in which to eat, sleep and merely sit, it may sound ludicrous that anyone would want to lie down for a nap on the dining room table. Each of the three tables on our messdeck was sitting and dining room for eighteen men and were only used for the purposes of eating, writing letters, playing cards or board games, sewing, ironing (providing it did not inconvenience too many others at the time) and so on. At breakfast it was a rule always to be properly washed and shaved beforehand and even in the hottest climates one could not sit down to a meal without a shirt on. You didn't clean equipment on the table or touch or use anyone else's belongings that were on it without permission, unless for example, to remove it in their absence to roll the oilcloth out, prior to a meal.

One always took one's hat off when coming into the messdeck and most holy writ of all, one kept clear of the mess when the tots were being poured

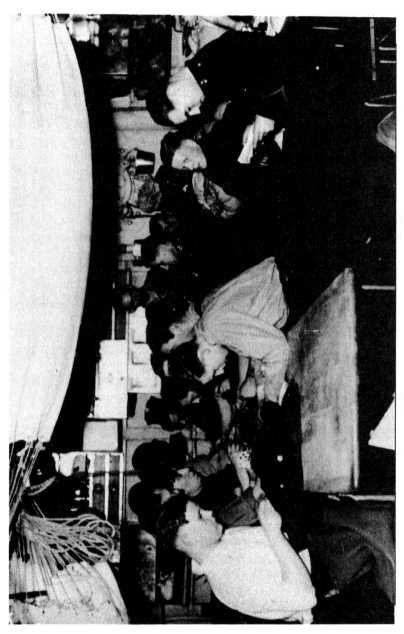

Typical scene in a Royal Marines 'barracks', ship unknown (*RM Museum*)

out by the mess rum bosun. The rough and ready dos and don'ts of behaviour were many and as hard and fast and more rigidly adhered to than a great deal of the received behaviour as practised in the wardroom.

There were also the formal rules as laid down by King's Regulations and Admiralty Instructions, the Articles of War and Admiralty Fleet Orders to be adhered to.

One example of a formal custom was the saluting of the quarterdeck as one came aboard or stepped onto it. As the quarterdeck was the domain of the officers it appeared at first sight to be an outlandish method of exacting respect to have to salute the very ground on which one's superiors trod. But as Wally explained, the custom went far back into history when there used to be a crucifix on the poop and one crossed oneself on coming aboard.

Naturally he could not remember everything or hold my hand all the time, so sometimes I found things out by experience. On watch one morning I must have been feeling cheerful and quite absent-mindedly started whistling, to be immediately jumped on by two people for totally different reasons.

'Stop that noise!'

Startled I looked round to find the Officer of the Watch standing behind me. 'Sorry, Sir!'

I must have looked mystified because he relented and told me that whistling was not allowed on a ship because it could be mistaken for a bosun's call. The other reprimand came from an older seaman who was greasing the guardrail bottlescrews nearby.

'Don't ever whistle on board a ship.' He glared at me menacingly, threatening to wipe his grease-filled hands on my face. 'You'll whistle up a wind or the Devil!'

When I told Wally about this, he said another reason why whistling was not allowed was because it had once been used as a signal for mutiny.

There were many other differences between life on a ship and that on land, particularly in the case of nautical terms and seamanship. There was also the Royal Marines' determination to show that, not only were they different from soldiers (referred to as pongoes) or sailors (matelots, dabtoes or sandscratchers) but they could perform both jobs with equal or better facility. It was a point of pride that a marine could do anything an experienced able seaman could do, whether boat handling, splicing, hoisting stores with derrick, whip and inhaul, or whatever. As a boy bugler I was not expected to practise seamanship to any great extent but it behove me to have at least a working knowledge and use seamanlike terminology. I learnt that to do something carefully and slowly was to do it 'handsomely', that pulleys and ropes were called 'block and tayckle' and time was counted in bells and watches. Ceilings were deckheads, walls, bulkheads and stairs, ladders. Marines have a habit of using terms that are out of context to their environment. Thus on land and in barracks, we did not go out, we had shore leave and had a run ashore. In obedience to the bugle call 'Come to the Cookhouse

Door, Boys!' we did not go to the dining hall we went to the mess where our food, often referred to as victuals, had been cooked in the galley. Now we were on board a ship things were the other way round. The Marine messdeck was called the Barracks. The Sergeant's Mess which was partitioned off from the main Barracks was called the Horsebox by reason of the half door at the entrance.

Many of these things Wally told me about, answering with great patience my never-ending questions on shipboard life.

As buglers we were put on the mess next to the Sergeant's mess which happened co-incidently to be the band mess. There were about eighteen bandsmen including a corporal; and a bandmaster who ranked as a colour sergeant and lived in the Sergeant's Mess. On the whole I got on well with most of the bandsmen, although one or two were quick to point out to me that as they were from the Royal Naval School of Music, they were an intellectual cut above the ordinary marine and very many cuts above a bugler. They inferred that Wally and I messed with the band on sufferance as intruders in their world of 'culture'.

Lack of diplomacy did not help matters when I told them (from a safe distance) that I could put more feeling into a bugle call than they ever did their music. In my turn I regarded them with mixed feelings because the bandsmen did not have the same ethos as the ordinary marine with whom I felt a rapport. I was after all not destined to be a bandsman. But the majority accepted me totally as part of their life and put up with my youthful boisterousness with a great deal of patience, particularly Bob Gronert the band corporal who, although naturally biased towards his fellows did much to keep the peace between me and the rest.

As buglers we came under the guard sergeant who was the NCO responsible for the ceremonial guard and all the sentry duties throughout the ship. For the first few months the sergeant was a disgruntled NCO , fat and red haired, called Harris. Disgruntled because he had been removed from a comfortable job in barracks which he had regarded as his 'square number' for the rest of the war.

Up until 1942 there were a number of people of all ranks who had decided that the best war for them was to stay in barracks for the duration and somehow make themselves indispensable on the permanent staff. The worst they had to endure were the jibes of those temporarily at home between bouts of contact with the enemy. Then somebody had decided that no one was exempt from active service and when the *Howe* detachment was made up, the bottom and crannies of the Eastney barrel were diligently searched for those embedded in the woodwork. The result was a number of individuals who, for years knowing only the *per Terram* side of the Marines motto suddenly found themselves faced with the prospect of doing the *per Mare* bit; and in wartime.

Sergeant Harris was displeased to find himself at sea and could think of no better way of showing his displeasure than to take it out of the smallest person he could find—namely me. Harris started very soon after we joined the ship. One morning at Reveille he was rousing out the marines quite normally until he saw that, like several others, I was awake but still in my hammock. From across the other side of the messdeck came a hysterical scream: 'DRUMMER! GET OUT OF THAT HAMMOCK! GO ON GET OUT IN ONE SECOND, OR I'LL HAVE YOU ON A CHARGE!'

It certainly had its effect not only on me but on all the other tardy marines who were still in their hammocks—those he would not dare to have shouted at. There was an embarrassed pause in the messdeck as he stood and ranted at me for about two minutes, until seeing he had made a fool of himself, he charged out of the messdeck. From that moment, as if to justify his initial stupidity, nothing I did was ever clean enough, smart enough or quick enough for him. His usual punishment was to have me parade in full marching order or to lay out my kit for his inspection. Both proceedings meant the maximum amount of work to ensure that all was clean and correct. He remained guard sergeant for some time and it was only when I was on watch or when we were at sea that I did not have to put up with him.

There were others who were also up-rooted 'barrack stanchions' (as the permanent barrack staff are called) and certainly not in their first flush of youth, sporting as they did the Long Service and good Conduct Medal. But most were philosophical about their lot and realised it was only fair for them to take their turn on active service. One such was the sergeant who had been in charge of the Eastney Sick Bay dispensary for many years, who had looked on everyone reporting sick as a potential malingerer but obviously had never thought of himself in that category until he found himself in *Howe*, protesting his age and indispensibility. However he settled down to life at sea and remained in the *Howe* for the full three and a half years of her active service.

As a boy I had a definite place in the social hierarchy on the messdeck. Royal Marines had a tradition of respect for those of long service and at one time a boy or a recruit would have had to stand to attention if he addressed a marine with three good conduct badges (indicating twelve years or more service). As it was I was expected to call them 'Trained Soldier' until by tacit consent I could use their names. As far as the pecking order was concerned I was the least among non-equals but the majority were kind and considerate in their way even though some disguised it heavily to preserve their hard-bitten image. Life was macho and of course the language down to earth. Lewd suggestions were often made not only to me but to any young and fresh-faced marine. But it was very rarely anything but crudity, or at worst humour at my expense. Propositions like 'Come with me, Sticks, and I will show you the Golden Rivet!'[2] or 'Sticky-blue, I love you!' or other more explicit suggestions were usually effectively countered by a 'Piss off!'—or words to that effect.

My relations with the marine officers could only be described as remote, because it was not permissible to approach them and one was only to speak when spoken to. Any communication had to be done through the intermediation of an NCO .

The Officer Commanding Royal Marines was a Major Ross who only spoke to me when I was brought before him for some minor misdemeanour or losing some piece of kit, which last I did on several occasions, mainly through my own carelessness.

Our first and typical encounter was such a confrontation and even then most of the conversation took place between him and the Sergeant-Major who stood to the left of the desk.

Having marched me in to the tiny office the Sgt Major shouted:

'Halt! Don't salute!'

For some reason wrongdoers may not use this mark of respect when hailed before their superior.

'PO/X 5136 Boy Bugler Rowe, Sir!' he continued, in the same pitch as if the OCRM was deaf. 'Investigation into loss of kit, namely one pair of gloves, Sir!'

'How did you lose them?'

'How did you lose them?' the Sgt Major repeated the question to me as if Major Ross and I spoke different languages.

'I only lost one of them, Sir! It went over the side when I was on the bridge during the Middle Watch, Sir!'

I had taken the offending article off and it had slipped from my grasp when I was looking over the side of the bridge. After a moment hovering in an updraught of air, like a seagull on a cliff face, it had avoided my despairing grab and plunged down into the sea.

'He only!—he lost them over the side on the bridge during the Middle Watch, Sir!' repeated the Sgt Major.

'That's no excuse and is very careless. You will have to learn to look after your equipment better than that! Will you pay the full cost or do you wish to have a Court of Enquiry to investigate the loss?'

'I'll pay the full cost, Sir!' I interjected hurriedly before the Sgt Major could interpret for me.

In theory I could have demanded a Court of Enquiry which was normal procedure when any loss of equipment was being investigated. But as they are more generally convened when someone happened to lose a ship rather than a glove, Major Ross's question was a rhetorical one designed to impress me with the seriousness of the occasion.

However I was not to know that and the idea of having to appear before one was a terrifying concept for a fourteen year old. I imagined being taken under escort aboard the Flagship, which would be flying the Union Flag for all the fleet to know that these dread proceedings were being held. There I would have to face a row of assembled officers in their formal dress complete with swords, as well as witnesses for and against, and explain to them how I came to lose a glove. I quickly opted to forfeit the cost of the gloves which was half a week's pay.

'He'll pay the full cost, Sir!'

'Very well, carry on, Sergeant Major!'

'Pay the full cost of one pair of gloves! Don't Salute! About Turn! Quick March!'

There were three lieutenants in the detachment, one of whom, rejoicing in the name of Willasey-Wilsey, spoke six words to me during the whole time he was in *Howe*. On that occasion I was on watch and was sent into the wardroom with a message for one of the officers. Contrary to what might be thought good manners, a marine on duty should only ever remove his headgear in church, or in court with the permission of the judge. On this occasion what had been instilled into me by my parents overcame discipline and I took my hat off as I entered the holy of holies.

I was at once confronted by an enraged W-W who hissed: 'Put your hat on at once!'

What with Major Ross threatening Courts of Enquiry and Willasey-Wilsey railing at me for displaying good manners I resolved from then on to avoid any future contact with my officers as far as possible.[3]

On the whole I had an easier relationship with the naval officers most of whom had no reason to acknowledge my existence. There were some exceptions including the Gunnery Officer, Lt. Commander Hammond who, seeing my extreme youth asked me how old I was and where I came from and what I wanted to be. In contrast was the Engineer Commander, a small monkey-faced man whose only ever contact with me was a kick on the ankle when once I was standing in his way. Whether it was accidental or not I don't know but his indignant look was so funny that I had difficulty in keeping a straight face as I limped to one side and apologised. Those with whom I had regular contact such as the Commander (Shaw-Hamilton, who was my boss at action stations) and the Watch Officers were generally much more helpful. Much of the knowledge I gained of naval routine and practice came from watching, listening to and at times questioning the more approachable ones.

As Wally was nearly eighteen and had been to sea before, he was regarded as a man already, whereas I was the boy and was treated as such.

But although theoretically subject to all rules applying to boy seamen, I was generally freer from supervision than they were. Whilst they lived on a segregated messdeck under the eye of a petty officer, I had the comparative freedom of the Barracks and could come and go as I pleased. There were three rules that I shared with the Boy Seamen. One was limited shore leave and having to be back on board by 9.00pm or earlier.

I was also supposed to use the boy's heads, which were separate from the men's, presumably to protect our youthful morals. It was Churchill who said that the old navy was run on 'rum, sodomy and the lash'—the lower deck version was 'rum, bum and baccy'—but what could possibly have happened in the heads was beyond imagination, as secret assignations in the toilets were highly improbable. Each tiny cubicle had just enough room for one human body and was fitted with a half door that hid the torso of the sitting tenant and nothing else. One sat in this complete lack of privacy like a broody hen in a nesting box whilst others strolled by looking for a vacant stall and greeting their friends as they came across them. There was no possible room for modesty whilst performing one's natural functions and the heads were used more in the social style of the Roman public lavatories. One could go and sit in a cubicle and chat to one's neighbours. I disliked using the boy's heads because there was seldom anyone in there to chat to.

Thirdly and because I was now under Naval discipline, as a boy I could be punished with the cane; something the podgy Harris delighted to threaten me with at the least provocation. At first I took his threats seriously, chiefly because as far as I could see discipline on board a big ship was maintained by punishment alone. On the quarterdeck I watched as a never-ending stream of offenders whose conduct had somehow been 'prejudicial to good order and naval discipline' was brought before the officer of the watch by the Crushers (Regulating Petty Officers). Then again hands were mustered on the quarterdeck after working hours for Evening Quarters and, with the sailors respectfully bareheaded, extracts were read out from the Articles of War[4].

We were warned in rolling cadences that anyone assembling mutinously or deserting or doing a multiplicity of other things whilst on active service '—shall suffer death, or such less punishment as is hereinafter mentioned'. It was hardly any wonder that for the first few months I lived in constant fear of dire punishment for some unwitting offence and would certainly not have been unduly surprised to see the odd sailor hanging by the neck from one of our yardarms.

In fact no boy was ever caned in the whole of the *Howe*'s active service and, as corporal punishment had long since been abandoned in the services—apart from hanging and shooting, which are about as corporal as can be—caning had probably even then fallen into disuse. However it remained on the books as a sort of ultimate deterrent for juveniles.

I was still learning these things when we left Fairfields Shipyard and the Clyde. And also Glasgow; a busy, dirty, generous city where in uniform we paid a penny to go anywhere on the trams, whose notorious Gorbals gangs forbade their members to touch a serviceman in wartime and where, on a run ashore with one of the marines, we were invited into a tenement flat by a man and his wife 'to hae a cuppy o' tea'. Apologising for the paucity of fare, they plied us with sandwiches, a crab salad; fruit cake and copious cuppies o' tea, which must have represented a pretty large chunk of their rations.

There was more Scottish hospitality in Rosyth our next port of call, where a family befriended me, not only inviting me into their home but taking me to Edinburgh and the zoo with their children, who were about the same

Dockyard 'maties' and families watch five years of work leaving Fairfields Yard at Govan (*IWM*)

age as me. I learned that Scottish people may be canny folk with their money but they are not mean.

At Rosyth the ship was fitted with radar—then called RDF—and also embarked our aircraft. These were Supermarine Walrus floatplanes, a biplane with a single pusher type engine. With a top speed of ninety miles an hour they were more familiarly known as Steam Pidgeons or Pussers Spitfires. On his way to the ship, one of the pilots force-landed in a field where he killed the farmer's prize bull, thus starting litigation that continued until after the war.

Not long after, the time came when we were finished with dockyards and on 26 August, nearly four months after I had joined the ship, we sailed to join the Home Fleet at Scapa Flow.

CHAPTER 6

Scapa Flow

Entering a naval harbour for the first time for any new ship was like being a new boy at school. Critical eyes watched her entry and poor seamanship was noted without fail, not only by admirals and senior naval officers who were quick off the mark with derogatory comments but by everyone from Able Seaman upwards. As the biggest gathering of Royal Naval ships in the world, the Home Fleet in Scapa Flow under the eagle eye of the Commander in Chief was the severest test of any.

Entering harbour is also an occasion riven with strict protocol as to which ship saluted which first. The pecking order was in terms of seniority of the rank of the officer on board, generally reflected by the size of the ship from battleship through aircraft carrier, cruiser, destroyer, frigate, corvette, submarine and so on down to the tiniest motor launch that sported a white ensign. Between ships of the same size it depended on which had the senior captain unless of course there was an admiral on board. Not only had he to be saluted first but rated a bugle call from those with buglers aboard.

As we entered the fleet anchorage in the grey light of a typical Orkney autumn afternoon Wally and I stood at our 'Station for Entering Harbour' above the bridge ready to pay any flag officer his due respects. On the compass platform, the Chief Yeoman of Signals (otherwise known as Chief Bunting Tosser) busily thumbed his way through various tomes, identifying ships as they hove into sight.

'*Cumberland* to port sir! Vice-Admiral 5th Cruiser Squadron!'

The distinctive silhouette of an eight inch gun County class cruiser with her three funnels loomed over to our left.

'Very Good. Sound the Alert!'

Wally and I came to attention smartly with bugles at the ready and duly sounded off.

'Attention on the upper deck, Port side!' The Bosun's Mate called over the SRE (Ship's Radio Extension).

From over the water came the answering Alert and call to attention followed after a pause by the Carry On, as *Cumberland* acknowledged our salute.

'Sound the Carry On!'

Wally and I obliged.

'*Anson* coming up to starboard!'

Our sister ship was older than us yet her captain was junior to Captain

Woodhouse and so we waited for her piped 'Still' before acknowledging it ourselves.

'*King George V* on starboard bow, Sir!' There was no need to add 'C in C Home Fleet'; everyone knew *'KGV'*, the senior of our class was the Flagship of Admiral Sir John Tovey.

Wally and I sounded off in strict tempo taking care not to make it sound too 'tiddly', in other words with no extra flourishes. It was not the Admiral we were worried about. In the flagship listening with critical ear would be Fleet Bugle Corporal Bert Wilkinson who was not averse to conveying his own brand of caustic comment to any erring bugler.

And so *Howe* threaded her way among the anchored fleet to her allotted mooring, proceeding more warily than through any rock-strewn channel, where she faced her next public examination.

This was coming up to the buoy and making fast; a test of seamanship for the Captain, Commander, the cable party under the Chief Shipwright and the ship's Blacksmith. But success also relied on the agility and skill of one seaman whose performance was watched with critical fascination by everyone in the fleet. His task was to leap from a boat on to the buoy and reeve a line through the ring to enable ship and buoy to be drawn together.

With the starboard bower anchor catted and a 'picking up' rope running out through the hawsepipe, the ship slowly moved up to the mooring, preceded by a pulled cutter carrying the blacksmith, the buoy jumper and the other end of the picking up rope[1]. From the bridge the buoy looked like a small oil drum to which a dinghy could tie up with her painter, its huge size only becoming apparent by contrast with the cutter as it drew near. Meanwhile, on the forecastle our 'painter' was being prepared. This was the anchor cable with anchor detached, a single link of which weighed over a hundredweight (50 kilos).

In the cutter the bow oarsman, alias buoy jumper, shipped his oar and with a line tied around his middle stood ready in the bows. The coxswain moved the boat warily up to the buoy in the stiff breeze, judging the right moment as buoy and boat rolled. Too far away and the jumper would land in the sea, too near and the rolling buoy could stave in the boat's bows. Meanwhile a large battleship slowly crept up behind them.

Then as the buoy rolled away and the cutter's bows rose on a wave the bowman leaped, caught hold of the rubbing strakes and climbed on to the top. As he rove the line through the ring an almost audible sigh of relief was expelled by everyone watching.

All went well; the line was through and the ship was hauled up to the buoy. With an outsize shackle the blacksmith made the cable fast—some three tons of it hanging from the hawsepipe—and *Howe* was safely at her moorings.

In traditional style, the jumping seaman got an extra tot of rum for his performance. On their part, the captain and ship got the unspoken approval of the fleet and we came to rest, swinging out booms and ladders in obedience to the 'Extend' whilst critical eyes returned to their normal duties.

As Wally and I finally stood down, tension relaxed on the bridge, for the only message received from Admiral Tovey was a welcome to his fleet. 'Finished with Main Engines,' was rung down on the engine room telegraph and all the bridge hierarchy from the captain down to the boy messenger went their several ways.

As it was still my afternoon watch I had to go and continue on the quarter-deck, whilst Wally went below. Nearly three o'clock, just time to get there. I raced down the starboard ladders, through the signal bridge, where, along with other flags, our identifying pennant numbers were being stowed, down to the catapult deck and through the passageway behind S3 and S4 gun tur-rets, leaving behind me a trail of imprecations from those I bumped into. The ship's bell was already back in its place and with a hurried salute to the quarterdeck and the Officer of the Watch, I raced passed him and rang six bells. The OOW, Sub Lieutenant Battersby turned a horror-stricken face towards the C in C's flagship wondering if they had heard. He had just turned back to me and opened his mouth to speak when every ship within earshot echoed my lead.

'My God, Drummer! You were nearly too early!'

His sigh of relief could well have been heard in *King George V.*

In my efforts to beat the Bosun's Mate to the bell I had very nearly set to nought all our good seamanship in entering harbour so faultlessly, by an-nouncing the time before the C in C.

Apart from being surrounded by islands with almost foreign sounding names the fleet anchorage could only be described as a bleak almost graveyard-like stretch of water. Which in a manner of speaking it was, be-cause some of the German ships scuttled there at the end of the Great War still lay at the bottom of the harbour.

In another part of the harbour not far from Kirkwall, there was a sadder resting place for another battleship.

In the early part of the war Scapa Flow was regarded as a secure harbour for the Home Fleet, until on Friday 13th October 1939 a U boat found a way through a passage hitherto thought to be unnavigable. In one of the more daring exploits of the war, U47 under her commander Kapitan-Leutnant Gunther Prien penetrated the anchorage and torpedoed the battleship *Royal Oak,* escaping by the way she came. There was great loss of life, only 424 saved out of a ship's company of over 1,200; made even worse, so I was told, by the fact that during the hours of darkness *Royal Oak* had swung right round on her moorings. As a result some of her company had leapt into the water on the opposite side to where the land lay, swimming out into the ex-panse of the harbour to die a cold and lonely death in supposedly friendly waters[2].

After the sinking, most of the sounds between the islands were blocked so that there were only two possible means of egress. An inner anchorage protected by anti-submarine nets was established wherein the larger ships gathered, each skirted with anti-torpedo nets; leaving *Royal Oak* by herself to the north, her masts and superstructure to be seen at low water.

As far as shore leave was concerned there was nowhere to go in Scapa except for one island, Flotta, the rest of the Orkney Islands being out of bounds. The main town of Kirkwall was quite near but would have been overwhelmed by the ship's company of a cruiser going ashore there let alone an entire fleet. The only place to go was the Fleet Canteen on Flotta. Run by the NAAFI this consisted of an eating place which could in no way be flattered by the name restaurant and a wet canteen which could hardly be termed a pub. Both places were more or less large halls set with trestle tables and chairs. Decor looked as if it owed much to the limited range of paint available in a warship. On the walls were one or two posters and pictures which were supposed to brighten things up but by their very cheerfulness emphasised the drear nature of their environment. There were two canteens of course to separate the ratings from the Chiefs and Petty Officers. There was also a cinema or theatre for the benefit of all.

Those were the entire social amenities available for several thousand men stationed at Scapa.

Life in harbour at Scapa can only be described as boring and monotonous. From eight o'clock in the morning—eight bells of the morning watch, when the colours were hoisted until four in the afternoon—everyone of the lower deck spent their time in cleaning, sweeping, scrubbing, polishing and painting under the eagle eye of a Petty Officer or, in the case of the marines, an NCO.

Even the wooden upper decks, having been darkened by the dockyard, were assiduously scrubbed and holystoned every morning to obtain the nearest that could be to the whiteness of the piping days of peace, in total disregard for camouflage. It was far more important that the admiral (and apparently, the enemy) should see how clean the decks were kept.

Amongst the very first pearls of wisdom Wally Waltham imparted to me was how to get paint off one's clothes because from the moment we first came aboard it was impossible to walk from one end of the ship to the other without seeing wet paint somewhere; nor was it difficult to brush some part of one's clothing against it; thus the importance of knowing how to remove it.

Repainting often had to be preceded by chipping off the old paint and getting down to the bare metal; and at any time in harbour there would be parties of men armed with chipping hammers, inch by inch and hour by hour tapping away at the superstructure like demented woodpeckers. They covered themselves and everything else with tiny particles of paint, often to the fury and frustration of other working parties nearby trying to scrub and polish some other piece of the ship.

Below decks the same thing happened. Besides scrubbing anything scrub-bable, any equipment made of polishable metal was stripped of its protective paint and buffed and polished until you could see your face in it. The amount of metal worn away by polishing in the Royal Navy must have amounted to many tons a year.

One of the buglers' jobs was to clean the ship's bell and so every day I went up to the quarterdeck with my tin of polish and cotton waste to wear away a bit more of the ship's metalwork. Early on in the commission it happened that despite my prodigious efforts word came back via the sergeant of the guard that the bell was filthy and with dire warnings ringing in my ear of being put in the OCRM's report I took my cleaning gear up to the quarterdeck and cleaned away at what seemed to me to be a pristine bell apart from some very slight tarnishing where it had been touched by the duty bosun's mate when ringing it. I reported back to Harris who said he would come up and inspect it. I waited by the bell for some time before he eventually turned up and asked me what the hell I was doing on the quarterdeck, the bells he was talking about were in the waist and on the foc'sle. Up to that moment I had no idea that there was more than one ship's bell and despite my explanations I was told that ignorance is no excuse and to parade that evening with full marching order 'and properly cleaned for my inspection!'

At first everything was a new experience for me but after a while the daily harbour routine became incredibly boring and frustrating not least because try as I might I never seemed to please authority. The highlight of the day should, I suppose have been the ceremony of colours in the morning. But taking part in ceremonial duties is only tolerable, even enjoyable, when there is a sense of occasion and circumstance. Parading with the Guard and Band for colours every morning in the dreary overcast of the fleet anchorage, with half a dozen seagulls as disinterested onlookers was not my idea of occasion. My growing lack of enthusiasm obviously displayed itself in my slapdash preparations for these ceremonials, giving Sgt Harris some justification for his attitude towards me. That he now had some reason for it was confirmed by Pete Medcalfe, the youngest musician and a good friend. Our kit lockers happened to be adjacent and, as we were getting ready for colours one morning, I opened mine and a cascade of my untidily stowed kit fell out on to the deck. He surveyed the resulting heap and watched my efforts to locate some necessary object from among the jumble.

'Sticks,' he said, shaking his head ruefully, 'Let's face it your lockers's a scranbag[3] and so are you!'

Fortunately it was about this time that another dimension entered my life which enabled me to acquire the philosophical outlook of the other marines and realise it was no earthly good questioning the senselessness of a life whose main objects appeared to be keeping a bell clean and going through various rigmaroles to hoist and lower a flag. The catalyst for this development was the ship's library through which I escaped into other worlds whenever the opportunity arose. At that time there was a scheme in Britain for people to send their unwanted books to servicemen and many ended up in libraries such as ours. Starting with Edgar Wallace, Agatha Christie, Ngaio Marsh and other thriller writers, I went on without direction to read Wilkie Collins, Dickens, T.H. White and Henry Williamson. *Tarka the Otter* brought back to me an old interest in natural history and, on finding a school text book on biology, I ploughed my way through the structures of amoebae and chlamydamonus to learn the difference between plants and animals and what a frog's nervous system and a cockroach's alimentary canal looked like.

In time there came to be plenty of the latter in the *Howe*, hiding in nooks and crannies around the messdeck and getting into the food if it was not well covered. My enthusiasm for the inner workings of the cockroach was not shared by the bandsmen particularly when I attempted to dissect one on the mess. The only implements I had were a needle and a razor blade which did not make the neatest job of it. It also happened that one of the bandsmen called Eliott who was not all that fond of me, was eating a late tea at the time. His cries of revulsion—which I thought rather overdone—caused me to be banned from the mess for the evening and my biological researches to be forcibly consigned to the gash bucket.

The text book must have been written specifically for the sea-going student because in progressing to higher animals another subject for study was the rat, always plentiful in a ship. There were very interesting illustrations of dissected specimens; but after representations to him from my messmates, led by Eliott of the delicate stomach, Corporal Gronert banned 'that disgusting book' from the mess, despite my promises not to dissect anything else.

From then on the interest displayed by the bandsmen in my current reading must have seemed quite touching to an outsider, hearing them ask about the title, author and contents and not realising it was a matter of self-interest.

Watchkeeping in harbour could have been another part of a boring day because, strictly speaking the bugler's job was merely to be on hand to blow the routine calls as well as sounding salutes to admirals who were either passing or coming alongside to visit. But there was a lot to learn from the others. On the quarterdeck the Officer of the Watch had overall charge then there was the duty quartermaster, usually a Leading Seaman, the bosun's mate an Able Seaman, the Corporal of the Gangway, a marine and last but not necessarily least the boy messenger. Theoretically the QM or the bosun's mate carried out a lot of the routine work like reading and logging barometer, temperature and wind speeds but it was often left to the messenger or, because I volunteered, to me.

Taking the sea temperature was done by the simple process of going down the gangway and dipping the thermometer in the sea and the wet and dry temperatures were merely read off from the thermometers. When it came to wind speed this was gauged by the indications in the Beaufort Scale which were all conveniently written out in the log book. It was Sub-lieutenant Battersby that taught me how to determine wind speed by its effect on the sea. For example 'large waves starting to form, white horses extensive everywhere; with some spray coming off the tops' meant force 6 on the Beaufort Scale, which was around 25 knots—an appropriate moment incidently, to set an anchor watch and raise steam on at least one boiler in case 45,000 tons of battleship dragged her anchor or broke loose from her moorings. In time I also learned to blow the boatswain's call properly and make many of the pipes (announcements) including the long and twittering 'Hands to Dinner'.

The main reason for watchkeeping was of course to keep watch; and everyone down to the boy and the bugler kept a weather eye open for any happenings that would impinge on the normal life of the ship. Anything out of the ordinary seen by anyone was immediately reported to the OOW, logged and if merited reported to the captain. It was always very competitive within the quarterdeck watch to see who could see and report happenings first.

Apart from ensuring that the harbour was not alive with enemy ships, U-boat periscopes or drifting mines etc (such excitements were in the main conspicuously lacking), there were also the movements of ships and boats coming alongside. But far more important than spotting the presence of an enemy was to be on the lookout for roaming admiral's barges or any captain's motor boats approaching or passing the ship.

Senior officers were very conscious of the respect that their rank merited in the way of salutes and ceremony from those they were visiting and, in the case of admirals, just passing by. Any admiral who failed to get a bugled salute during daylight hours would, as soon as he got back aboard his flagship, dispatch his flag lieutenant to the signal deck to send a reprimand to the captain of the erring ship. The message would be sent by semaphore or general light signal so that all ships in harbour would read it, thus not only adding to the discomfiture of the captain but, in line with the age-old Admiralty principle, 'pour encourager les autres'.

On receipt of the signal a furious Captain would then send for the Commander who would reprimand the Officer of the Watch who would return to the quarterdeck and tear a strip off the Quartermaster who would give a 'right bollocking' to everyone including the bugler.

Fortunately admiral's barges and captain's motorboats were fairly easy to spot and a close eye was always kept on the various flagships to make sure that their transport was safely secured to their respective booms.

The greatest danger came from one ship on whom an eye could not be kept. *HMS Iron Duke* was a venerable battleship who in her heyday, flew Jellicoe's flag as Commander-in-Chief of the Grand Fleet at Jutland. The Second World War found her in Scapa and 'partly demilitarised', where she was bombed twice by her old enemy and forced to beach to prevent sinking. Concreted in to the side at Lyness she became flagship of the Admiral Commanding Orkneys and Shetlands, out of sight of the main anchorage but certainly not out of mind. We had been warned to keep a sharp lookout for ACOS because he did not necessarily use a conspicuous barge and but would often tour his domain in a small motor dinghy, descriptively known in the navy as a 'skimming dish'. He also had a habit of running under the bows of the ship and around the stern in order to surprise an unwary watch. If he could arrive on deck without having been spotted it made his day, at the same time unmaking that of the Officer of the Watch. It seemed to me that ACOS cheated in the game of Spot the Admiral with his underhand methods but on the other hand the security of the anchorage was his responsibility and he had a duty to test our alertness. A previous ACOS had been made to take early retirement after Gunther Prien sank the *Royal Oak*.

If a flagless boat was spotted coming alongside then the next move was for the boat's coxswain to indicate whose it was. Four fingers placed across his sleeve indicated a captain, who had to be piped aboard, otherwise a shake of the head would indicate that he carried only junior ranks. Generally speaking coxswains of motorboats responded only to enquiring looks from quartermasters and above and boy messengers and buglers were ignored.

After dark, boats were challenged which was much more fun because anyone could shout the inquiry: 'Boat Ahoy!'

To which the answer might be 'Flag!', or the name of a ship, indicating its Captain or 'Aye, Aye!', 'No, No!' or simply 'Passing!'

There were also other shouts we would hear as we 'swung round the buoy'. The smaller ships, busy escorting convoys across the oceans, would formally salute us as they went on their way; but from somewhere below would come the shout:

'Get some sea-time in, you great big bastard!'

Such insults, however, were as nothing compared with those hurled at the battleship *Rodney,* after one of her number was court martialled for having an amorous adventure with a sheep. Since that time whenever she passed, or was passed by another ship the waters would echo to the sound of bleating. At one stage the practice became so bad that a Fleet Order was promulgated threatening dire punishment to anyone caught baa-ing at her. After this it was no longer done openly but still continued to a lesser extent when a face would appear at a port or doorway utter a loud 'B-a-a-a-a!' and rapidly retreat into the bowels of the ship, to the frustration the ship's regulating staff who were supposed to catch the culprits.

All these things helped to alleviate the boredom of harbour routine but the best break was getting out to sea and every week I would eagerly scan the fleet training programme to see when we were due for exercises.

CHAPTER 7

Battle Practice Target

We had a full programme of training to get through in working up to fighting efficiency. Gun drills, Asdic, RDF, damage control and other exercises were carried out almost daily; but for me the most exciting part was going to sea for firing practice. Not only did this mean that I could watch the guns firing but more important as far as I was concerned, we usually slid out of harbour way before Colours was due and came back after sunset. Even the bells were unshipped before going to sea so I did not have to clean them.

At first everyone closed up for any type of firing and getting the whole ship at action stations was a regular exercise, the aim of which was to get the time down to less than five minutes. The bugle call was never used for exercise so the Bosun's Mate would pipe 'For exercise, Action Stations.' Action Stations!'

As the senior bugler, Wally's action station was on the bridge whereas mine was in the after conning position with the Commander. Although after conning position sounds a grand name it was in fact a small bridge about four feet by ten on the after funnel from which the ship could be commanded, or conned, in the event of the main bridge being wiped out. On either side of the funnel there was a 44 inch searchlight platform and the whole was completed by a catwalk going around the funnel. As well as the Commander there was the Chief Boatswain's Mate and a boy messenger in the position. But what with all the phones and voice pipes in the conning position itself there was precious little room for all of us, so the messenger and I normally stood outside the enclosed bridge on the catwalk by the searchlight, usually on the leeward side. There were disadvantages to this because the fumes from the funnel would sometimes eddy around us and, in order not to suffocate we would have to move to the windward side and face the weather. Our perch was excellent for observing anything going on around the ship although it offered little protection but God, in the words of the Naval Prayer, to 'preserve us from the dangers of the sea and from the violence of the enemy'.

The most spectacular shoots were during the night encounter exercises when an 'enemy' ship had to be detected, brought within range and fired on. As the ship came into range the 5.25s would open up using starshell, the parachuted flares illuminating the whole area around it, slowly descending into the sea and as the ship became visible the searchlights would stab out into the night lighting up the enemy against the night background.

Another interesting shoot was the Close Range Weapons practice. These consisted of multiple two-pounder Pom-poms and 20mm Oerlikons firing a mixture of tracer, incendiary and HE shells. For this an aircraft would tow a drogue target over the ship whilst the various groups would fire at it. At first the marksmanship left a lot to be desired but each gun's crew always tried to be the first to hit the drogue. Such was their eagerness that one trigger-happy Pom-Pom fired a burst in front of the aircraft causing the furious pilot to painstakingly flash on his Aldis signal lamp.

'I am pulling the bloody thing not pushing it!'

Many shoots were carried out with sub-calibre guns; that is with a smaller calibre barrel fitted inside the larger gun, thus saving wear and tear as well as expensive ammunition. But it was by no means as spectacular as the real thing.

At first I was nervous of the full calibre firings, particularly of the 14 inch, and both the messenger and I used to seek the shelter of the conning position whenever the 5.25s or the fourteen inch were fired. However as the platform was open with half doors there was little protection from the blast and it seemed to me that it was worse inside. So in time I got used to standing and watching from the catwalk.

When a battleship fired salvoes, half the guns from each turret were fired at a time whilst the other half were loading. The effect of five 14 inch guns going off on anyone standing in the open was like being in a London Underground station when a fast train goes through. On the catwalk I was buffeted from side to side by the blast. The first concussion to reach me came from Y turret aft as it was nearest, followed almost instantaneously by that from A and B turrets. It was more of a push from side to side as 338 lbs of cordite threw a shell weighing three quarters of a ton out of each gun. The tension was heightened by the delay between the order to shoot and the guns firing, as they would only fire when the ship was on an even keel. Thus, if the ship was rolling, which it usually was, there was a pause of uncertain length between the firing bell and the guns going off. From where I stood I could hear the fire orders from the director and when I heard the order 'Shoot!' followed by 'Ting-ting!' on the bell I would brace myself for the crash. Sometimes it seemed ages before the ship level led off and the guns fired, but at others the blast followed immediately after the bell and before I was ready.

Strangely the effect of the big guns on my ears was not nearly as bad as some of the smaller calibre. On occasions concussion from the 2-pounder pom-poms was quite painful, particularly when they were trained right round towards one.

Much of the exercise action was also to check damage control, firefighting and watertight doors. On these occasions the Commander and Chief Bosun's Mate would go on a tour of the ship leaving the messenger and me to man the conning position. As we stood there answering calls from the voicepipes and phones, usually only telling whoever it was that the Commander wasn't there, I would imagine the bridge wiped out and the Boy Seaman and me left in sole command to con the ship. It developed into a

The silent guns. A and B turrets trained to port (*RG* HMS Howe *Assoc*)

The sound and the fury. A remarkable picture catching the instantaneous
flash as the shells leave the muzzles (*RG* HMS Howe *Assoc*)

game with one of the messengers, a boy called Coates who was about eighteen months older but with an imagination like mine. Having listened to the orders given on the bridge, I knew roughly what to do and Coates was au fait with gunnery commands and using the various unmanned voicepipes and phones I would steer the ship into action whilst Coates would be the Gunnery Officer.

'Starboard ten, Quartermaster,' I would shout down a voice pipe.

'Steady as you go.'

'Three zero revolutions!' down the engine room phone.

I would bring the ship around so that all guns would bear on the enemy fleet.

Meanwhile Coates would be giving orders to the turrets, the transmitting station and directors having been put out of action.

'Range one four thousand yards.'

'With full charge and SAPC, Load! Load! Load!'

'Shoot! Ting-ting!'

'Up two hundred. Shoot! Ting-ting!'

'Down one hundred. Shoot! Ting-ting!'

'Cease fire! Tr-r-r-ing!'

This last being the sound of the Cease Fire bell as another German ship went to the bottom.

The game came to an abrupt end one day when I shouted down the Emergency Steering Position voice pipe.

'Port ten, Quartermaster!'

And a voice answered, 'We haven't taken over yet, Sir!'

I had forgotten that part of the day's exercise was to test the auxiliary systems.

'Oh! Just testing communications' I said hurriedly and slammed the lid shut, to the accompaniment of giggles from Coates.

A break in our working up routine occurred when one day we steamed out of Scapa seemingly for a rendezvous with a Battle Practice Target but then kept on going out to sea and down the west coast of Scotland. As we went on our journey the captain announced that we were on an extremely hush-hush mission and for a change we ourselves were to be the practice target for our two man submarines who needed experience in attaching their explosive charges to a battleship under realistic conditions.

The choice of *Howe* for this particular duty must have been due to our availability but it was nevertheless, a historical co-incidence.

In 1776 the first ever recorded submarine attack was carried out by a craft closely resembling an oversized barrel. Named the *Turtle,* this forerunner of the modern submarine was invented by David Bushnell from Connecticut during the War of Independence, with the express purpose of attacking the British fleet.

Considering the knowledge and materials available at the time the little submersible was a remarkable piece of technology. The controls were crude and the single crewman, originally Bushnell's brother Ezra, had a busy time of it. Sitting with his head on a level with the conning tower windows, he cranked an Archimedean type screw in the front with one hand for propulsion whilst with the other he controlled depth with a screw on the top. Steering was by means of a tiller tucked under his arm and there were also two hand pumps and an inlet valve for controlling the ballast tanks. Air was supplied whilst on the surface by an intake and exhaust pipe on the conning tower. The idea was to get underneath a ship and with a sort of auger worked from within, attach a mine with a clock-work time fuse to the ship's hull.

On the day before an attack was planned, Ezra was taken ill and so brother David called for a volunteer from the army. A Sergeant Lee—also named Ezra and also from Connecticut—stepped forward. Almost within long cannon shot of the British fleet, which was at that time engaged in the attack on New York, Ezra No.2 was given a crash course in submarinership.

The attack finally took place at ebb tide on an August evening. The *Turtle* was towed down the East River by three canoes until they came in sight of the British fleet, whereupon Sergeant Lee took his place at the controls, battened down the hatch and cast off. He selected as his target the flagship *HMS Eagle* (64), anchored on Diamond Reef at the mouth of the river and, although aided by the ebb tide, it was hard work keeping the wayward craft on course. The run-in to the target was carried out hull down with the conning tower windows just above the surface; although the *Turtle* could dive if detected.

With perfect timing Sgt Lee arrived unseen under the *Eagle's* counter at dusk and slack water. He then flooded his ballast tanks, manoeuvred the *Turtle* under the ship and got to work with the auger. But try as he might he could not penetrate the hull. The reason was that the *Eagle* had only recently been in dock and her bottom re-coppered against the depredations of the toredo worm. For hours he manoeuvred up and down the flagship's bottom trying to find a crack in the copper in which to drive his auger. Yet despite the noise he must have made bumping and boring under the hull in the small hours of the night, no alarm was raised. Eventually short of air and tired out from his all night effort he came to the surface just as dawn was breaking and laboriously cranked his way towards friendly shores. Now in the full light of day, he was spotted from the redoubts of British-held Governor's Island and a boat was sent out to investigate.

When it got within two hundred feet of him, Sgt Lee created a diversion by pulling the lever which freed the mine and started the clockwork fuse. The sight of their quarry dividing into two was enough for the British and suspecting some diabolical Yankee trick they turned tail and raced back to base. In retrospect it was a wise decision because half an hour later, with the gallant Ezra Lee and the British safe ashore, the mine exploded with a great bang and a spout of water.

The Admiral who, but for a thin sheet of copper, might have gone up with it was Lord Howe; and now one hundred and sixty six years later, his namesake was to be attacked, albeit for exercise only, by the modern equivalent of Bushnell's infernal device.

There were already rumours that we had been developing manned torpedoes after the Italians had attacked some of our ships in the Mediterranean with their own version, which they called the Pig. The British 'Chariot' was an improved version of the Pig; one or two of which had been recovered after operations in the Mediterranean. Shaped like a torpedo, powered by electric motors and with a detachable warhead, two men sat astride dressed in diving gear and closed circuit breathing apparatus. The bowman, usually an officer was the pilot and steersman whilst his companion attended to the trim and the handling of the warhead. By all accounts the chariots were nearly as unwieldy to trim and manoeuvre as was the *Turtle* in its day.

Anchored at the extreme end of a lonely Scottish loch[1], *Howe* was surrounded by anti submarine nets as well as torpedo nets directly alongside. Special sentries were posted each night to try and spot the attackers as they in turn tried to get under or through the nets and attach their explosives to our hull.

The loch itself was surrounded by hills towering on every side and was one of the wildest, most restful places to be imagined. Because of the secrecy of the trials our presence was to be kept from the local inhabitants and no shore leave was allowed. Not that there was anywhere to go apart from the nearest village, said to be Inchnadampf, which was some miles away. However anyone in the vicinity who was not actually deaf could hardly miss hearing the bosun's calls, bugles and tannoyed announcements that emanated from the normally silent loch. To cap it all for some reason best known to those in charge it was decided that First and Last Post were to be blown each evening and when Wally and I sounded off in the still night air our bugles seemed to be amplified by the hills. What the highlanders made of the sad notes of Last Post echoing around their hitherto peaceful hills is anyone's guess.

Our stay in this sanctuary from other ships and admirals was marred by an accident among the charioteers. One night as I lay in my hammock there came the sound of much activity alongside on the upper deck. Curious, I hastily slipped on trousers and shirt and went up into the waist where I saw an unmanned chariot made fast alongside. In the light of two torches shadowy figures carried something limp and heavy up the after gangway. I was not supposed to be out of my hammock but I slipped quietly from the waist to stand in the shadow of P4 turret where I could get a better view of the quarterdeck. As they laid their burden on the deck a torch briefly lit up a tableau of four people standing around an inert body. In contrast to the black diving gear and hood the face was white. As the onlookers stood there, water slowly spread from the body smudging the scrubbed deck. I did not wait to see any more and, shivering I ran below to the warmth of my hammock where I tried to get back to sleep. I had seen a dead body before, that of my grandmother when she had been laid out as if just sleeping. But this was something entirely different. The stark reality of sudden death had impinged on my Boy's Own Paper outlook of the war. As I lay in my hammock the image of that white face and the water seeping from the body kept coming between me and the deckhead above me.

Two days later the body was buried at sea, the ceremony taking place from a motor launch. Wally went as well and once more the rugged coast echoed to the sound of Last Post.

It was not long after this incident that the charioteers departed to wage their particularly hazardous brand of warfare, whilst we returned to Scapa to continue our work-up.

Another departure for which I was very sorry was that of Wally. On his eighteenth birthday he had decided to turn over to the ranks. This meant that after seeing the captain he was rated Marine and, when a relief arrived, drafted back to the recruit's depot at Deal to start his marine's training.

Wally's relief was Eric Payne who, in common with all Paynes in the marines was nicknamed 'Whacker'—quite why nobody knew. He had been in the class of buglers just after mine and was, despite being a year older, the junior bugler—I had been in at least three months longer!

Much to my chagrin he took over Wally's action station on the bridge. As he was older and looked it he was assumed to be the senior; but this non-recognition of the true state of things did nothing to boost my ego. My only consolation was that he couldn't take charge of the bridge like Coates and me in the after conning position. But I had the satisfaction of teaching Whacker all the things I had learned from Wally and I regarded myself as quite an old sea-soldier with my three months sea time.

Our working up continued satisfactorily but, as it seemed to me, we swung around our buoy uselessly for inordinately long periods like the other battleships in Scapa Flow.

The reality of our present situation was that our very existence kept the German battleships moored to their buoys in their harbours.

At sea the Atlantic convoys brought food and war weapons into Britain and there were also those we were sending to Russia with much needed war materials. On both routes the ships had to run the gauntlet of the submarine packs and the possibility of German raiders breaking out into the open ocean. Whilst the convoy system covered by escorts lessened the U-boat menace, there were also the powerful German ships lurking in the Baltic ports and the fjords around northern Norway. Had they been able to get out no convoy would have been safe. The fact that there were four modern fast King George V class battleships in the offing did much to deter the Germans raiders from coming out.

Occasionally *Howe* was ordered to be on short notice for departure and I usually got to know fairly quickly when this was happening. Captain Woodhouse would write the order in the confidential Order Book which had to be signed by those required to take action. The book was taken round by the Captain's Messenger, a three-badged Able Seaman called 'Nippy' Knee. Nippy was of course part of the bridge party at sea and so I spent many a watch with him and, when he came through our messdeck with the book under his arm, my hopes would rise.

'What's the buzz, Nippy?'

He would glance around conspiratorially to see no one else was looking and flash the open book at me showing the order to raise steam for whatever notice was required. Usually my hopes were dashed as nothing happened.

As the weeks rolled on I looked forward to the time when *Howe* was fully worked up and operational. I daydreamed about the Germans coming out as they did at Jutland and imagined the Home fleet headed by our sister ships *King George V, Duke of York, Anson* and of course *Howe* ranging against the *Tirpitz, Scharnhorst, Gneisenau, Hipper, Scheer, Deutschland* in a glorious ding-dong battle in the North Sea. Naturally I would play a prominent part somehow, probably emulating Boy Jack Cornwell who won a Victoria Cross at Jutland. I would of course prefer mine not to be posthumous like his.

CHAPTER 8

A Rum Christmas

Christmas 1942 was highlighted not only by Christmas dinner but by an episode stemming from the nefarious activities of a marine that nearly proved fatal to some of the participants.

Amongst the watchkeeping duties carried out by Royal Marines was that of Keyboard Sentry. Situated right aft near the admiral's cabins the main keyboard held the keys to all the important stores and magazines throughout the ship. A twenty-four hour guard was kept and the sentry was responsible for making sure that all keys were signed for and issued to the persons authorised to have them. Extra security was ensured by the fact that no unauthorised person was allowed in the keyboard flat.

Royal Marines have a tradition of trustworthiness but there always is the occasional black sheep, one of which, a marine called Charlie (fictitious name) got in amongst the Keyboard Sentries. He was a burglar in civil life; an occupation that he had quite naturally not thought fit to mention on joining up. As he sat on duty all alone in the small hours of the night it occurred to him that here was an ideal opportunity to keep his occupational hand in, pending his discharge on the world's return to normality. On hand he had the means of entry to all the most important and valuable stores in the ship.

How to go about it was another thing; but Royal Marines, including black sheep, are known for using initiative. He rejected the obvious idea of just taking a key, leaving his post when all was quiet and burgling some store. Nor could he take a key off watch with him because the other sentries would be bound to notice and report it. Even if he forged a signature, the removal of a key in the middle or morning watch was so unusual as to be noticed immediately. But he was not a craftsman in his trade for nothing and, bringing on watch some small files and odd blanks of metal, he whiled away the small hours of the night watches making duplicates of every key he thought might be useful.

With these Charlie could break into places like the Slops Stores and help himself to just one or two items at a time. A pair of socks or a vest or a couple of tins of tobacco would not be immediately missed nor would it cause much of an uproar at stocktaking. In any case the supply branch would get the blame, for who would ever think of the Keyboard Sentry.

Things continued smoothly and without incident until Christmas Day 1942.

As was customary on that day, His Majesty the King expressed his usual wish that the Navy should Splice the Main Brace, which is to say all those entitled to rum should receive an extra tot. Deciding that he and a few friends should honour King George's wishes he fashioned a key for the ready use Rum Store and in the quiet of the Christmas afternoon took a gallon jar of rum, which he shared with a few of his messmates. As the afternoon wore on the marines invited the stokers from the neighbouring messdeck. All might have been well at this point but Charlie's duty as host overcame his normal discretion and as time went on and thirsts increased he went again and again to the store and took altogether thirteen jars. In terms of navy rum that is a lot of alcohol, even allowing for the considerable ability of marines and stokers to imbibe liquor and it was inevitable that the theft should be discovered. Charlie was sober enough to realise this and made some attempt to make it look as if the door had been forced rather than opened with a key. But later in the evening, one of the marine officers, Lieutenant Day, noticed the damage to the door and reported it. A quick round of the messdecks revealed that the lower deck Barracks and the adjoining stoker's messes were in a rather jollier (or more comatose) state than that normally associated with splicing the mainbrace. As a result the lower deck was cleared of marines and stokers, who were mustered on the quarterdeck. Three stokers were missing and after a search were discovered completely unconscious in the middle deck Seaboot and Oilskin Locker. Fortunately they were found in time and their lives were saved by the prompt use of stomach pumps, without which they would certainly have died of alcohol poisoning.

I knew nothing of all this at the time, although I had unwittingly become slightly involved.

After the Christmas Dinner, duly attended by the Marine officers, I had wandered down to the middle deck marines barracks to see how they were doing down there. On looking back I can see that although to all intents and purposes they were pleased to see me there was nevertheless a certain furtiveness about them.

As I sat down on one of the mess stools one of the marines, held out a mug half full of rum.

'Here you are, Sticks,' he said, 'seeing as it's Christmas, have sippers!'

'Oh, thanks,' I replied

'Sippers' means literally to take a sip of rum.

'Go on, have gulpers!'[1]

I looked at him in surprise because gulpers from someone's tot was a very great favour indeed. However I could see that the offer was made because he had already had too much rum and was feeling in a generous mood. I duly took a gulp and next minute, to the amusement of the whole mess, was coughing and spluttering as, like liquid fire, the rum went down my throat.

'Jesus Christ,' I gasped, my voice little more than a hoarse whisper 'That's neaters!'

'Yeah, don't you tell any bastard about it, okay?' one of the other marines chipped in.

'Course I won't,' I replied with tears streaming down my cheeks. I was well under age of course and, although most of the NCOs would have turned a blind eye to someone giving me sippers at Christmas time, one or two including Harris would have put me on a charge had they known.

'Thanks!' I continued 'Haven't had neaters before.'

As I left the messdeck I heard someone say 'You shouldn't have given him it!'

'Oh that's all right. Sticks won't say anything.'

I thought no more about this incident until about twenty to eight that evening, when the pipe was made to "Clear lower deck of Royal Marines and Stokers!". It happened that I was due to go on watch at eight and I asked the sergeant-major if it included me.

He looked at me keenly.

'Do you know anything at all about someone pinching rum?'

'No, Sergeant-major!'

I must have looked quite shocked as the truth dawned on me why the marines in the lower messdeck had been uneasy.

'You are sure?' he persisted.

'Yes, Sergeant-major!' I replied, edging away in case he smelled my breath.

'OK,' he decided, misinterpreting my shocked expression for innocence. 'There's no need for you to attend. Go and get ready for your watch.'

Relieved that I had got off any further interrogation I thankfully prepared for the First Watch.

The final chapter of misdoings did not emerge for some time because other events overtook us. As a result of very good detective work the truth came out about Charlie's keyboard activities. In due course we were mustered on the quarterdeck whilst the warrant was read out giving details of his crime and the punishment awarded. He was given six months in detention and dismissed the service.

Charlie served his sentence and was no doubt delighted to return to his civilian occupation rather sooner than he expected.

After this excitement we settled back into our normal routine; but not for long, because in the dog watches of the 30th December Nippy came through the messdeck with the Order Book. I knew there was no shooting for us the next day.

'What's up, Nippy?'

He showed me the Order Book which said: 'Raise steam on all boilers for immediate notice.

CHAPTER 9

Northern Lights

Cable Parties and Special Sea Dutymen were called at 0530 the following morning and at 0600 *Howe* slipped her moorings and steamed out of Scapa Flow. It was dark and colours had not been hoisted so there was no ceremony or saluting of other ships and as we passed out of the Hoxa Gate we picked up our destroyer escorts and went on our way. We also picked up *King George V* and the cruiser *Bermuda*.

Despite knowing that we were definitely going somewhere the actual destination was still not known. There was however the certainty that it was not an exercise.

At 7 o'clock as usual there was the pipe:

'Hands to breakfast and clean. Rig of the day, Number 3s.'

Then as the messes settled down to breakfast : 'Do y'hear there!' and then a different voice.

'This is the Captain speaking.'

And he told us that a convoy had been attacked by surface vessels and we were on our way to the Arctic.

We were unaware of the details at the time, but the actual reason for our sudden promotion was an attack on a convoy on its way to Murmansk. Made up of fifteen merchant ships, their escort was typical of such convoys, consisting as it did of six destroyers, two corvettes, two armed trawlers and a minesweeper called *Bramble*. Thirty miles to the north of them were the cruisers *Sheffield* and *Jamaica,* whilst in the distance lurked our sister ship *Anson* and the heavy cruiser *Cumberland.*

On the 31st December the convoy was attacked by the heavy German cruiser *Hipper,* the armed ship *Lutzow* and six destroyers. The distant cover was too far away to intervene but like sheepdogs in defence of their flock, the British destroyers and corvettes took up positions between the merchant ships and the raiders, whilst *Sheffield* and *Jamaica* raced to the rescue. The *Hipper* opened fire on the destroyer *Onslow* which sustained heavy damage and casualties as did the *Achates* which went to her assistance. Three other destroyers then engaged the *Hipper,* which, fearing a torpedo attack turned away. Meanwhile *Bramble,* which had previously been despatched to round up some stray merchantmen and was trying to close the convoy, inadvertently came upon the *Hipper* which opened fire, badly damaging her. The German destroyer *Eckholdt* finished her off and sent her to the bottom.

By this time the British cruisers had arrived on the scene and the *Hipper,* coming under fire from them, broke off the engagement and retired, calling on her consorts to follow her. At this point the *Eckholdt* got her come uppance for sinking little *Bramble*. In the middle of a snow squall, she closed on the *Sheffield*, mistaking her for the *Hipper* and was promptly sunk for her pains.

The final outcome was that the convoy was saved with the loss of *Bramble* and the destroyer *Achates*, which finally sank and damage to the other destroyers, particularly *Onslow*.

Besides being the deciding factor in our becoming involved in the Arctic before being properly worked up, the consequences of this comparatively minor action were important. The *Hipper* was damaged to such an extent that she had to return to Germany for repairs and was out of action for some time. The failure of the German ships to make more of this operation infuriated Hitler and ultimately led to the removal of Admiral Raeder, the Commander-in-Chief and the German surface fleet being laid up, for the time being at least.

Although too late for the action we steamed out into the Atlantic in line astern of our sister ship, heading north to the Arctic and into one of the coldest and stormiest assignments of the *Howe*'s service.

As we went the sea colour changed from the grey green of the continental shelf to the blue-green of deeper waters; and the waves became longer making the ship roll slightly in the fresh wind. Noticeably the number of seagulls diminished the further away from land we went. Ever hopeful of a meal from our gash shutes, a very few persevered for about two days not realising that HM ships in wartime only ditched gash once during the dark hours, in order not to leave a convenient trail for U-boats to follow. Usually at some time around four bells in the Dog watches the pipe would be made 'Do ye hear there! The starboard gash shute is now open!' starting a procession of cooks of messes, galley staff and anyone with rubbish to throw over the side to the appropriate shute.

With the German raiders back in harbour our task now was to take over from *Anson* providing heavy ship cover, both for the Russian bound convoy and another of fourteen ships returning to the UK. We were also to stay up north to cover future convoys for that winter.

From about the fourth day on the first trip, while we shadowed the convoy a Focke-Wulff Kondor, the German four engined reconnaissance aircraft, shadowed us. The captain announced over the tannoy that if there was a chance we would have a go at it with fourteen inch shells fitted with time fuses[1]. Meanwhile there was no harm in the Huns knowing that there were now three fast battleships in the area.

U-boats were still on patrol in the North Atlantic and several times during our shadowing duties we had ASDIC (now called SONAR) contact with submarines. A battleship is too cumbersome for offensive action against submarines and carries no depth charges. But it is a large and desirable target for any U-boat captain (which is why we did not sail with the convoys) and so while our destroyer escort attacked with depth charges, *Howe* turned away and fled at full speed. Once or twice investigation proved the contact to be a pod of whales, in those days a common occurrence in the North Atlantic and it was a spectacular sight to see the great backs coming out of the water and to watch the whales blow before they up-tailed and sounded.

Another hazard that appeared regularly were floating mines. Presumably they had broken adrift from the German minefields around the Norwegian coast which were subject to the full force of Atlantic gales. They provided an opportunity for the close range weapons to put in a bit of target practice and for everybody else to watch. But the onlookers were doomed to disappointment if they thought to see anything spectacular because, contrary to expectations, unless hit on the detonator horns they very rarely exploded and, if hit at all, sank most unspectacularly.

After a few days we were within the Arctic circle and as we travelled further north I watched the gradual disappearance of the sun from the sky. There were two things that I had always felt were reliably permanent in life, the first the feel of terra firma underfoot and the second the light and warmth given out by the sun in the heavens for at least some part of the day. We had already lost the first and, as if heralding the end of the world, the sun, when it put in an appearance from behind the dark grey clouds, became progressively weaker and lower on the horizon as if weary of rising into the sky at all. Eventually the only sign of its presence was a lightening of the sky to the south for two or three hours a day and the world became a place of perpetual gloom.

Meanwhile both convoys reached their respective destinations safely at Kola Inlet in Russia and Loch Ewe in Scotland. Apart from the odd Asdic contact and our friend the Focke-Wulffe who kept an eye on us our journey had also been uneventful and we repaired to Iceland.

Iceland is an inhospitable land in winter for visitors and at that time so were the people as far as the British were concerned. Because of the pro-Nazi attitude of the Icelanders and the island's commanding position over the Atlantic and Arctic convoy routes, the British occupied Iceland in 1940. An act that did not exactly endear us to the inhabitants.

The occupation was carried out by 650 Royal Marines with their own field battery and support from a naval howitzer battery. There was no opposition except from the German Consul's wife and daughters who, dressed in their nightgowns, were found frantically burning documents in the consular bath filled with paraffin. An enterprising marine saved most of the secret papers by smothering the fire with the bedclothes from the Consul's double bed.

At that time it was reported that the inhabitants were friendly but the impression was chiefly due to the helpfulness of the British residents. Before we were allowed in Reykjavik in 1943, we were told that they were distinctly unfriendly and such was the case.

On going ashore in the dark winter afternoon it seemed to us that Reykjavik, with its crowded streets and covering of early snow had the superficial air of a small English town open for late night Christmas shopping in pre-war days. The shops were brightly lit and full of goods and food, in sharp contrast to Britain's austerity and that of the European countries occupied and pillaged by those whom the Icelanders admired. Things were expensive and when I paid my one and only visit to the capital, all I could afford to buy was a beautiful Danish pastry, sticky with icing and fruit. It cost me two days pay and was a luxury I could not really afford but I had not seen one before the war let alone since rationing and so I indulged myself.

The girl in the patisserie who served me was about seventeen or so. Fair haired and with a peaches and cream complexion and lips that needed no embellishment with make-up, she was attractive as were most of her sisters. When I asked for what I wanted she looked straight through me as if I was not there. She put the cake in a paper bag, took my money and gave me my change without a word or a smile. It was an interesting experience to be treated as an unwanted invader. There was no contact whatsoever between us and the inhabitants despite the fact that they could nearly all speak and understand English perfectly. If you attempted to talk with or ask a simple question of anyone they would ignore you completely. On the other hand it was different for the Americans despite the fact that they were also an occupying power. The Icelanders' high principle of socially ostracising the invaders was rapidly forgotten when it came to lavish spending Yanks. The US Navy escorted the convoys from the United States to Iceland, bringing with them luxuries from their country in short supply even in Iceland. So whilst the girls totally ignored us they fell over themselves to be seen on an American's arm wearing the price tag for their favours, nylon stockings.

Americans had an unwitting habit of causing at best amusement, or at worst resentment with their luxurious living standards compared with ours. Such was the case when, as a gesture of goodwill it was decided to entertain a few of our allies and show them around the ship.

The main problem was finding suitable refreshments for our guests. There was no fresh food available, our normal menu consisting mainly of whatever the galley staff could make out of such things as corned beef, frozen meat and tinned or dehydrated vegetables.

Under pressure however the victualling staff astounded us all by producing a small quantity of ham which they issued to the galley, with the proviso that it was for the Americans only. Some of our meagre ration of butter was also sacrificed and along with our white bread mounds of ham sandwiches were made.

The band mess was one of those detailed to act as hosts and, having shown the Americans around the ship, the bandsmen brought them back to our messdeck where there were just enough sandwiches available to give to our guests. So whilst we had tea only, professing not to be hungry, we handed round these forbidden and delectable luxuries. On the mess table there were bowls of mustard, that is English mustard. Unfortunately the Americans were more used to their own weaker variety which they spread on their food like jam, and despite our warnings they did the same with ours.

'Jeez, that's real hot mustard!' one of them said to me as he took great gulps of tea.

'Say, Charlie!' he turned to a sailor nearby, 'Try this Limey mustard on your ham. It's real good!'

'Oh, right!' said Charlie helping himself liberally.

To the delight of the first sailor, Charlie turned purple but nevertheless roaring with laughter he turned to his neighbour and told him to try the mustard. As the joke was tried on the unwary, to the vast amusement of those who had been caught, we watched with barely concealed horror whilst, after one bite out of each sandwich the ham was consigned to the gash bucket.

'Shall I get you another sandwich?' I asked Charlie, looking around to see the last one being spread with mustard.

'Hell, no,' he said 'We had ham and eggs for breakfast today, yesterday and probably tomorrow so I guess we get pretty fed up with it anyway!'

When they were finally called to the gangway to catch their boat, Charlie came up to me and shook hands.

'I guess we've had a real swell time,' he said and putting his hand inside his short peajacket he presented me with a package. 'Thanks for showing us round—and for the tea!'

As he walked down the ladder to the boat, I felt a little less resentment at their terrible waste of what was to us a luxury. It showed at least some thought to bring gifts for us in exchange. With a final wave to the Yanks as they sped away I looked down at his gift—Spearmint Flavoured Chewing Tobacco.

The northern weather was unpredictable at this time of the year with high winds and storms interspersed with comparative calm. But even with light winds the ground swell was nearly always high, telling of gales elsewhere in the region. At sea in the next few weeks I was to learn how to interpret the top end of the Beaufort Scale when, together with Convoy JW53 to Russia, we experienced what was deemed afterwards to be the worst weather conditions to hit any of the convoys in the war.

Starting with a strong breeze the wind rapidly climbed through Force 7:

'Sea heaps up and white foam from breaking waves blows in streaks along the direction of the wind. finally mounting to Hurricane Force 12 and off the scale.'

'Exceptionally high waves, wave crests blown into froth, air filled with foam and spray, visibility very seriously affected (small to medium sized ships might be lost to view behind the waves).'

Above Force 12 is not described by Admiral Beaufort but the white horses are whipped off the tops of the waves before they have time to break, the force of the gale actually starts flattening the tops of the waves, whilst the surface becomes covered with a white spume running before the wind.

Long before it reached this stage the pipe had been made to clear all hands off the upper deck and close all upper deck doors and hatches. As we ploughed through the heavy seas, *Howe* staggered as her forecastle buried itself into each successive wave and the green water cascaded over the forward breakwaters, rushing past 'A' and 'B' turrets in a great wall to dash against the superstructure. Every so often the ship's stern juddered as the screws came clear out of the water, threshing the air before submerging again.

As predicted our escorting destroyers were duly lost to view as they played hide and seek in the enormous waves, popping up occasionally as dim shapes seen through the whipped up spray. What life must have been like aboard these small ships in that weather I could not imagine. Whereas the battleships cut through much of the sea the small ships followed the contours of the waves, climbing and dipping some forty or fifty feet.

In our galley cooking became hazardous in the extreme with soup and whole meals cascading over the deck whenever the ship turned broadside on to the wind. After one or two such accidents occurring in the Wardroom galley, the bridge gave warning of sudden course changes. At mealtimes the movement was often enough to send one's plate down the other end of the mess table like the Chaplin film of two people eating the same bowl of soup on a rolling ship.

Answering the calls of nature was quite an ordeal with the heads situated right forward on the main deck. With the ship pitching heavily, sitting on the toilet became at best an uncertain activity. The movement up and down of some thirty feet or more meant that on the downward swoop it was difficult to keep in contact with the seat, experiencing as one did a sensation of near weightlessness; whereas on the upward movement the G force applied clamped one firmly in position. To add to the discomfort of some, at the height of the storm a non-return valve failed with the result that the occupants of the starboard side cubicles found their toilets converted with startling suddenness into bidets. Word got around that this was happening and a number spectators gathered in the heads to witness the phenomenon. Doubtless the unwary victims must have vaguely wondered why there were so many loafers hanging around in the heads until they received their Arctic-cold douche and their ankled trousers filled with water, to the great amusement of the onlookers.

On watch on the bridge everything was dank and cold in the little caboose under the ADP. There was an electric heater on the bulkhead that gave out little heat. The best one could do was to put one's hands on it and get some warmth in them before putting gloves on again. The door was constantly being opened as people went up and down to the chartroom below and so little heat was ever retained. In the background there was the continuous shrieking and moaning of the wind around the superstructure and in the mast stays and halyards, together with the thumps and shudder of the bows burying themselves into the waves.

In the midst of all this turmoil the gale suddenly dropped to Force 1 'light airs' as we went through the centre of this deep depression whilst the sea still ran high with dark lead-coloured clouds overhead. Off duty I went up on deck to stand in the shelter of the after 5.25 turrets to breathe some fresh air. As I watched, the huge waves towering above me when the ship went into the trough in contrast to looking into a watery chasm when the stern rose on the next crest, I saw a flight of birds skimming the water within inches of the surface. They were stormy petrels, an astonishing sight to see these frail little seabirds so far out at sea, yet perfectly at home swooping up and down the sides of the waves. It was hardly to be wondered at that sailors held these little birds in superstitious awe, calling them Mother Carey's chickens.

Then out we came on the other side of the eye and back into the raging winds again. A day later the storm blew itself out leaving us with Carley rafts missing and a whaler stoved in on the boatdeck.

Another series of storms awaited us for our final convoy, RA 53 of some thirty ships homeward bound from Murmansk and the last of that season. Fierce and deadly cold winds swept down from Greenland and the polar ice cap and scattered the convoy giving the U-boats their opportunity. Three ships were torpedoed whilst another foundered in the heavy seas.

A further complication arose when it became known that the battleship *Scharnhorst* had left Gdynia in the Baltic bound for Norway. The Home Fleet was put on immediate notice and our sister ship *Anson* proceeded with all speed from Scapa to Hvalfjord. In case the Germans attempted a breakout into the Atlantic, patrols were restarted in the Faeroes-Iceland passage and the Denmark Strait where, in some 500 fathoms lay the remains of HMS *Hood,* victim of their last foray.

But the weather was ill-suited for surface action by either side and whilst we all stood by, both convoy and *Scharnhorst* studiously ignored each other and went about their separate businesses.

Ice was a particular hazard at this time of year. We encountered quite a lot of pack-ice and one or two large ice-bergs. Spray froze onto the upper works-increasing the weight of the superstructure by many tons. In these conditions ships are in constant danger of capsizing due to the extra weight of the ice and it was noticeable that, as it built up, recovery from a roll got more and more sluggish, even with as large a ship as ours.

Whenever they could, all ships kept working parties busy chipping away at the ice. On the *Howe* the guard rails became about eight inches in diameter and the turrets had to be chipped free before they could move. Working parties could only work at this when the weather moderated because it was too

Howe and County Class Cruiser *Berwick* covering Arctic Convoy JW53, February 1943 *(WM)*

dangerous to be on the upper deck. Anyone going overboard would not have stood a chance for not only would the ship not stop to pick him up in hostile waters but no-one could live for more than three minutes in the Arctic winter sea.

CHAPTER 10

Sea Change

The base for ships involved in the distant cover was Hvalfjord on the north coast of Iceland, not far from Akureyri the second biggest town. Hvalfjord, or 'whale fiord' in English, was surrounded by hills with a background of the larger mountain ranges. The countryside was like most of Iceland, a land of windswept treeless moors, rocks and crags having the same chill attractive beauty as the shop girls of Rekjavik and, as we discovered, those of Akureyri too.

Several times when we were in harbour the marine detachment landed for marches and weapon training and once or twice I went with them.

For these exercises I was issued with a Thompson Sub-Machine Carbine, or to give it its familiar name, a Tommy Gun. It was the same gun as those I had seen in gangster films without the round magazine and was a fairly heavy weapon for me to carry around. It was also pretty inaccurate, which was why nobody else wanted to be lumbered with it. But I was delighted to tote this piece of ironmongery around and actually fire it on the range. I was not allowed to spray bullets around as in the films because the only way to obtain any accuracy at all with the Tommy was to fire single shots, or at most a burst of two rounds. In time I became a fairly good shot with it from the hip at close range.

Another weapon in our armoury was the Boys Anti-Tank Rifle, a large gun with a bolt action like the familiar SMLE and firing a 0.5inch armour piercing round. It had its own built-on bipod and was fired from the prone position. The name comes from the designer of the weapon and did not imply a use by juveniles. Nevertheless it was thought it might be appropriate for me to have a go with it and, goaded on by the marines who had been firing them, I volunteered. The target was roughly fifty yards away and as I lay down Sergeant Aris, who was in charge of proceedings, said: 'Right, now get your shoulder right into the butt and pull it hard into your shoulder.'

The rifle was just a bit longer than me and the butt had a large rubber pad into which I pushed my shoulder as hard as possible.

'With five rounds. Load!'

'Target to your front, range 100 yards! In your own time five rounds, fire!'

It was surprising that Sgt Aris did not give me any other instruction than that, considering that the only rifle I had ever fired before was a little Diana air gun I had when I was small. However a strict parental discipline had taught me about guns and their handling and safety. I had known since I was six that one lay down at an angle to the target, legs apart for steadiness, elbows on the ground, forearms forming a triangle and so on. Seeing that I had taken up the correct position, Sgt Aris assumed that I had fired weapons before.

Wondering what on earth I had let myself in for, I set the range on the sights (100 yards is normal for any distance below that). Taking careful aim I took first pressure on the trigger. All was OK as I took a deep breath, held it and squeezed the trigger. The next instant with my ears ringing from the explosion, I was propelled backwards along the ground for about three feet. What had happened to the bullet I had no idea.

'Dig your toes into the ground!'

Sgt Aris said, taking not the slightest notice of my shocked face and putting his feet firmly behind mine.

'Now try again!'

Using both hands, I worked the bolt back and forth and took aim again. The gun roared and this time instead of going backwards I was half lifted off the ground by the kick.

'Good shot!'

The projectile could have gone anywhere for all I knew, or cared. All I wanted to do was to get my five rounds off and remain in one piece. But after the third round, having got used to the kick and the explosion I actually found I enjoyed the last two shots, despite the fact that my ears rang and my shoulder ached when I finally stood up.

'Well done, Sticks!' One of the marines applauded my performance, as I thankfully reclaimed my Tommy gun from him. 'You can carry the Boys on your other shoulder!'

One particular hazard in the extreme cold that I discovered was the danger of touching metal with bare skin. On one occasion as we returned to Hvalfjord after one of our Arctic outings I was as usual at my station for entering harbour. The main reason for my being in this exposed position was to pay due respects to any flagship we might happen upon. The fact that the nearest admiral was probably six or seven hundred miles away in Scapa Flow had escaped everyone's notice and I had been standing there, strictly at ease without moving feet or hands, for some time. Despite thick underclothes including Arctic type Long Johns, gloves, duffel coat and all else I could reasonably pile on, the cold had begun to seep through and I was longing to get down into the warmth of the messdeck. On coming at last to our anchorage I was told to sound the Extend, which is to say 'Out Booms and Ladders'.

Two bugle calls that were very much alike were the Extend and the Close and I always had to think carefully before blowing either. But my brain was too numb with cold and I managed to start with the Close, change halfway to the Extend and finally stop altogether quite lost as to what I was actually blowing, to the amazement of everyone on the bridge. Fortunately booms and ladders were duly run out in the right places; but as I took my bugle away from my mouth the skin came way with it.

My lips had frozen to the bugle, so I hastily drew attention to the blood on my mouth and the skin left on the mouthpiece as an excuse for my error; but it really had nothing to do with the extraordinary noise that echoed back and forth in the fjord.

Some good did come out of the incident and from then on in these sub-zero temperatures, buglers did not go up on top of the ADP but stayed in the comparative shelter of the lookout positions for entering or leaving harbour. Also instead of wearing our bugles whilst on watch in harbour they were kept in the warmth of the quarterdeck lobby to prevent the same thing happening.

In harbour it was only when high winds were blowing or it was snowing that the cold really became apparent. In the dry cold of very low temperatures conditions were tolerable. Occasionally, when the air was still and there was not a cloud in the sky, the brief daylight seemed quite beautiful. The fishing boats would make their way down Hvalfjord, their bow wave forming a chevron right across the glassy water from shore to shore. Astern they left a white wake and an ascending line of perfect smoke rings from their little funnels Through the still air could be heard the sound of their one-stroke engines, making the noise which gave the tubby little boats their Scandinavian nickname, Tok-a-toks.

Daylight only lasted three or four hours at the most which meant that colours were hoisted at 11.am and sunset was sounded at 1.00 pm. As darkness descended in these cold clear conditions the northern night sky was occasionally lit up by the Aurora Borealis, sometimes like white flashes and searchlights probing the sky, once making me think there was a battle going on over the horizon. At other times it would be like ephemeral curtains of green or red incandescence, sometimes appearing suddenly in full display then almost as abruptly disappearing or at other times building up and fading away gradually.

As the winter wore on the weather grew colder and colder. In Hvalfjord the sea froze. Starting from the innermost inlets the ice crept along until it reached our anchorage. The same thing was probably happening to the German battleships in Norway but, whereas we had the freedom of the sea they were unable to move out without being spotted and chased by us and they became locked in for the winter. Before the same thing happened to us we steamed out of Hvalfjord and made our way back to Scapa Flow. Thankfully we left behind the storms, ice and snow of the Arctic Circle, the bare, barren landscape of Iceland. And the ice maidens, whose frigid hearts could only be melted by nylon stockings.

As the days got lighter and spring advanced routine was broken by the arrival of two visitors. The first was Winston Churchill who, despite having a severe cold, cheered us all up by telling us that he could see the beginning of a silver lining in the dark war clouds. He wore a plain yachting cap as well as the one-piece rig like an overall known as a siren suit.

The second visitor was the King who inspected us at Divisions with a large entourage of gold braid following in his wake.

Then in early May a buzz started that something was happening. As we sat at dinner one day, one of the musicians said he had heard from a Marine on the victualling party that they had been bringing kegs of lime juice aboard that morning.

'Well, so what?' I asked

'Limers[1] is issued to everyone in the tropics. It keeps your blood cool,' was the reply supplied by Pete Medcalfe.

'Do you think we're going foreign then?'

'Can't see any other reason for getting limers on board,' said Bill Tribe.

'I expect they'll start putting bromide in the soup soon,' he continued. 'You'll see, one day you'll notice a funny taste and that'll be what it is!'

Bill was the band drummer and a very good one at that. He was also a great joker. When I first arrived on board he said that he had only just taken up drumming and perhaps I could give him a few tips. With the knowledge gained by my four months training I was all set to teach him everything I knew, until I saw him performing not only with the military band but also in the dance band and orchestra. He could make a drum speak as I would never be able to. So I never really knew when Bill was serious and I did not know how to take this latest piece of information.

'Why do they do that?'

'Oh, never you mind!' he replied vaguely, which appeared to amuse the rest of the mess.

Nobody would enlighten me as to what he was talking about so I had to ask one of the bosun's mates when I was next on watch.

'It stops you getting a hard on!' he replied 'The heat in the tropics makes people very randy!'

'Especially the women,' he added ruminatively.

Shortly after, events started to take shape and we went down to Rosyth dockyard for a minor refit and also five days leave.

My parents were still in Birmingham but had moved to King's Norton. Due to my father changing jobs in Air Raid Precautions (Civil Defence) and later with the Ministry of Home Security about the only reliable feature of my home leaves throughout the war was a different house to go to each time.

The new house had a large garden with a vegetable patch which my father was busy cultivating. Like many others his enthusiasm for gardening had started when the nation was adjured to 'Dig for Victory'. As there was a pond in the garden my parents had bought some ducklings as a further boost to the food output. Unfortunately what they did not realise was that this particular type, Khaki Campbells, were bred more as land birds and were prone to get cramp and drown if allowed in the water. After the loss of the first batch the next lot were kept in a chicken coop away from the water. Even so instinct overcame breeding occasionally and when they escaped their confinement, the whole family rushed down to the pond where they were recaptured with the aid of my small sister's fishing net.

Another problem was the rabbits from the neighbouring fields that came in by way of some holes in a dilapidated fence. It seemed to me that as they were getting fat on our produce they could also supplement our diet if we could catch them.

Neither my father nor I really had any idea about making snares (or setting wires, the proper term that I learnt many years later from a poaching friend) but after one or two experiments I found that the best materials were brass picture wire I found in the garage and some two foot iron rods as pegs.

The overall result of my bid for supplementary food was an indignant cat from next door and a very large hedgehog. Apart from having lost a little fur around its neck the cat showed no signs of being any the worse for its experience, indeed it was positively grateful for being released.

The hedgehog had a bit of a rub around its middle and so was taken in and treated with Germolene on the parts that could be reached. After a bowl of bread and milk it seemed to be none the worse for its experience. In time he became very tame and would wander into the kitchen in the evenings for a meal. Trapping for food was abandoned after this in favour of blocking up the holes in the fence.

My parents were obviously aware that *Howe* was off to foreign parts—why else the five days leave—but I could not tell them where because I did not know myself. Nor could I have written and told them when once we knew because censorship was very strict and all our letters were posted unsealed to be read by a duty officer before leaving the ship. Sometimes bits were cut out that seemed to me to be quite unnecessary. I once happened to mention in passing that I got soaked to the skin in the rain when I was on watch because I had left my oilskins below. This was struck out of the letter because it mentioned weather conditions. That it happened about a week or so beforehand, that rain is a universal phenomenon and that the ship could have been anywhere in the world did not come into it. Anything relating to general conditions on board, climate, anybody else leaving or joining the ship or a host of other things that might be considered of use to the enemy were taboo. It goes without saying that ship's movements were also forbidden territory. Generally this information was kept secret for some time, probably until enemy intelligence had found out anyway or when it was released for propaganda purposes.

All in all it left a poor letter writer such as myself very little to write about so, in order to keep them informed of my general whereabouts I arranged a simple code with my parents. It consisted of varying the endings of my letters, normally a down to earth 'Love from Robin'. 'With love from' would indicate somewhere west of Suez (Mediterranean most likely), 'from your affectionate son' would be east of Suez (Indian or Pacific Oceans) and finally 'with love from your affectionate son' would mean that we were coming home.

On returning to Rosyth we found that victualling went on apace and we were ammunitioned and fuel led for what looked like a long trip. There were also forty more Oerlikons, 20mm close range anti-aircraft weapons, that had been brought on board.

We sailed from Rosyth expectantly, eagerly anticipating the announcement telling us where we were going, to find ourselves disappointingly back again at Scapa Flow. But about a week later, Nippy Knee came through the messdeck with the Order Book showing 'Raise steam on all boilers for 0600 hours'.

Once again we set off but this time as we got out into the Atlantic we turned south and on hearing the captain's announcement I wrote a letter home ending 'with love from Robin'.

CHAPTER 11

Mediterranean Episodes

The journey to Gibraltar was a gradual transition from the grey dreariness of Scapa Flow through the Atlantic with the weather getting warmer and warmer as we progressed south. Like most of the wartime passages undertaken by ships we kept as far as possible away from land. This meant going out into the Atlantic to avoid not only being spotted from land but also avoidance of the usual convoy routes which would be patrolled regularly by German aircraft and submarines. It was a pleasant break and with the fresh breezes it seemed that cobwebs were being blown away from the mind with the promise of new experiences to come. I had last been this way when I was six years old, coming back from India with my parents in the luxury of a P&O liner, with quoits and deck chairs and fancy dress parties. A special treat was to be allowed by the steward to beat the dinner gong at lunch time. Now I blew 'Cooks to the Galley' and 'Rum Call' for the same purpose.

We had actually left the UK with such haste that there had been no time for the dockyard to mount our new guns and, as we journeyed south the shipwrights and carpenters were busy installing the Oerlikons on the upper deck and in the upper works.

I looked forward with great anticipation to the first sight of Gibraltar partly because it was my birth place and after two days I began to wonder how far we had travelled and where we were at that stage of our journey.

On the third day as I reported for the forenoon watch on the bridge I saw Nippy Knee gazing over the side by the port lookouts so I went over and joined him. It was a bright morning, the sun was high in the sky and the sea reflected its deep blue.

Most old sailors could hazard a good guess as to where they were in the world by the colour of the water combined with the types of waves and the weather. The colour of the sea is affected by the depth of water but of course allowance has to be made for the reflections from cloud cover. The size of the swell depends on the 'fetch' or distance the wind has to build up the wave height. Their behaviour and pattern are also affected by the proximity of land as they are reflected back off the coast. Nippy, with his three badges and Blue Peter had been at sea for most of his eighteen years service so he would know.

'Where are we now, Nippy?'

'Seventy five miles north of the Azores, on course West by South.'

'Seventy five miles?' I was astounded that he could be that accurate. 'How on earth can you tell that?'

'Easy, I've just been in the chartroom!'

It was during the course of bridge watchkeeping hours that I heard about the places we were likely to be visiting. In the small hours of the Middle and Morning Watches I listened to Scottie, the Bosun's Mate, Nippy Knee and the rest talking about the attractions of Gibraltar, as well as Malta, Algiers and Alexandria.

Because of the small size of the Rock, the war and large garrison there did not appear to be very much to do on Gibraltar, The main attraction on Gibraltar was the Trocadero, a bar on Main Street where one could get a drink and be entertained by flamenco dancing. Occasionally when the American navy was in port fights broke out in the 'Troc' and elsewhere but even this diversion was short lived due to the Naval patrols of both countries that wandered the few streets of the town. One or two of my companions had been involved in the past and advised me to get out fast if a fight developed with the Yanks. It was not so much the fighting that I was to avoid but the enthusiastic use the US Navy patrols made of their nightsticks on both participants and bystanders alike when restoring order.

On my first run ashore I inevitably ended up at the Trocadero, having persuaded Scottie to take me with him.

The room was about thirty foot long with a bar on one side and a few too many tables crammed onto the floor space. In one corner there was a couple of guitarists on a small dais who seemed to be more interested in chatting and drinking than entertaining the clientele. Drinks were ordered via the waiters who, of course expected a tip, which made drinking much more expensive and cut my choice down to one glass of cheap red wine.

There were several of our ship's company seated around the room.

'Hullo, Sticks! Enjoying yourself?'

I turned to the next table to find one of the Marines, Jerry Maile, grinning at me. With him was another Marine, Barney Marshall, who gazed cheerfully at me with slightly unfocussed eyes, looking for all the world as if he was going to burst into one of his songs—he always spent hours in the bathroom singing away whilst doing his dhobi-ing.

'Just having a wet,' I replied casually, trying to look as if I were used to this sort of life.

'You be careful. A sniff of the barman's apron and you'll be pissed!'

Despite this insult I was determined that I should see all that there was to see and waited patiently, sipping my wine slowly not only to make it last as long as possible but because it tasted like watered down vinegar.

After we had been there for about half an hour, the guitarists put aside their drinks and strummed one or two chords, whilst from under the dais on which they sat a small stage was pulled out, displacing the nearest table and its occupants. From a door at the back came two dancers dressed in flouncy red and orange dresses. One was small fair and somewhat podgy and the other about a head taller, dark, middle-aged and thin. To cheers from the audience they mounted the stage and stood for a moment poised with castanets in hand and disdainful looks on their faces before starting on what appeared to be a frenzied attack with their feet on the woodwork of the little stage. As this was my first experience of flamenco I was not sure what to expect but it was patently obvious that these two were not top flight practitioners in whatever they were doing. Nor did they have sufficient room in which to do it for as the thin one gyrated in one direction the plump one bumped into her going the other way nearly knocking her off the stage. Cheered on by the audience the thin one elbowed the other to her own side of the stage whilst both continued their stamping and clattering of castanets. They next turned their backs and promptly reversed into each other to more cheers and shouts of 'Ole' from the aficionados. Their haughty looks had now changed to anger as they glared alternately at the each other and the audience. The guitarists meanwhile were having a little race on their own to see who could finish first and gradually the tempo got faster and faster with the dancers trying to catch up. At one time the thin dancer lost one of her castanets when the string broke. As it clattered to the floor the plump one gave a smirk of triumph as she continued to fire on all four castanets whilst the thin one could only operate with her right hand. With a final flourish and pose the girls hurried off the stage, chattering at each other, to the accompaniment of laughter and cheers from the audience.

Our stay in Gib was only brief, for which I was glad because after two or three runs ashore there was not much left to do. I had seen the apes and climbed to the top on about the only day when the Rock was not crowned with a fluffy cloud, often the only one in sight from horizon to horizon. It was a depressing place in wartime with its blackout (in contrast to brightly lit Algeciras across the bay in neutral Spain). All night from the harbour came the sound of explosions as patrol boats dropped small charges to deter the Italian charioteers who had already tried to penetrate the harbour. Excitement was provided one day by a red air raid warning. *Howe* was guard ship and was fully manned for such eventualities. For the first time I was called upon to sound off Repel Aircraft for the real thing and having done so, I raced up to my action station, eager to experience my first action and to see *Howe* fire her guns in anger. The result was anticlimactic and ignominious to say the least. A solitary German reconnaissance plane came over and, together with the Rock's anti-aircraft batteries, *Howe*'s 5.25s opened up. But in their eagerness the gun's crews apparently did not set the fuses with the result that our fine barrage splashed harmlessly into the sea. Captain Woodhouse was ashore at the time and was not well pleased when he returned aboard.

Not long after this incident we left Gib without our partner *King George V* which went elsewhere. In fact we seldom seemed to be together in the same port for very long all the time we were in the Mediterranean.

As we sailed further east it got warmer and it became very apparent that *Howe* was not a ship built for hotter climates. Even at sea when there were fresh breezes, below decks it became unpleasantly hot.

Numbers of people started coming out in heat rashes, the worst of which was dhobi rash. This usually appeared around the genital area as a raw rash so irritating that it could drive grown men to tears. Very little will relieve it except perhaps some cooling type of ointment like calamine lotion which was not carried in our sick bay. The two most common ointments for external use in the navy seemed to be gentian violet or Whitfield's ointment. Gentian violet was usually used on dhobi rash, as well as other skin complaints such as scabies and impetigo and the sufferer would be painted a bright violet. Whether the colour had anything to do with the cure or, because the last two complaints were contagious, it acted as a visual leper's bell was debatable.

As we left Gibraltar I was afflicted with a small spot on my chin rather like a gnat bite. At first I took no notice of it but within two days it formed a weeping scab that began to spread until it was about the size of a fifty pence piece. Realising that it was impetigo I was determined that I would not be painted violet nor, if it got any worse, suffer the indignity of being confined to the CDA (Contagious Diseases Act) mess. Known as 'Rose Cottage' it more commonly housed people with venereal diseases. So I went to the bathroom where I scraped the scab off and liberally plastered the area with Germolene. Amazingly, it had more or less cleared up the next day leaving only a small area of pink skin.

In England dawn is a leisurely progress from dark to light as the sun sidles along the horizon in its ascent of the sky, whereas nearer the tropics it comes straight up over the earth's edge, heating the air in a few minutes. The ship never really cooled down at night having been heated during the previous day by the sun and her engines, generators and other machinery. But there was a time just prior to sunrise when the temperature was at its most bearable. On the upper deck, when the movement of the ship or the proximity of land produced a breeze, for a brief moment one had the sensuous luxury of actually shivering, before the sun leapt into the sky to banish the breeze, disperse the mist and scorch the air.

It was at such a moment in the morning watch when mist still shrouded the seascape that we first arrived off Algiers.

Poor visibility could not disguise the fact that we were where we were. As I stood on the after bridge with shirt sleeves rolled down over goose-pimpled arms, my nose was assailed with a mixture of French cigarettes, camel dung fires, perfume, fuel oil and maybe stale humans, brought out to sea on the land breeze and bringing to mind as nothing has ever done before or since, the phrase used by so many who do not know what they are talking about: 'This place smells like a brothel!'.

Then as the sun rimmed over the horizon, drawing away the veil of thin mist covering the glassy sea I caught my first glimpse of the fabled city of bars and licensed prostitution.

From the jetty at which we berthed the town spread out and upwards to the hills, with the European town in the foreground but dominated by the white squat buildings of the Arab quarter and the casbah on the hills beyond. The word casbah means a fort and it was in fact a walled Arab city. It was out of bounds to all allied service personnel. Not that we needed any warning about the dangers of entering it. One had heard of the famous casbah in Morocco, on film at least the romantic haunt of Charles Boyer who invited maidens to 'Come with me to the Casbah!' and where tourists seem to be quite safe as they wandered around the souks. The Algerian Casbah was an entirely different kettle of fish where Europeans did not enter unless either completely foolish or accompanied by an armed guard. The chances of coming out unharmed were very slim.

Berthed on the other side of the jetty from us was an old French light cruiser called *Le Terrible,* a name that aptly described her appearance. The contrast between her and *Howe* was startling, with the latter's clean paintwork, gleaming white decks with all lines cheesed down, gangways with canvas scrubbed white and guardrails decorated with turk's heads. Even after a spell in the hands of the dockyard our ship could not have got so dirty. It was a thought provoking sight to those of us who had become so frustrated with the neverending cleaning and polishing, to see what a ship would look like without it.

The Frenchmen were intrigued by our cleanliness and our early morning routine of scrubbing decks, an activity they obviously had not thought of judging by their own decks and the way they lined the side. They watched this spectacle at first with amazement then amusement as not only the quarterdeckmen who were doing the work but we of the quarterdeck watch discarded our shoes and socks whilst the hoses sluiced the cool salt water around our feet. We bore their smirks and comments for some time until one of the quarterdeckmen could stand it no longer.

'Yer frog-eatin' bastards!' he shouted, waving a broom at the watchers 'You could do with a few of these to get the shit off your crap heap!'

Both the French deck officer and our own could not have failed to hear his comment and the look on the French officer's face showed that he understood English. He glared at our Officer of the Watch as if expecting some action on his part to punish the offender. The Officer of the Watch, wise man, after a reciprocal stare at his opposite number, tucked his telescope under his left arm and strolled, with his hands behind his back, to the opposite side of the quarterdeck.

The other side of the jetty was often occupied by one or the other of our allies whilst we were in Algiers and occasionally with one of our own. The most intriguing was an American ship, the USS *Ancon.* She was an Assault Headquarters Ship and had numbers of landing craft along her sides, which seemed to indicate what was forthcoming. Unlike *Howe* with her camouflage *Ancon* was painted the uniform grey of the American navy. As she came alongside and I sounded off the Alert, she responded to my surprise with the same four notes heard from some American car horns.

'ATTENTION PORT SIDE!' boomed a bored voice in response to our more restrained 'Attention on the upper deck, starboard side!'

Everything *Ancon* piped over her tannoy was at least ten times as loud as anything we could produce and the informality of all their announcements and orders was further embellished by one or more of the quartermasters having a Brooklyn accent. We were all delighted to hear:

'Liberty guys muster abaft the after smokestack!'

American naval officers appeared to drink quite a lot of coffee, possibly because their ships were 'dry' and on many occasions the pipe was heard:

'De guy dat makes the awficer's cawffee, lay aft!'

Once again the striking differences between their ideas of hardship and ours was highlighted when we talked to the Yanks ashore. Like us they complained about the food they had to put up with on board.

At that time we were very restricted in the variety and amount of food available as supplies were only just then becoming more plentiful in the Mediterranean. Despite a small amount of frozen beef that we acquired (reputedly having been in store for two years) we had been living off tinned meats made into fritters, hash or stew accompanied by dehydrated vegetables. The worst thing of all was the dehydrated potato, which unlike the later powdered variety was grated and dried. When boiled up it became a glutinous mass like wallpaper paste.

As an alternative boiled macaroni was tried, which on the face of it sounds reasonable. Unfortunately our flour stores were infested with weevils at the time so one either had to eat without looking too closely, blow though each little tube individually to get rid of the insects, or go without. Our bread and even the navy's old stand-by, currant duff, not the greatest pudding in hot climates, contained small crunchy insects despite the flour being sifted.

Meanwhile the Americans, in commiserating with us complained that they too had their problems, what with chicken three times in a week, shortage of maple syrup for their waffles and only chocolate or vanilla ice cream.

As far as most of the ship's company were concerned a run ashore in Algiers was like any other foreign port and consisted of much the same thing. Probably the order of priority was first a bar for a drink, sometimes many never getting beyond that, secondly female company. Food came a very poor third due to the innate conservatism of the British serviceman. Foreign muck was definitely out and only English type food would do. In our middle watch discussions the only place mentioned for food was the Fleet Club in Alexandria where one could get chicken, egg and chips. In normal times, Valetta and the Gut, or Straight Street to give it its proper name, was a good place for the satisfaction of diverse appetites but since the siege, drink and food at least were in desperately short supply. Algiers had the drink and females but even with our restricted diet nobody would try the food.

As far as sampling all the delights of Algiers were concerned the constraints applying to me were neither moral nor the dire warnings given us about the evils of drink and loose women. Indulgence was limited only by a pay scale of a shilling a day.

On my first run ashore, once again with Scottie as my mentor, we went to one of the nearest bars and sat at a pavement table drinking Muscatel; a sweet wine much more to my taste than the dreadful vinegar of the Trocadero.

As we sat there in the warm sun we discussed what to do.

'Tell you what,' Scottie said 'Let's go to one of the bag-shanties.'

'Which one?' I asked.

'Any of 'em. There's the Black Cat, the Sphinx, the Half Moon, the New Moon, Number Twenty-Two—' like the old hand he was, Scottie rattled off the names of all the licensed brothels in town.

'I haven't got any money, though,' I objected.

'That's all right we'll only have a shooftie! Come on, the Sphinx is just up the road.'

My excuse of not having sufficient money, whilst wholly true was also a cover for vague misgivings about going to a brothel. However at this stage I thought there would be no harm in just looking, so I followed Scottie to a large house with open double doors through which we passed.

Inside was a wide hallway with a staircase facing the door leading up to the first floor. On the left of the entrance crouched a sphinx, twice life-size, from which the establishment took its name. Like the original in Egypt the inscrutable expression gazed with a lofty indifference over the heads of those passing beneath. But where there was a beard flowing on to the chest in the Egyptian version, here were aggressively jutting pink-nippled breasts. Together with the expression, they seemed concentrated on some distant point on the horizon. To the right a cashier's desk stood in which presided a large middle-aged woman who was busy taking money from a queue of American, French and British servicemen. She was what the Americans politely called the Madam, which is to say the owner or manager of the establishment. More down to earth but cumbersome, the British sailor's term was 'Mother-Judge-of-Pricks'.

As prospective clients we were quite entitled to view the goods before purchase and so Scottie and I climbed the stairs and walked around to have a look at the girls. There were probably about ten or so rooms along the landing and corridor. Open doors proclaimed that the occupants were at that moment disengaged whilst behind closed doors the occupants were busy. I found this out when I inadvertently opened a door, to be greeted by an indignant yell from the uppermost naked figure on the bed. Hurriedly shutting the door, I realised that the only reason I knew he was an American sailor was because he still had his hat on.

Having made our tour of inspection, we went downstairs again.

'See that blonde at the top of the stairs?' Scottie asked. 'I rather fancy her. Which one did you like?'

'Oh, I don't know,' I answered evasively.

'Well, you must have fancied one of them!'

'Yes, well,' I replied, trying to act like an old hand 'I liked the small ginger one in the last room. I could go her.'

She did look quite nice and also seemed to be nearer my age than the others.

'Well, I'm going to have a go,' Scottie announced as he got the money out of his wallet. 'How about you?'

'I can't, I'm broke!'

Scottie looked at me and at the money in his hand. 'Here you are! Pay me back next payday!'

My jaw dropped as he thrust the money into my hand.

'But I—'

'Oh yeah', and here's one of these!' he interrupted, putting a pusser's issue condom on top of the notes. 'Come on!'

He turned away to the cash desk leaving me gaping after him.

'I'll just go and see if she's still free!' I called out. Being thrown into this sort of situation at the age of fifteen needed a bit of mental preparation. There was a vast difference between this and exploratory fumblings in Milton Park.

I wandered up the stairs along the corridor to see the door still open. She was sitting in a chair beside the bed, filing her nails.

'Ullo, Darleeng!' she said invitingly.

I looked at her and at the bed and hurried back downstairs, passing Scottie on the way up.

'She free?' he asked

'Yes,' I replied 'just going to pay the Mother-Judge!'

About twenty minutes later I met Scottie in the hallway.

'OK then?' he asked

'Fine,' I replied

'What was she like?'

'Oh pretty good. How about yours?

'Not bad,' he replied, thoughtfully. 'Bit like throwing a banana up an alley, though.'

'Yeah, that's what I thought,' I agreed, not quite getting what he meant.

As we walked out of the door I felt the sphinx's stare on the back of my neck and, putting my hand in my pocket, touched the fold of money and the condom. Next payday I'd give Scottie his money back; but not the condom, otherwise he might suspect!

After a week or so in Algiers we sailed again, this time west along the coast to Mers-el-Kebir, the port of Oran. Mers-el-Kebir consisted of a large harbour protected by a long mole to seaward to which we made fast. On the inner wall of the mole facing the town a huge message was written: 'Un seul but la victoire', the words of General Giraud who was the Free French commander in North Africa. It was put up as a boost to French morale after the capture of the Vichy held naval base in 1940. As a result of the bombardment by British ships and the casualties caused there were obviously people who were resentful over this affair. Ruffled feelings had still, in 1943, to be smoothed over and to play our part we staged a parade and a Beating the Retreat ceremony in Oran in conjunction with the French civil and naval authorities. The finale was held in the town square in front of the Hotel de Ville, and as *Howe*'s Royal Marine detachment presented arms, the French, British and American flags were hauled down. There is no doubt it is a moving ceremony but I was still surprised to see so many French people in tears as, with the sun getting low on the horizon the flags were lowered whilst Whacker Payne and I played Sunset accompanied by the band.

We continued our seemingly aimless wandering around the Mediterranean with a visit to Alexandria, where Scottie was able to indulge himself with chicken, eggs and chips at the Fleet Club. At the same time I went with some of the boy seamen for an organised three days leave in Cairo. We stayed at a hotel and were taken on various outings around the city. One of these was naturally to Gizeh where we climbed Cheops' pyramid and saw the other Sphinx.

Cairo was full of servicemen, hoards of beggars and small shoe-shine boys offering various services. They were particularly persistent and had an ingenious method of drumming up business. Whilst you were not looking they would throw dog or camel dung at your shoes and then offer to clean them. Others offered a shoe-shine or their sister, both purporting to be 'verree hygienic!'

On our next call at Algiers there was a different ship next to us, the USS *Savannah,* an American cruiser; and her stay coincided with a visit from the King. Once again he seemed to arrive on the scene when things were about to happen for us, although in fact his visit was in the aftermath of the German surrender in North Africa.

For security reasons he had flown out under the name of his Guardsman batman, T. Jerram and landed in Algiers on the 12th June.

Both King George and Queen Elizabeth commanded a tremendous respect not only from the British but from our allies too. They were closely involved with the people throughout the war and genuinely set a great example to everyone.

Everywhere he went on his North African tour the King was greeted with enthusiasm. He paid an unscheduled visit to a large convalescent centre by the sea, where thousands of British soldiers were recuperating from wounds or illness. As word got around that the King had arrived, the men raced to greet him, crowding around him, laughing and cheering; many of them dashing out of the water to be among the first to shake his hand. In the midst of this someone started singing the national anthem, which was taken up by everyone with genuine fervour and emotion. When it had finished the cheering just went on and on.

Despite all the spit and polish and hoo-ha surrounding his visit to *Howe* we too were pleased to see him again.

Afterwards he crossed over the jetty to visit the *Savannah* and as he left, instead of three cheers, the Americans shouted in unison 'The King! The King ! The King!' A remarkable display of respect from another people.

As with all the other Mediterranean seaports there was a great deal of activity and build up of shipping going on in Algiers, which gave one a feeling that Winston Churchill's words about 'light at the end of the tunnel' were true. Since the surrender of German forces at Cape Bon in North Africa, just a week before we had arrived in Gibraltar, there seemed generally to be more of a sense that we were now shaping events rather than being overtaken by them.

Things started reaching a climax as June gave way to July. We were in Algiers at that time with the *Ancon* on the other side of the jetty. Around the ship and indeed the whole harbour there was an air of expectancy. No-one, not even the enemy, could doubt that we were going to take part in the next phase of the war, an invasion of Europe itself. The burning question was where? It could be anywhere from the south coast of France through Sardinia, Sicily, Italy or Greece. However anyone in *Howe* who could know anything was saying nothing and the less people knew the more knowing and mysterious they were. During one quiet afternoon watch on the quarterdeck, when I asked the Officer of the Watch about all the activity going on, he told me sternly he could see nothing unusual and firmly discouraged any further enquiries. Even Nippy Knee assumed an air of mystery when asked for the latest buzz. But despite authority's blind eye, oilers sidled up to ships to refuel them; and stores and ammunition barges went alongside anyone requiring them. At the gangway we manned the side for the pre-occupied comings and goings of the Captain, the Navigating Officer and others such as the Captain's Secretary carrying confidential books, complete in weighted bags in case they had to be thrown over the side if the ship sank.

There appeared on deck floats made of wood with metal buoyancy tanks. Each carried a rocket with yards of slow burning fuse and, although they were lashed down on the quarterdeck in places where we could hardly avoid falling over them, they remained firmly unacknowledged by anyone approached on the subject.

If there were spies in Algiers they too could not have avoided tripping over the obvious signs of activity and would doubtless have been busily reporting to their various controls. What they made of Noel Coward coming on board in the midst of all this activity, I could not guess. On a quiet afternoon he seemed to suddenly appear on the gangway, dressed, looking and deporting himself so much like Noel Coward with that disdainful expression. It was only when he arrived on deck in our midst and after several double-takes from the officer of the watch that he was ushered with great circumspection to the Captain's cabin. Having seen him in the film 'In Which We Serve', the quartermaster wondered if we were going to be in a film but the corporal of the gangway said that he was probably taking over command of the ship and the war was as good as won.

Then one day things began to happen.

On board *Ancon* it was noticed that, instead of liberty guys mustering abaft the after smokestack, wisps of smoke appeared from it and its forward counterpart. The following morning, to the accompaniment of shrill piping and dipping of flags from all the other ships, and my bugled salute alerting the whole of Algiers, she sailed out to sea together with a number of other ships, to the sorrow of all the brothels, bars and other places of entertainment in the town. Their disappointment was tempered to a certain extent by the almost immediate arrival of *King George V*, but even that was short lived for two days later, on the 9th July, both *Howe* and she cast off and with six attendant destroyers we made our way out to sea, leaving the harbour almost empty of warships.

CHAPTER 12

Operation Husky

As far as we were concerned everything pointed to the fact that this was the big operation. The day before, Nippy's order book had required steam to be raised on all boilers for the morning so it could not be an emergency. There was also a purposeful air in the way we were bowling along faster than our usual economical steaming speed.

Our suspicions were confirmed when, after we had been at sea for about four hours, the Captain announced that in the early hours of the following morning, British, Canadian and American troops would be landing on the south coast of Sicily. Together with *King George V* and the destroyers our job was to protect the western flank of the landings from possible intervention by the Italian fleet. Being the fastest battleships, we were also acting as a reserve and a diversionary squadron. On the eastern flank and nearer to the Italian mainland was the remainder of Force 'H' consisting of the battleships *Rodney, Nelson, Warspite* and *Valiant,* the fleet carriers *Indomitable* and *Formidable,* six light cruisers and eighteen destroyers. Detached as we were from the others, we were known as Force 'Z'—a strange choice considering the fate of *Repulse* and our sister ship *Prince of Wales.,* the last Force 'Z'.

All the ships taking part received a signal from Admiral of the Fleet Sir Andrew Cunningham who was in overall command:

'Our primary duty is to place this vast expedition ashore in the minimum time and subsequently to maintain our military and air forces as they drive relentlessly forward into enemy territory. In the light of this duty great risks must be and are to be accepted.'

Operation Husky was, as Admiral Cunningham said, a vast expedition, consisting as it did of a total of 3,226 craft of all types from battleship to motor torpedo boat and landing craft. What he had not said and what was not immediately apparent to us was the precision with which the whole operation was timed. Many ships including troop carriers and supply ships had to come from Britain. Some ships were faster than others and so they were divided into fast and slow convoys. Thus there were ships setting off at different times from British and Mediterranean ports to arrive as and when they were wanted at the beach heads for the initial landings and afterwards.

At ten o'clock on that Friday night as we steamed to our destination, allied troops were being landed by glider behind enemy lines followed quickly by paratroops. Their job was to seize special objectives and capture the coastal defences from the rear. Four and a half hours later, at 2.30 on the morning of

Saturday 10 July, the main seaborne landings of 60,000 troops started on the south-east corner of Sicily, to face an estimated total of 400,000 enemy troops on the island.

The Germans and Italians were taken by surprise, having expected that the Allies would come from the North African ports of Bizerta and Tunis and land in the west, with the result that the actual landings achieved their immediate objectives in a remarkably short time.

By 5 am complete air superiority had been established, all the beach heads along a seventy mile stretch of coast were secured and the allies were advancing into the interior.

Meanwhile, as we patrolled the western basin there were one or two alarms when unidentified targets appeared on radar. The first occurred on the Saturday, a typical sunny Mediterranean day. I was standing on the after bridge talking to the bosun's mate when the Navigating Officer called from the compass platform

'Drummer, sound off Quarters!'

For a moment I had no idea what he meant, as we were not taught any call by that specific name. It could not be Evening Quarters nor could it be Quarters Clean Guns. Fortunately I remembered having read of the drummers 'beating to quarters' in the days of Nelson and I realised that he could only mean Action Stations.

As I sounded off, the drama of the moment was heightened by the ship increasing to full speed. When Whacker relieved me on the bridge I had quite a way to go to the after conning position and, as I climbed the ladder to the platform the whole funnel was shaking with the speed. As usual I was ever hopeful of seeing some real action but was once again doomed to disappointment as the radar contact turned out to be a group of our own MTBs returning from some mission.

On the Monday (12 July) it was decided that we should carry out a bombardment on the west side of Sicily, for which operation we were joined by the cruisers *Dido* and *Sirius*. The enemy had already thought that we were going to land there and the object was to simulate landings so that troops would be kept in that area.

We went to action stations about an hour before arriving on the scene and, as I stood on the catwalk of the after conning position, I could see signs of activity on the horizon as the Royal Air Force carried out a heavy raid on the towns of Trapani and Marsala on the mainland and Favignana on the nearby island of Levanzo. We were timed to commence firing immediately after the RAF had finished and as we got nearer searchlights probed the sky over Trapani. Airbursts of AA fire twinkled over the town where I could see flashes of exploding bombs and the glow of fires.

The night was still and fairly calm as we glided into position, the sounds of our movement through the water overlaid by the distant rumble from the targets. Ahead of us I could just make out the loom of *Kind George V* whilst further inshore the cruisers moved unseen.

As Trapani crept steadily from our starboard bow onto the beam, the bombers ceased their work and turned for home. Out of the corner of my eye I saw the guns of Y turret swing outboard onto the target. At that moment I suddenly realised that they would probably be firing full broadsides rather than salvoes and, deciding that discretion was the better part of valour I hurriedly moved into the conning position. Being an open bridge there was no better protection from the blast but I felt a little less vulnerable. I had just got inside and shut the half door when from the after director came the sound of the firing bell. The next moment the whole ship was lit up by huge orange tongues of flame in the staggering violence of one and a half tons of cordite throwing seven and a half tons high explosive shells into the air.

As the acrid smelling cordite smoke eddied around us my ears rang, despite the cotton wool I had put in them and, having stupidly forgotten to close my eyes, I was temporarily blinded by the flash, so for the first two or three broadsides I could not see the fall of shot. When I regained some night sight I saw that over Trapani the searchlights were still looking for aircraft overhead and the AA guns firing, unaware that the assault was now coming from the sea. I could now also see the gun flashes of the cruisers and hear the boom of the broadsides from *King George V*. As the bombardment proceeded the Italians realised that the enemy was not overhead and the searchlights were switched off but if any coastal defences realised the truth and fired at us at all we were unaware of it.

When finally we ceased fire there were quite a few more fires burning, lighting up a pall of smoke over the target areas. Astern of us I was amazed to see a number of explosions and rockets going up into the air, until it dawned on me that they were our 'secret weapons', so long the cause of speculation and caustic comment. The fused rocket floats had been dropped over the side so that after we left the scene there were explosions and fireworks going on as if a landing were imminent. As we steamed away from the coast the cruisers left us to carry out a further bombardment of Marsala whilst we turned away to resume our patrol of the western Mediterranean.

On the order to cease fire, one of 'Y' turret's guns had still been loaded and the following day the time-honoured permission was granted to 'unload through the muzzle'. Although it was announced the gun was going to fire, one of the shipwrights obviously had not heard the pipe because he walked onto the quarterdeck just as the gun fired. Fortunately he was behind the muzzle when it went off otherwise he might have been blasted off the ship. As it was he was quite severely shaken up.

Following the bombardment we returned to Algiers together with the *King George V* and whilst being mainly based there we continued our role as deterrent and reserve battle squadron whilst the campaign in Sicily proceeded to its conclusion when, on August 17th the town of Messina, on the north east point capitulated.

During this time there were a number of alarms when it was reported that the Italian fleet was on the move. Once when we were ordered to sea in a hurry, the tugs were tardy in coming alongside, so Captain Woodhouse, with great skill took the ship out from the jetty and negotiated the narrow entrance without any assistance at all.

Our time in Algiers was not without incident, one of them proving to be disastrous for one of our ships. It happened when *King George V* was away and our companion alongside was the destroyer *Arrow*. She was duty destroyer that day and was called away to assist with a fire that had broken out on an ammunition ship in another part of the harbour. At about 3.30 there was an almighty explosion, the blast of which we felt on the quarterdeck, as the ammunition ship blew up. *Arrow* was alongside the burning ship fighting the fire and over a hundred of her crew were killed in the explosion. Many were blown overboard, some in pieces and unrecognisable as human beings. The ship itself was badly damaged with the forecastle and superstructure stove in. The remaining ship's company could not cope with the disaster and help was sent from all the naval ships. Later a call went out for all the fleet sailmakers for the job of sewing the remains into canvas for burial. To help them through their gruesome task they were liberally plied with rum.

For some time after bodies or parts of them were recovered from the harbour waters. About two days later one of our picket boats returned from a routine trip towing two nearly whole bodies. On the same day as I was on watch I saw a largish piece of flesh, like a piece of pork, pale and edged with shreds of ragged skin, undulating by at the bottom of the gangway. Feeling sick, I walked quickly away to the other side of the quarterdeck unable to report it to anybody. A few minutes later I felt that I had to do something about it and I went to look again before reporting it. Thankfully it had gone.

In the explosion a tanker caught fire and was towed out of the harbour by tugs where it remained anchored off shore and burning for over a week.

During the first week of September, when both *King George V* and ourselves were in Algiers the Germans launched an air raid with some sixty bombers. I closed up at my action station as usual, although it seemed silly to man the after conning position whilst in harbour. After all we were not going anywhere, so even if the bridge was hit there was nothing to take over for. The Commander and the Chief Bosun's Mate were on the bridge so that there was only the messenger and myself. Not long after we had donned our anti-flash gear and steel helmets there came the sound of aircraft overhead and searchlights from the land began to probe the sky. At the same time our port 5.25s, pom-poms and Oerlikons opened up a blind barrage of continuous fire. Because they were next to the jetty, the starboard batteries could not join in as *King George V* was on that side. As part of the harbour defence smoke canisters were ignited around the harbour which effectively screened the ships. On the other hand our close range weapons were unable to see much either.

The noise and concussion of the anti-aircraft fire was so great that neither the messenger nor I heard any bombs at all, although some must have dropped in the harbour. As we watched there was a sudden burst of flame in the air and burning debris fell into the sea not far from us to the accompaniment of cheers from the pom-pom crews below us, convinced that they had shot down an enemy plane.

The raid could not have lasted more than half an hour and as our guns blazed away there was a misfire in P2 5.25 turret. Normally a misfired gun should be left for at least half an hour before the breach is opened; but the gun's crews were loading and firing so fast that, before it was realised, the breech was opened and the undischarged cordite case ejected on to the empty cases below. The case burst open pouring the cordite onto the hot cylinders and a searing sheet of flame filled the whole turret and casemate. A petty officer and a boy seaman were killed and the whole gun's crew was badly burned.

Howe was credited with half a plane—in other words with having a hand in shooting one down—probably because of the incident we saw when burning debris fell out of the sky. However the messenger and I were convinced that it was one of our own barrage balloons that came down because the descent was too slow for a burning aircraft and, having watched pretty well all the action around the ship, we had not seen anything else come down. But we both decided to keep our counsel as it would seem churlish to take away this small consolation after the death of our boy comrade, who both of us knew well.

Other incidents during our stay were less gruesome, like the time when there was a Polish destroyer tied up to us. Their libertymen had to come across our quarterdeck to go ashore. It was strictly forbidden for anyone to bring their own alcohol aboard one of HM ships but whether it was the same with the Polish navy we did not know. Be that as it may, their libertymen came merrily up the gangway with bottles under their arms to be halted by our Officer of the Watch. Neither side purported to understand the other of course as the quarterdeck staff tried to convey in sign language that they could not come aboard with their bottles. The Poles were loath to be parted with their booze and if they understood at all did not take kindly to the threat of being put on a charge for bringing it on board a British ship. Meanwhile time was getting on for the end of liberty and, as more and more Polish sailors plus bottles arrived, the gangway and pontoon became quite crowded. Some of them realising the situation hid their bottles in their clothes and tried to bluff their way past with bottle-like lumps sticking out of their jerseys and trousers. But our OOW would have none of it and told the Corporal of the Gangway to search all coming aboard. Finally the Polish Officer of the Watch was sent for, who summoned his Commander who asked to see ours.

After some polite and diplomatic exchanges it was decided that in this instance the Poles were to be dealt with by their own officers on their own ship but in future they must be warned that they could not bring drink across the *Howe*. So the, by now, nearly complete Polish watch ashore trooped over to their own ship, bottles and all, where they probably went down to their various messes to drink their booze.

King's Rules and Admiralty Instructions and allied relations were satisfied the following day when the Polish destroyer was moved to another berth where no doubt, a blind eye could be cast over their returning libertymen.

Our own libertymen were not a great deal of trouble chiefly because any unsteadiness in coming on board over the brow was rewarded by an escort of a 'crusher' down to the cells to await sobriety and the Commander's report in the morning. Occasionally someone would try their luck with a concealed bottle of hooch; but usually when they saw people were being searched there would be a discreet splosh into the water as they climbed up the gangway. On one occasion a cheery matelot arrived at the top of the gangway to have his concealed bottle fall down inside his bell-bottomed trouser leg and smash at his feet. As the RPO and OOW closed in on him he looked all about him in surprise.

'Oo the 'ell threw that?'

There were a few who could be relied upon either to return to the ship considerably the worse for wear or else not turn up at all. Memorable runs ashore were usually extolled by them according to the condition in which they returned.

'Wonderful run! Big eats, got pissed, filled in and caught the boat up too!'

Catching the boat up meant contracting VD.

The worst of these were well known to the Master at Arms and to any of us who were regular quarterdeck watchkeepers and in the First Watch, from 8.00pm to midnight, we would always check to see if any were ashore by looking through the watch cards. Sometimes called liberty cards, these were handed in by anyone going ashore and retrieved on return.

One such person was a Canadian stoker, predictably nicknamed 'Canada', whose drinking bouts ashore were prodigious. In his late twenties or early thirties, Canada had the most battered face that I have ever seen, suggesting a singularly unsuccessful career in the boxing ring. His nose was a flattened mess, his eyebrows split with scar tissue and his right ear well cauliflowered. Even when sober his eyes seemed half closed. He was tattooed virtually over the whole of his upper body, with a crucifixion scene on his back, a tiger on his chest and incongruously under one nipple 'milk' and the other 'cream'. His arms bore various sentiments like a dagger entwined with 'Death before Dishonour' as well as two arrow-pierced hearts professing undying love for someone whose name had been obliterated and replaced by 'Maisie'.

His return from his first run ashore was typical. As the evening wore on and people started coming back on board, we saw a figure staggering its way through the gate and along the pontoon, weaving so much from side to side it was difficult to see if it was making for *King George V* or us. But as he got to the ship and climbed the nearest—and wrong—gangway we knew it was Canada.

In port we usually had a gangway from the forecastle for the ratings and one from the quarterdeck for officers. The pontoon in Algiers however was not long enough for the whole ship to lie alongside so there were two gangways virtually next to each other on the quarterdeck. The after gangway was fresh painted and decorated with turk's heads and scrubbed canvas panels whilst leading on to the deck was a footplate emblazoned with the ship's name. Use of this splendid stairway was, of course strictly reserved for officers whilst the plain one rigged forward next to P4 turret was for the tread of common feet.

Oblivious of the shouts from the Officer of the Watch and the duty Regulating Petty Officer, Canada hauled his way up hand over hand by means of the guardrails. Arriving at the top he was confronted by the RPO who barred his way.

'This is the officer's ladder. Now go back down and use the other one!' he ordered indignantly.

Canada swayed and looked from the RPO to the gangway up which he had so laboriously climbed.

'Aw, piss off, you stupid bastard!'

'Call the Duty Sergeant!' the OOW ordered.

While the bosun's mate, messenger and myself were standing back enjoying the entertainment, the RPO and the Corporal of the Gangway restrained Canada as best they could, until the arrival of the sergeant with two marines. It was not an easy job and it finally took the sergeant, two marines and the Corporal of the Gangway to remove Canada from the quarterdeck. Things were not quite finished. Noticing my grinning face Canada shrugged off his escort and came over to me

'Say, you're de guy dat blows the bugle in the mornings!' he exclaimed and with that took an almighty swing at me. However it was so ponderous and well signal led that I just stepped back and he fell flat on the deck. The Sergeant and the marines hauled him on to his feet again and they all staggered their way forward to the cells, cannoning off the sides of the passageway as they went.

Despite punishments of increasing length and severity, Canada always went ashore again as soon as he had liberty and funds. He would have his one evening's outing, with the same performance on his return—even down to threatening the bugler as he was carted off to the cells—and then spend the next week or ten days under punishment. The quarterdeck watch gave up trying to stop him coming up the after gangway a) because it was more convenient to deal with him separately and b) it was hopeless trying to stop him.

And, as with any other user of that august ladder, the side was manned for Canada's arrival, albeit by the Officer of the Watch, the Duty RPO, a marine sergeant, the Corporal of the Gangway and two marines.

One of the few things Canada seemed to remember of his runs ashore was threatening the bugler, because whenever he passed through our messdeck and spotted me he would say, 'You're the guy that blows the bugle, huh?'

Then take out all the change in his pocket and present it to me.

July, August and September were good times as far as the war was concerned. As well as our own part in great events, the Russians were pushing the Germans back around Bryansk, Kharkov and Orel, inflicting casualties at the rate of 4,000 a day and the bombing of German cities continued with the heaviest raid on Berlin occurring on 31 August. In common with the people at home we were grimly pleased with the idea of repaying the Germans with interest for their bombing of our towns and cities. From the wind they had sown with attacks not only on Britain but places like Warsaw, Rotterdam, Amsterdam, Brusseis, Paris they were now reaping their well deserved whirlwind.

Another item of news, greeted by us with some amusement, was the fall of Benito Mussolini on the 24 July. Il Duce had provided the comic relief in an otherwise bleak war, with his posturing and strutting. His only praiseworthy act during his leadership of the Italian people seems to have been to make their trains run on time.

The beginning of August saw the Germans evacuating Sicily across the Messina Straits, whilst the RAF pounded away at the beaches ferries, barges and lighters as they tried to escape.

From the landings of the 10th July it had taken 39 days for Sicily to fall and, after a pause of fourteen days the Straits of Messina were crossed and allied troops were back on the mainland of Europe on 3 September

Three days after the Messina landings *Howe* and *King George V* were suddenly ordered to Malta. Stopping in a bomb-battered Valetta only long enough for one run ashore to collect two beer tickets each, drink the ration in a dungeon-like NAAFI bar from glasses ingeniously cut from the bottom half of bottles, and pick up Vice-Admiral A. J. Power, we put to sea again

As we left harbour the captain came on the air, telling us that Italy had signed an armistice and their surrender was to be announced to the world the following day (8 September). Also we were to be joined by six cruisers which had already embarked elements of the 1st Airborne Division and we were going to land them at Taranto. The main object of the operation, (Slapstick), was to seize the town and harbour before the Germans could consolidate their position in that area. The paratroopers were to hold on until re-inforcements arrived.

Taranto was the great naval base situated in the instep of the Italian 'boot' where elements of the Italian navy were based, an important prize to be taken before the Germans could do so.

On the afternoon of the 9th we were joined by the cruisers which took up their positions in line astern of the *King George V* and, with the flag of Admiral Power flying at our maintop, *Howe* led the fleet into Taranto Bay as we went to action stations.

The weather was clear and from the after funnel I could see the coast about eight or ten miles to port. As I looked there were a number of explosions all along the coast which continued as we progressed. They seemed to be in the sea and looked like mines being set off. So intent was I in watching this spectacle that I was unaware of anything else until there was an exclamation from the messenger who had wandered over to the starboard side.

'Jesus Christ, Sticks! Come and look at this!'

I followed his pointing finger to just off the starboard bow where there was a line of Italian warships coming towards us.

As they came nearer we made out that they were headed by two battleships and three cruisers, their guns all fore and aft but still looking as if they were aimed at us. With the rumbles of explosions from the land on the port side, everyone who was on deck watched silently as they approached and passed down our starboard side whilst, just in case of treachery, our main and secondary armament trained around following their every move. Apart from the tension of the moment the silence was also due to admiration of these beautiful ships with their rakish lines, like racehorses compared with our no-nonsense carthorse appearance. As they passed us the *King George V* turned out of line and took up a position astern of the Italians to escort them to Malta.

Taranto harbour was huge with a protective wall to seaward and deep water jetties alongside the town. With minesweepers going ahead and the American cruiser *Boise* leading us in we entered the harbour. The minesweepers were a wise precaution because the Germans had sown the harbour with mines. I was told that they were also being floated down in the current from the river; but whatever the case the mines appeared to be very sensitive because there were numbers of explosions going on most of the time we were there. Captain Woodhouse had a large barge removed from its moorings and we secured to the vacated berth possibly because he deemed it safer than most.

From where we were I could see the masts and superstructure of a ship sticking out of the water. It was one of the Italian battleships that had been sunk in the great Fleet Air Arm triumph of 1940. On a memorable night 11 November, Fairey Swordfish—the biplane torpedo-bomber, known affectionately as the Stringbag—from the carriers *Eagle* and *Illustrious* carried out an attack on the ships in Taranto with such success that the whole balance of power in the Mediterranean, which the Italians fondly called Our Sea, was altered in our favour. Three battleships were left partly under water with another badly damaged together with two cruisers and two fleet auxiliaries.

As we secured and settled down at defence stations, around the harbour there was a good deal of activity both on our part and that of the Germans. At one point a Heinkel 111 bomber flew across the harbour but we had no means of knowing whether it was Italian or German manned. As it flew into the distance the Italian AA batteries opened up on it which proved it was in fact a German plane; but with everything in a state of flux we were in a most difficult position to know who was now friend or foe.

As the evening wore on the cruisers started landing the paratroops but at about 11.00pm there was another explosion. One of the cruisers had struck a mine while disembarking her troops. By an ironic stroke of fate, it was the *Abdiel,* herself a fast minelaying cruiser. In a very few minutes she broke in two and sank taking about 300 of her crew and the paratroopers with her. With all the ships' boats called away to pick up survivors, some two hundred of the troops were brought on board *Howe.* They were made welcome by everyone and having been cleaned, fed and given a tot of rum they were re-kitted from the Royal Marine stores and armoury. The following morning Major Ross suggested that the Marine detachment should land with them to make up the numbers but the captain refused to let us go because it would leave unmanned too much of the ship's armament. So, having been blown up the day before, the paras disembarked that morning and the ship's company lined the side and gave them three cheers to speed them on their way. Sixteen hours after their ordeal they were in action against the Germans and I wished good luck to whoever had the Tommy gun I had fired in Iceland. I doubt if they took the Boys anti-tank rifles though.

Earlier on the same morning another mine blew up close astern of us which emphasised the risk to all the ships within the harbour. There was actually nothing more *Howe* could usefully do now that the big Italian ships had departed peacefully, apart from being a large target for floating mines, so Admiral Power transferred his flag to a destroyer and sent us back to Malta.

On the 11th we arrived at Bighi Bay where we anchored for the night. There being no room in Grand Harbour, the following morning we joined the *King George V* anchored outside. Inside the harbour there was an astonishing sight. All the day before, from Italian ports like Spezia, flying black pennants which were the agreed recognition marks, four battleships, six cruisers and seven destroyers had steamed into Grand Harbour. During their trip they had been attacked by German Stukas and torpedo bombers in the straits between Sardinia and Corsica in an attempt to prevent them reaching Malta. The battleship *Roma* was sunk by a direct hit which split her in two.

After the siege and continuous air attacks the Maltese had suffered, they were ecstatic and came in their thousands to view the fleet of their fallen enemy. Every Italian ship that entered the harbour was greeted by a cacophony of sound from any vessel that happened to have a siren or klaxon.

With the arrival two days later of the battleship *Guilio Cesare* from Venice, Grand Harbour became so congested that on 14 September the *Howe* and

Taranto. Arms and supplies for the paratroopers who survived the sinking of the *Abdiel*, author centre picture (*IWM*)

KGV were ordered to escort the battleships *Vittorio Veneto, Italia,* four cruisers and four destroyers to Alexandria.

We arrived there to the full orchestra of sirens and klaxons and people crowding every viewpoint to see the Italian ships with their black pennants of surrender. Ironically Alexandria had been the scene of the Italian Navy's greatest triumph, brought about not by these powerful ships but due to an action by a handful of very courageous sailors on the tiniest craft in the Italian navy, the two man torpedoes or 'pigs'.

In December 1941 Lieutenant Luigi de la Penne had led an expedition of three pigs in an attack on Alexandria harbour. He had attempted one on Gibraltar in 1940 but had been detected before getting into the harbour, hence the boat patrols and their continuous depth bombing whilst we were there. At Alexandria he successfully gained entry by coming in when the boom was lowered for three ships entering the harbour. The two prime targets were the battleships *Queen Elizabeth* and the *Valiant.* Lt de la Penne's target was the *Valiant.* As he approached in the early hours of the morning, the current took his craft into the *Valiant's* side with a tremendous crash, knocking out his companion's breathing gear and forcing him to the surface. Surprisingly this evoked no response from the battleship but the pig was immobilised by a fouled propeller. Undeterred Lt de la Penne dismounted and manhandled it under the battleship and set the time fuses for 6.00am.

Meanwhile on the second pig Engineer-Captain Antonio Marceglia and PO-Diver Spartaco Schergat had attached their warhead to the *Queen Elizabeth* whilst the third, with Gunner-Captain Vincenzo Martellotta and PO-Diver Mario Marino busied themselves under a tanker.

By this time the alarm had been raised and Lt. de la Penne was picked up by a patrol boat at 3.00am and taken on board the *Valiant.*

Despite intensive questioning he refused to talk and so was locked in a hold way below the waterline with some cigarettes and rum. His watch had been taken from him so he had to calculate the time and at 5.50 he asked to see the commanding officer, Captain Morgan. On being brought into the captain's cabin he told him that he only had a few minutes in which to save his crew. He refused to say any more so Captain Morgan had him returned to the hold. At some time after six the charge underneath the *Queen Elizabeth* detonated followed by that under the *Valiant* which caused an injury to de la Penne's knee. The lights were out in his prison but he found his way to the door which had been left unlocked and made his way to the upper deck. There was a great deal of activity going on with the Damage Control Parties working to save the ship; but as he came up on deck the officers and men saluted him as a very brave man. The *Queen Elizabeth* and *Valiant* settled on the bottom and remained there until they were refloated only a few months before the Italian ships were brought into Alexandria.

The Italians as a whole had not distinguished themselves in the war. Their land forces had managed, not without difficulty, to overcome tiny Albania after which they had bitten off far more that they could chew by attacking Greece; from which dilemma the Germans had rescued them. In early 1941 they retreated from Mersa Matruh in Egypt 500 miles to el Agheila in Libya, leaving behind 140,000 prisoners, including 19 generals, in the hands of the 30,000 British Army of the Nile So renowned were they for running away that when it was announced that Italian troops were being sent to the Russian front, the *Daily Mirror* published a cartoon depicting Mussolini in running shorts and with spiked running shoes in his hand, fearfully passing a sign reading 'To Russian Starting Line'.

At sea they had been the same with their vastly superior numbers relying on their speed to extricate them from trouble. One class of Italian cruiser was even built with two gun turrets forward and three astern.

The courage of Lieutenant Luigi de la Penne and his companions did much to restore some honour to the Italian armed forces.

Now with the Mediterranean cleared of all but a few small enemy units, there was no reason for us to remain, so together with *King George V* we departed for Scapa Flow, there to relieve our stand-ins the USS *Alabama* and the *South Dakota* which were wanted in the Pacific.

CHAPTER 13

Refit

During our absence from Scapa the Home Fleet, augmented by the American battleships and under the new C in C Admiral Sir Bruce Fraser, had carried out a number of minor operations in the Arctic.

One of these, codenamed Operation Gearbox, provided cover for two separate activities. The first was a convoy to Russia to deliver supplies and mail to the merchant ships marooned in Murmansk for the long summer day, whilst the second carried men and stores to the isolated Anglo-Norwegian weather station at Spitzbergen.

Prior to and during the landings in Sicily, another two operations were carried out to occupy the German mind and divert attention from our Mediterranean activities. Various units of the Home Fleet, escorting a motley collection of trawlers and motor launches paraded up and down the Norwegian coast to simulate major combined operations against Southern Norway. Despite attempts to draw the enemy out to investigate, like breaking radio silence and making quantities of smoke, the Germans remained unimpressed and stayed firmly at home.

Following the withdrawal of the American battleships, the *Tirpitz* and *Scharnhorst* ventured to sea and bombarded the long-suffering Spitzbergen weather station. By the time Admiral Fraser had received the news and sortied from Scapa Flow the Germans were safely back in harbour. 'Safely' not for long however, because on 22 September the Royal Navy returned the compliment with a raid on Altenfjord by the tiny X craft midget submarines. The result of this daring raid was serious damage to the *Tirpitz* which remained unseaworthy until March 1944. The German squadron was further reduced when *Lutzow* was sent back to Gydnia in the Baltic for a refit, leaving *Scharnhorst* as the only effective capital ship.

The Home Fleet meanwhile had been augmented by the modern 43,000 ton French battleship *Richelieu,* so that, by the time we arrived back with the *King George V* Admiral Fraser was in the happy position of outnumbering the Germans by five to one, enabling him to send *Howe* down to Plymouth for a refit in December.

Like all the major seaports, Plymouth had had its share of attention from the Luftwaffe and when I first went ashore into the city I was horrified to see the destruction in the city itself as opposed to the dockyard. Although Portsmouth had also been badly hit I had never really been into the centre and so Plymouth was the first bombed city I had walked around. In some places it was difficult to see where the streets had been, let alone the build-ings. The shopping centre and its the surrounding residential areas were piles of rubble and gaunt shells of buildings which told the tale of an imper-sonal war of bombing, but the human desolation was brought home to me by the signs of deserted habitation within the empty shells. Typically, two floorless storeys up in what had been a block of flats, a cooker clung crazily to a wall. Flowered wallpaper surrounding a fireplace showed where a bedroom had been. On the mantelpiece amongst broken masonry were the remains of a clock.

As I wandered through the town in the late December afternoon, I came across one of our marines who came from Devon.

'How can I get to the Hoe from here, Jan?' I asked.

Being a Devonian his nickname was Janner. Had he come from Cornwall, just two miles further west on the other side of the Tamar, it would have been Jacker.

'It's up there,' he replied pointing out a street to the south. 'But to tell the truth Sticks, I can hardly tell where we are exactly and I come from hereabouts!'

'Ah now, there's Dingles.' he continued, pointing to the ruins of what was once a large department store 'When we was kids we used to come shopping here with Mum. Sometimes when she felt flush, we'd have a cuppa tea and cakes in the restaurant in Dingles.

He sighed 'It's all a bloody mess and no mistake.'

'I wonder what Coventry's like, then,' I mused, then realised my mistake as an indignant look came over Jan's face.

'Coventry!' he spat out the word, as he glared at me 'Coventry's had bug-ger all compared to Plymouth! They only had a couple of night's blitz and just because their cathedral was bombed they sit back and lap up all the sym-pathy.'

He swelled with something like civic pride.

'We've had more bombs down here than they've had hot dinners—and we've cleared up more rubble than they'll ever have—and we've got on with plans for rebuilding.'

Suitably chastened I went on my way leaving him to look around moodily at the shattered reminders of his boyhood.

Later, in the early evening as I was walking back through Union Street I met Jan again in more mellow mood.

'Come on, Sticks,' he called 'Come and have a wet!'

It seemed he had forgotten my gaffe in mentioning Coventry and, nothing loath, I followed him into a pub.

As we sat there with our glasses in front of us he asked, 'What did you want to go to the Hoe for?'

'Well it's the only place I know of in Guzz and I wanted to see where

Drake played his bowls before the Armada,' I replied 'There was a statue of him and also a big war memorial with a lot of names on it.'

'I expect there'll be a lot more by the time this one's over.'

He took a swig of his beer.

'Y'know, some people say that Drake never played bowls before the Armada.'

'Oh well, it's a good story,' I said, picking up my beer 'Here's to Sir Francis anyway.'

'Yeah, and balls to Lady Godiva!'

Obviously I wasn't quite forgiven.

Two days later the ship's company, all bar a care and maintenance party, were sent to our respective barracks' whilst the ship went into dry dock. Whacker and I arrived at Eastney to find a few changes had taken place. Cpl Cripps had become Bugle Major as Dick Newman had at last retired allowing the upward movement of the hierarchy. Our old room in A block had been vacated due to the increase in the number of boys who now occupied two rooms. The biggest change was of course in ourselves. We were sixteen, had been to sea and were now old soldiers, to be looked at with envy by the sprogs! To add to our status, Whacker and I, together with about three other buglers in barracks at that time, were wearing the ribbon of the first war medal to be issued, the 1939-43 Star (subsequently renamed 1939-45 Star). It was not only the younger boys who were impressed but also the marine recruits who would come up and, addressing us as old soldiers would ask us what it was. We invariably replied 'Oh, it's nothing really!' with all due modesty. Which of course it wasn't.

We were allowed to smoke now as we had been to sea and to that end I had come ashore suitably prepared. Not only did I have my allowance of two hundred cigarettes but one of the first things I did on getting into barracks was to take my drum apart to extract the eight hundred more that I had secreted within. So that the package didn't rattle about I had tied it to the inside of the shell with a bit of cod line; and at a pinch the drum could still be played although it would have sounded a bit odd.

As I was doing this I noticed one of the real old soldiers watching me with a knowing look. Nick 'Boon' Carter was one of two pensioner buglers that had rejoined at the outbreak of war after twenty five years of service. Employed mostly on general duties, neither of them played bugle or drum now, although in their time they had been around the world and both sported 'Mutt and Jeff' the Great War medals, as well as the 'Blue Peter' or Long service and Good Conduct Medal.

'When I was in the Far East in the twenties I bought a little monkey,' he told me 'and when I came home I wanted to smuggle it into the country, so I put it inside my drum.'

'What happened?' I asked

'Well, it was quite all right, because of the air hole in the shell. But at the last moment it was decided we were to march the detachment back to the barracks with the band.'

The monkey remained quiet and nothing untoward happened until they came to march off. There is a brief moment between the orders 'Band Ready!' and 'Quick March!' when all is still and silent.

'Just before the order was given to move off,' Boon continued, 'the monkey took it into its head to start leaping and rattling about and there was I standing there with my sticks in line with my mouth and my drum beating a tattoo of its own and jumping about all over the place!'

'Bandmaster must have heard it because although he didn't have time to do anything I saw him look over his shoulder.

'So we played from the dockyard right through Portsmouth to Eastney with me trying not to hit my drum and the drum banging away all by itself. When we got to the barracks, Bandie asked me what was wrong and I told him I couldn't play properly because I had hurt my wrist!'

'What happened to the monkey?' I asked.

'The poor little bugger died a few days later but whether it was the march or the change of climate or something else I don't know.

Boon looked so sad as he told me his tale that I gave him a packet of Senior Service from my ill-gotten gains.

As we had been abroad, Whacker and I went home on foreign service leave for a fortnight. My father now worked in a government ministry in London so home was now Purley in Surrey from whence he commuted to town every day.

When I got home I found my mother busy knitting tiny matinee coats and drinking vast quantities of raspberry leaf tea in expectation of another offspring in January.

As if sensing the calculations that were going on in my head my father told me that they had planned to have another child to take the place of my elder brother. Hitherto we children could all attribute our conception to some celebration nine months beforehand. My elder brother was conceived on the wedding night whilst I was the result of my mother's twenty second birthday party. Richard and Tessa, the next two, were the result of *ad hoc* celebrations. That it was a planned decision was as startling as the actual advent of the baby itself.

As usual father took me down to the local where I was introduced to a new circle of friends, the Purley equivalent of the Birmingham 'war cabinet'. Consisting of the same sort of people, mostly veterans of the Great War, about the only differences were the southern accents and doubtless their sitting room maps, whose coloured pins would now be concentrated around Naples in Italy and the Arakan in Burma.

My medal ribbon was admired by all and gave me some sort of standing as an expert on the Sicily and Italy campaigns. As my source of information was much the same as theirs, namely the BBC, I could add very little to the main picture so I held forth on the bombardment of Trapani and the surrender of the Italian fleet. To add a bit of colour I also told them about the explosion in Algiers harbour, which I believed, erroneously as it happens, to be the result of sabotage.

'I'm not surprised!' exclaimed one of my audience 'Never could trust the Frogs in the last war!'

The American complaints about having chicken and only vanilla ice cream sparked off other reminiscences.

'When they came into the trenches in '17, they were very full of themselves,' commented another 'Thought they were the cat's whiskers until the Boche started shelling, then it was a different matter! Dug-outs weren't deep enough then!'

'Have another beer?'

As father and I declined and got up to go, the discussion had gone on to the difference in the sound of Gas and HE shells and the bar echoed with imitations of whistles, whooshes and crumps.

'Oh, just off then? Best of luck, old man!' they all wished me well; and as we went out of the door I heard:

'By George if only I was thirty years younger I'd be going with him!'

Back from leave in barracks we were kept quite busy with the divisional band. At the time there had started the enormous build-up for the invasion of Europe, or the Second Front as it was called and there were numerous units scattered around the country training for the event. The band visited many of the camps which, I would have thought, regarded our ceremonial displays with mixed feelings, chiefly because they often had to take part.

One such unit was a Royal Marine Commando, at that time inflicted on the small community of Hatch End in Middlesex. Dragged from their billets on a Sunday morning, they took a reluctant part in a church parade through the village street for the benefit of the inhabitants, many of whose homes had been commandeered to house their unwelcome visitors. I doubt very much whether either locals or commandos were much heartened by the display but for two days we of the band thoroughly enjoyed 'roughing it'; walking a mile or so with knife, fork, spoon and mug in hand from our billets to the village hall where we took full advantage of the extra rations that were then being issued to the special forces.

Despite the enjoyment of travelling with the band around southern England Whacker and I were very pleased to get back to *Howe*, which we rejoined on 15 April 1944 after a four months sojourn on land.

Howe had been refitted for a different type of sea warfare in which the role of capital ship had been taken over by the aircraft carrier. Although not realised at the time, the last battleship action by the Royal Navy had been fought on Boxing Day 1943 off North Cape, when the Home Fleet and the *Duke of York* had sunk the *Scharnhorst*. From now on sea-battles were to cover far greater ranges, with carrier-borne aircraft capable of delivering a punch the equal of a cruiser's broadside. The battleship, whilst still available in the increasingly unlikely event of ship to ship engagements, was now to be used as anti-aircraft protection for the fleet and for heavy bombardment.

As we walked up the gangway we could see that much had been changed in our four months absence.

The catapult deck and hangars were gone as were our Walruses, the space now being taken up with messdecks, on top of which were the boats. The old boatdeck now sported extra Pom-poms and quadruple Bofors guns, together with their directors.

The ship's complement had been increased from the original fourteen hundred or so to over sixteen hundred. With three hundred marines now embarked *Howe* boasted the largest Marine detachment ever to put to sea. They were to man all the after main and secondary armament.

I was still on the same mess, 106, and Whacker was on 104 both marine's messes and needless to say I was delighted. The band had grown in size so now had a small messdeck to themselves. Many of the new draft were very young and had not been to sea before so it behove Whacker and me, as old hands at sixteen, to become sea-daddies to the nineteen year olds.

There were many new faces, including a new captain, Henry McCall. Like our last captain he was involved with the battle of the River Plate. He was the Naval attache in Buenos Aires and Montevideo and when the German Battleship *Graf Spee* took refuge in Montevideo he played a prominent part in trying to persuade the authorities to delay her departure. Meanwhile, off Montevideo and just outside territorial waters three cruisers, including Captain Woodhouse's *Ajax,* waited for the re-emergence of the powerful German.

Captain McCall's last ship before *Howe* was the cruiser *Dido* which he commanded during the evacuation of Crete in 1941. He won the DSO in this action, *Dido* being heavily bombed and lucky not to be sunk.

We also had a new Commander by name Christian-Edwards, who was as short as the last one, Commander Shaw-Hamilton, was tall. As my boss at action stations we were to be together quite a lot in the near future.

Having completed our refit in Devonport we sailed for Scapa Flow and a further period of working up. The Fleet anchorage had not changed at all apart from the fact that, in common with most other harbours we had recently been in, there were now anti-chariot patrols with duty picket boats dropping small depth charges. During our stay there were a couple of scares when it was thought midget submarines had penetrated the anchorage. With most of the fleet's boats charging around dropping depth charges, the battleships, including *Howe* got up steam and fled out to sea, like old ladies running from a mouse. Meanwhile in the anchorage, a suspected contact was depth bombed with such enthusiasm that one boat went over a charge just dropped by another, thereby nearly getting her stern blown off. However it was all a false alarm and after a while the big ships returned somewhat sheepishly to their buoys.

We were still in Scapa Flow when the allied landings took place on D-Day 6th June 1944. I was disgusted at not being there during what was probably the most decisive event of the whole war. Nine allied battleships were taking part in the preliminary bombardment of the Normandy beaches and here we were, the most modern battleship in the Royal Navy skulking in Scapa. To my mind it was a further missed opportunity for taking part in some action but the reason why we did not take part might have seemed obvious. During her refit *Howe* had been 'tropicalised' indicating that we could be destined for hotter climates. However such signs were taken with a pinch of salt because eighteen months previously, we had taken on stores suitable for a hot climate and had promptly gone off on Arctic convoy duties in mid-winter.

So we carried on with our work-up ignoring the great events going on in Europe, until on 1st July, having achieved some degree of efficiency, we sailed out of Scapa Flow—in the event for the very last time—and actually bound for the Far East.

CHAPTER 14

East of Suez

Our journey from Scapa to the Indian Ocean took in all 39 days, going as we did through the Mediterranean in quite a hurry and only stopping in Algiers on the way through.

Algiers always seemed to be an eventful place for us and despite the shortness of the stay this time was no exception. As we came up our to old berth there was little room for manoeuvre, for on the other side of the jetty was an ancient French battleship called the *Paris*. With the help of two tugs and the harbour pilot we managed to collide with the French ship, doing some minor damage to one of our screws. Although not serious enough for any major repairs, the damage did subsequently affect our maximum speed slightly.

The French ship, a relic of the Great War—or perhaps even earlier—was a museum piece in itself, with her 12 inch turrets and secondary armament mounted in barbettes along the sides. The most noticeable embellishment was an enormous dial, like a clock on the forward superstructure, giving her the appearance of an *hotel de ville* that had somehow lost its *ville*. In the not too distant future *Paris* was to fulfil her ultimate destiny by being sunk in position as part of a temporary harbour structure; bringing the wry comment from Captain McCall that it was probably the best thing she had ever done in her existence.

The Mediterranean in July should have been an ideal introduction for the newer members of the ship's company to warmer climates but unfortunately our quick trip was not long enough for gradual acclimatisation. After only a day in Algiers, when only the non-duty watch got ashore, we were off to Port Said and the Suez Canal.

As the biggest ship ever to go through the Canal up to that time *Howe* was particularly difficult to handle. A large vessel going along a narrow waterway tends to push all the water in front of it like a loose-fitting plunger in a pipe and the ship has to travel slowly enough to allow the water to pass around its sides and underneath. Steering becomes a problem because any deviation in the ship's head will cause more water to pass down one side than the other thus swinging the head further round. A knot or two faster could damage the canal banks, whilst on the other hand if the ship is too slow she becomes unwieldy and will tend to yaw from side to side and hit the banks.

From the bridge I watched our stately progress along the narrow waterway with our escort of two tugs, one ahead and the other astern. With Egypt to starboard and the Siniai to port it looked almost as if we were sailing across the desert. The mill race created by our passing caused panic on quite a few Arab feluccas, some breaking their moorings and their furious owners engaging in heated altercations with our pilots and the captains of the tugs Several times on our way through we grounded on the mud from which the tugs pulled us off. No damage was caused and it says a great deal for the experience and skill of the canal pilots that we did not hit the banks more often.

The advent of a battleship going through the Suez was a welcome diversion for the troops stationed in the Canal Zone—a posting that was the land equivalent of Scapa Flow as far as amenities, entertainment and pure boredom were concerned. Word got around the various camps and our passage was watched by hundreds of soldiers and airmen lining the banks. Our progress was enlivened by shouted comments such as:

'Get your knees brown!'

'How's Blighty then?'

'Yer going the wrong way!'

Getting stuck in the mud on the sides would be greeted by ironic cheers and hoots of laughter.

'Didn't know it went on land as well!'

'Ain't you got a steering wheel, mate?'

'Your driver's pissed!'

All in all the pilots must have been glad when, after two days we sailed into the Gulf of Suez; not however, before getting both bows and stern stuck across the dredged channel in the Great Bitter Lake, where we moored for the intervening night. Fortunately this crowning ignominy was out of sight and shouting distance of our land-based fellow servicemen.

If the passage through the canal was entertaining for some of us, the journey down the Red Sea was horrendous. The month of July is the hottest time of year in the Red Sea and this is where we found out that 'tropicalisation' carried out during the refit applied to machinery only and not to the benefit of the ship's company. Under a glaring sun and with a following wind that did nothing to cool the ship, temperatures soared. The worst sufferers were the stokers in the engine room and the cooks who had to work in temperatures of 130 degrees Fahrenheit (54°C). In the galley, temperatures in the proximity of the ovens reached 170 degrees F (76°C). About the only tropicalisation that had been done with the ship's company in mind was the opening up of the main and middle deck scuttles—hitherto sealed in the interests of water-tightness—and the provision of wind scoops to fit in them. Large canvas scoops were also made by the sailmakers and fitted into various hatches in an endeavour to force some draught below decks. But as the wind was roughly the same speed as the ship, no relief was forthcoming from these provisions. At sea we were not allowed to sleep on the upper deck and night time down below became a period of restless sticky dozing from which it was almost a relief to get up in the morning.

Old and new in the Suez Canal. *Howe* and an Egyptian felucca *(IWM)*

Watchkeeping on the bridge, although still very hot, was a pleasure compared with being down below and when I was not on watch I stayed on the upper deck during the day, going down only for meals. Sweat evaporated immediately, leaving the skin dry and clothes salty and as soon as I came off watch I went below, showered and washed my shorts, shirt and socks. Five minutes on the upper deck at the most would dry the clothes ready for ironing. This simple routine was so convenient that, from then on whilst we wore tropical rig, I got into the habit of always 'dhobi-ing' and ironing my shift immediately on coming off watch. The rest of my kit simply stayed clean and untouched in my locker.

It was with relief that we arrived in Aden, supposedly one of the hottest places in the area but which had the great advantage of being stationary and therefore subject to the cooling effect of the breeze that had followed us down the Red Sea.

I was on the bridge as we were getting ready to enter harbour and talking to the Chief Bosun's Mate. He was telling me about the delights of Aden, which appeared to be precisely nothing.

'It's all sand and Wogs,' he informed me 'The best thing about Aden is leaving it, or better still, not going there in the first place.'

'Still I expect we'll be led in by George as usual,' he added.

But before I could ask who George[1] was, he went down below; but it was not long before I found out.

As we approached the harbour we were accompanied by a school of dolphins, one of which was larger and quite scarred around his head and nose. He stayed just ahead of our bows until we were right inside the outer mole as if he had the job of guiding us to our allotted mooring and almost as if he knew which one it was. This great old dolphin was George, a familiar sight to all sailors who came in to Aden and who apparently seldom failed to turn up to do his duty.

Aden had a smell of warm fuel oil mixed with wood or camel dung cooking smoke and although not quite so pungent or far-reaching as that of Algiers, still peculiarly its own. The first element came from the fuelling jetties whist the other ingredient seemed to emanate from an island in the middle if the harbour, on which there were a number of people wandering aimlessly about. Someone on the bridge told me that it was a leper colony and I went to look at them through the powerful lookout binoculars, to be promptly—and quite rightly—given a dressing down by one of the officers.

'Those people are put on that small island to live out their lives whilst parts of their limbs and faces just drop off. How would you like it if you were in the same boat with every idle gawper looking at you through binoculars?'

Feeling 'lower than a worm's belly' with shame I went red-faced about my business. I never stared at them again but still watched covertly when I was on deck not because of curiosity but because I wanted to know more about them. The words leper and leprosy still conjure up in my mind that bare island with little huts and people waiting to die—and an unthinking boy who wanted to stare at them.

The journey across the Indian Ocean was uneventful and we finally arrived in Trincomalee in Ceylon (Sri Lanka).

The Eastern fleet had been much neglected since 1942 with all of the best ships withdrawn to be engaged in the European theatres of war. The C in C, Admiral Sir James Somerville had been left with the battleship *Warspite* and the ancient *Ramillies, Resolution, Revenge* and *Royal Sovereign* to face the might of the modern Japanese fleet with their newly acquired base at Singapore. Fortunately the powerful fast Japanese carrier task forces became too heavily embroiled in the Pacific and made only one foray into the Indian Ocean to attack Ceylon. Having had a good deal of success—sinking the cruisers *Cornwall* and *Dorsetshire* and the aircraft carrier *Hermes* as well as bombing Colombo and Trincomalee—the Japanese retired to Singapore and never again entered the Indian Ocean.

Admiral Somerville's venerable ships meanwhile, acting in a more or less defensive role and carrying out convoy duties, covered the whole of the Indian Ocean from the Arabian Gulf to the East Indies.

In 1943 the old 'R' class battleships had been sent home for badly needed refits. 1944 saw something of a build-up and, when we arrived we joined the battleships *Queen Elizabeth, Valiant, Richelieu* and the battle-cruiser *Renown* as well as two fleet carriers, two escort carriers, seven cruisers and a number of destroyers which were already there.

'Trinco' was a large natural harbour on the east coast of Ceylon whose small entrance made it ideal for a fleet anchorage. Surrounded by lush tropical vegetation, it was also hot and humid, a condition that we were to experience in the Far East from now on. There was precious little ashore except one or two buildings that had been taken over by the navy and some playing fields for cricket, football and hockey.

Our first night with the fleet proved eventful. I happened to be duty bugler and was down for a 'shake' at 0530 to call the hands and was fast asleep when the Corporal of the Gangway came down and, giving my hammock a tremendous shake called out:

'Come on, Sticks, up on the quarterdeck at the double!'

I had great difficulty in waking up which was unusual for me in the mornings. But he persisted and I finally came round.

'OK, OK, for Christ's sake, Geordie,' I recognised him as one of-our many marines from Newcastle, as he all but tipped me out onto the deck.

At that moment the pipe came:

'Emergency Party muster on the quarterdeck!'

'What's up?'

'Come on quick, there's a flap on, its something to do with the *Valiant*,' Geordie replied as he disappeared between the swinging hammocks.

As I hurriedly put on shirt, shorts and shoes and grabbed my bugle I looked at the time, 11 o'clock—six bells in the first watch. No wonder I felt tired; I had only been asleep for about half an hour.

On the quarterdeck the commander and the officer of the watch were conferring, the last of which I heard.

'—and have the duty part of watch stand by and muster all power boat crews. They might need some help over there!'

'Quartermaster!' the OOW turned round and repeated the order.

'Aye-aye, sir. Come on Sticks.'

As we raced round to the SRE I asked what was going on.

'It sounds like the dry dock has sunk from under the *Valiant*. Don't know how though.'

I got to the microphone housing, pulled down the lid and switched on.

'Who's duty watch, for Christ's sake?'

'First of starboard!'

I sounded off 'Both Watches of the Hands' preceded and followed by one G, indicating the part of watch.

'Hands muster on the quarterdeck,' the QM piped 'Away all power boat's crews! Coxswains report to the quarterdeck.'

As we walked back to the gangway there came the thump of an underwater explosion. Startled at first, I had forgotten about the anti-midget submarine patrols. It was the duty boat dropping depth charges but it reminded me of our visit to Alexandria in 1943, after *Valiant* and *Queen Elizabeth* had been attacked.

'Do you think the Nips have got in with chariots?' I asked

'No, if they had there'd be a bloody sight bigger flap than there is now,' the QM replied.

Looking over to where the floating dock was moored I could see one or two lights but nothing of any significance. If there had been midget subs in the anchorage they certainly would not be flashing lights around a stricken ship.

The boats' crews were manning their boats on the after and starboard booms and a sleepy 'duty part' were on the quarterdeck awaiting events.

There seemed a lot of uncertainty as to whether we could help at all but after a time the duty watch was sent below, the boats' crews were told to man their boats and the Commander told the ship's company over the SRE that the floating dock had sunk from under the *Valiant* causing some damage to her.

Morning brought the whole scene to light; the floating dock's superstructure was just visible above the water whilst not far away lay the *Valiant* considerably down by the bows. There were no casualties but the ship was so severely damaged that she was shortly afterwards sent back home for repairs, thus negating the advantage in numbers occasioned by our arrival.

Whilst we stayed most of the time in Trincomalee, the fleet also had an anchorage in the Maldive Islands to which we repaired occasionally between exercises at sea. The Royal Navy had a remarkable flair for finding the remotest and dreariest places in which to park its fleets and Addu Atoll was probably the pearl of them all. Described as 'Scapa Flow with effing palm trees' it did not even have a canteen on its tiny islands, whose highest points were—and still are—six feet above sea level.

Addu Atoll had been the hidey hole from which Admiral Somerville's inadequate fleet sortied when the Japs ventured into the Indian Ocean.

Luckily for us time spent in either of them was mitigated by the exercises and other activities we engaged in.

One unusual diversion was a landing exercise by our detachment on the jungled shores near Trincomalee. The whole detachment was involved, including me complete with bugle and a new Tommy gun; although the idea of bugles sounding off in the jungle and giving away our positions was ludicrous. The enemy was to be a Troop of 42 Commando Royal Marines who at that time were engaged in various activities in Burma. Borrowing a few decrepit looking landing craft from some local organisation, we set off for a distant shoreline that appeared to be a nice place for a landing.

At that time the only marines who had had any real training in beach assault were the commandos and although the theory of down ramps, out troops—centre row, port row, starboard row in that order—was known, little attention was paid to it.

The captains of the landing craft, on the other hand knew all about the dangers of getting stranded on a beach and, reluctant to get too near dry land, their normal drill was to cut off engines before driving onto the beach then as soon as they touched, gun the engine astern and to safety. The result of this manoeuvre was that the first troops out may get a fairly dry landing whilst the unfortunates who were last quite often leapt into water up to their waists or higher. It was the same with our skipper, a Marine NCO , and on seeing the gulf rapidly widening between ourselves and dry land we all dashed off at once. Fortunately the water was only up to thigh level at that time.

One of the other landing craft was not so lucky. They grounded on an unseen sandbank about fifty yards from the shore.

In the boat were most of our rations for the day including a large kettle full of lime juice. Since embarkation it had been held upright against the roll and pitch by a very large colour sergeant called Hodge. At the moment of impact the landing craft with its ramp open came to a dead stop and Sgt Hodge was forcefully decanted into five feet of water. With remarkable agility and strength he kept to his feet and waded ashore head, firearm and 'limers' only above water, to be greeted by cheers from those already landed. Not a drop was spilt or contaminated with salt water and, had it been a 'live' landing he would undoubtedly have gained at least a Mentioned in Despatches for his feat.

Having got ashore I lost all idea of what was going on and so, I suspected did everyone else in the HQ party. The sections under their various officers and NCOs went off into the interior to contact the enemy and that was the last I saw or heard of them until their return in the evening. Meanwhile I wandered down to the mangrove-like swamps and became engrossed in the wild life. One of the most interesting things were the mud skippers pattering along across the mud at an incredible speed. Not having known about them before I was astounded to find that on closer examination they were actually fish that could exist out of water and run about on their pectoral fins. There were also large butterflies and high up in the trees a troop of monkeys swung from branch to branch.

The detachment Second in Command's brief on this landing was to look for and report on anything edible and the possibilities of living off the land. Whether Captain Glossop was a biologist or not was a moot point but he gathered some things together including rancid coconuts from the ground and an extraordinary fruit that looked delicious at first. About the size of a coconut it was a red colour and grew in a palm-like tree. Inside it was very fibrous but to me after one lick only, had a quite pleasant sweet tasting juice[2].

Whether or not the exercise was a success is a moot point but it did us all a power of good to get away from the ship for a while. As to the 'enemy', they turned up just as we were about to re-embark on the landing craft and wished us God Speed.

Besides regattas in the harbour and inter-fleet football competitions, other matters occupied us showing that we were on more serious business than hitherto.

Only sixteen days after our joining the fleet we took part in an operation, together with *Renown,* two cruisers and five destroyers providing cover for carriers *Victorious* and *Indomitable* in a strike against various targets around Padang in south-west Sumatra. At the same time we closed the town and bombarded what was said to be the Jap's only cement works in south-east Asia. A few weeks later we set out again on the same sort of mission in the same company for strikes on Sigli in north Sumatra. Aircraft from both carriers carried out photo reconnaissance of the Nicobar Islands and northern Sumatra. Although actual operations, these jaunts were regarded as combat training for the young and inexperienced pilots of the carrier aircraft. They were also attempts to distract Japanese attention away from the Pacific on the eve of the American invasion of the Philippines.

Throughout this time there was a sense of something impending and on the messdeck arrivals of ships and people were noted and discussed with great interest. Lord Louis Mountbatten was Supreme Commander, South East Asia Command; Admiral Sir Bruce Fraser, the victor of North Cape had taken over as C in C Far Eastern Fleet. Various ships started arriving.

Then just after my seventeenth birthday in November, I inadvertently gained some information from an unusual source.

For some time I had noticed a lump that came and went in my right groin. It did not hurt at all but as time went on, maybe due to the heat, it got larger

Howe leaving Colombo bound for the Pacific *(IWM)*

usually disappearing at night or when I lay down. More out of curiosity than anything else I reported to the sick bay where the doctor informed me that I had a hernia.

'You will have to have an operation,' he added, 'but it's nothing to worry about and there's no immediate urgency. The best thing to do is to wait a few weeks when we will be in cooler conditions.'

Back on the messdeck I announced that we were off out of the Indian Ocean soon.

'Oh yeah?' someone said 'and where're we going then?'

I had no idea but said the first thing that came into my head.

'Australia!'

'How do you know that?'

'Through my contacts,' I replied enigmatically.

'Oh piss off, Sticks!'

They had all had enough of buzzes.

But almost as if on cue things started hotting up. On the 22nd Admiral Fraser hoisted his flag in *Howe* as C in C British Pacific Fleet and we moved down to Colombo. The aircraft carrier *Indefatigable* joined the fleet, bringing with her someone who was always in the thick of the action, Rear Admiral Sir Philip Vian. Finally as if to cap it all, our old partner *King George V* turned up on 15th December.

Then on the 18th December, with Admiral Fraser's flag at our main truck, we steamed out of Colombo.

As soon as we were at sea the familiar pipe came over the SRE 'D'ye hear there!' followed by a short pause and then the captain's voice told us we were bound for Fremantle and then Sydney.

On the messdeck I was of course insufferable.

'Told you so!'

CHAPTER 15

An Australian Experience

A day out from Colombo a messenger came aboard to make an important announcement. For the occasion a perforated hose had been rigged athwartships on the fo'csle forward of the breakwater, which produced a spray concealing the hawsepipe by which the visitor was to arrive.

At about four bells in the dog watches I heard one of the bridge lookouts call 'Dolphins ahead!'

The Officer of the Watch reported to the captain.

'Very Good,' Captain McCall acknowledged the sighting. 'Sound the Still, Drummer!'

As I sounded off, from the bows behind the spray screen a voice shouted, 'Ship ahoy! What ship is this?'

'His Britannic Majesty's ship *Howe*,' the captain replied 'Who are you?'

'I am the Herald of His Majesty King Neptune, Emperor of the Seas.'

The spray died down to reveal Neptune's Chief Herald accompanied by two assistants and four bears, the latter looking remarkably like four of our crew in grass skirts and cloaks of oakum.

'Welcome, Herald,' said the Captain 'I have sighted the dominion of your Royal Master and request his permission to clear the Line and proceed south'ard.'

Messages of goodwill were then exchanged with both captain and herald breaking into verse, apparently the normal mode of conversation on the ocean floor. Having made arrangements for his master's reception, the herald and entourage disappeared behind the resurgent screen of seaspray, the captain bidding them 'Farewell until the morning!'

Later, as I went off watch at eight bells, there was a crowd around the notice board in the canteen flat and, when I got near enough I saw it was a message from Neptune.

> 'By command of His Majesty King Neptune, Monarch of the
> Oceans, Emperor of the Seas, Knight Commander of the Ancient
> Order of Shellbacks and Grand Master of the Brotherhood of
> Deep Sea Mariners.

A PROCLAMATION

Know all Men by these presents that His Majesty King Neptune will hold court aboard His Britannic Majesty's Ship *Howe* on December 6th at 0900 hours.

And hereby commands that all those who have not been granted the Freedom of His Domains shall present themselves before His Court to undergo such initiations as Ancient Usage and Custom do demand.

All such of His Subjects who have already been duly initiated and have received the Freedom of His Royal Domains are hereby Commanded and Enjoined to render every assistance to the end that the Ceremonies may be rightly and properly ministered.

By Commandof His Majesty,
Signed: DAVY JONES
Clerk of the Court
Keeper of the Royal Locker.

At the Court of King Neptune
At War Stations
Dated December 5th 1944

We had of course almost arrived at the equator and were about to cross the line. In fact *Howe* had twice crossed over on our recent excursions to Sumatra, but on both occasions Neptune took a precedent from his most famous son and turned a Nelsonian blind eye, it being wartime.

As well as initiating greenhorns, Neptune also takes the opportunity to confer awards and punishments on older members of the Ship's company and the summonses left by the Herald made ominous reading for those addressed. With the same preamble and signature as the proclamation and addressed to various individuals they stated:

'You are hereby summoned to Present yourself before His Majesty at His Court to be held on board His Britannic Majesty's Ship *Howe* at 0900 to receive such punishment or reward as shall be judged fit and proper to your conduct.'

The next morning started as usual with Calling the Hands at 0530. Ever since being in the tropics we had been working what was called the long forenoon routine, the working day starting early before the heat and finishing at 1300. Today, after 'Both Watches of the Hands' had scrubbed decks the 'Secure' was sounded prior to the breakfast time 'Cooks to the Galley', which meant that work had finished for the day. However having had the Dogs and Middle watches, I was still due for the Forenoon so, when at 0750 the watchmen were called to muster, I once again made my way to the bridge.

It was a beautiful day, with brilliant sunshine and not a cloud in the sky. Odd zephyrs of breeze riffled the otherwise smooth sea which had just enough swell to keep the ship gently rolling. Flying fish skittered away from the foot of the bows, leaving a ripple as they used their tails to speed over the surface. Neptune was in a benign mood.

From a vantage point by the lookouts I could see the forecastle where the chippies and sailmakers had been busy erecting a dais, complete with thrones all gaily bedecked with bunting, in front of which was a large canvas pool of water. On a sort of platform at the edge of the pool they were busy putting the final touches to a chair that faced the dais and hinged so that it tipped backwards over the bath.

A crowd had already gathered around and others were climbing on-to the tops of A and B turrets, some sitting astride the length of the huge 14 inch guns.

At about 0830 the Royal Marine Guard and Band fell in on the starboard side aft of the fo'csle, all dressed in full ceremonial rig and the guard with fixed bayonets. Last of all the Captain strode forrard on to the fo'csle, immaculate in white drill uniform and sword.

Then, dead on time at 0840, with bears roaring and savaging everyone in the way, King Neptune, accompanied by Queen Amphitrite, the Lord Chamberlain, the Royal Doctor, His Majesty's barber (complete with huge wooden razor) the Royal Policemen and a bevy of lissome mermaids, made his very dignified progress up to Commander Christian-Edwards and the reception committee.

'Guard, Royal Salute Pre-sent ARMS!'

The Marines stood rigidly presenting arms and the band broke into the chorus of 'Rule Britannia' as a royal salute.

The guard was duly inspected by Neptune and Amphitrite after which the bears cleared a passage through the spectators, roaring and biting at anyone in the way and the royal entourage proceeded to the dais. Quite why Neptune has to have bears, and brown ones at that, is not clear. Neptune, crowned and dressed in flowing robes and beard acknowledged the crowds appreciation with gracious gestures, exchanging one or two remarks with them, as did his Queen and the mermaids who, with their long tresses and ample bosoms moved to the accompaniment of howls and whistles of admiration. Most of the male members of the Royal Party had long and luxurious beards, which made me wonder why they really needed a Royal Barber. But I was to find out.

After the captain's address of welcome who, for his service at sea was made a Duke of the Indian Ocean (rhyming with promotion), there followed the awards for those who had received summonses. Some of Neptune's police meanwhile disappeared below to scour the ship for particular people. Nobody knew whether they were to get an award or a punishment which added to the enjoyment of the onlookers. Most of those on watch could be seen craning their necks around doorways and corners when their duties allowed. The only ones concentrating on their jobs were the lookouts at their binoculars. I had nothing to do except in possible emergencies, so I watched and listened to most of the goings on.

One of the early victims was Lieutenant Commander the Viscount Curzon, next in line to the Howe earldom and Close Range Gunnery Officer. He was indicted for littering the ocean with practice sleeves.

> '—Untidy, Your Majesty. We think that he oughter
> Be shown what it's like to be shot in the water.
> Up bears and at him. He's in for the high count
> It's rare that we lather the face of a Viscount.'

In between the celebrities numerous first timers were dragged from the crowd and brought before Neptune, coming away from their ordeal bruised of face and half drowned after being lathered, shaved and ducked. Once they had been through the mill, the newly initiated were eager to see that everyone else shared their fate and most of them joined the Royal Police in their hunt for other victims.

Like African driver ants they went through the ship seeking anyone who had not been initiated. Nobody was safe no matter where they hid, except those on duty. Or so I thought as I watched the proceedings from on high.

But then the ants arrived on the bridge and asked for the duty bosun's mate. As there were plenty of people, including myself and the boy messenger who could use a bosun's call and make the pipes, he was dragged away.

Then it was the messenger's turn and, as they took him away, Neptune's policemen eyed me.

'You're next, Sticks!' said one, the letters CID painted on his shiny black helmet.

'I can't leave the bridge. Nobody else here can blow a bugle!'

With smug satisfaction I watched as the messenger was taken and given the treatment.

I was still looking over the side when the he came back from his ordeal. Turning round to greet him my grin froze on my face. There right behind him were the police plus Whacker Payne with his bugle.

'You've been relieved, my son. Your oppo's volunteered!' CID announced.

Grabbed by the policemen, I glared at Whacker, his hair still wet from his own dunking.

'You're a bloody good friend, I must say!' I yelled as I was bundled down the ladder, frantically stripping off my web belt, shirt, bugle and shoes as I went.

Arriving at the dais, King Neptune looked at me with distaste.

'Aha! here's another of them as wakes me from my slumbers with his row! Give him a good shave and a couple of pills!'

'Pills is finished,' said the Doctor.

'Well, an extra good bath then!'

I was seized from behind with my arms behind my back and placed in the barber's chair. A fearsome great coir haired brush was dipped into a large bucket filled with foaming lather and applied all over my face. Stupidly I opened my mouth to squawk a protest to have it promptly filled with soap. Next the Royal Barber shaved, or rather scraped the great razor around my face, neck and anywhere else the lather happened to be.

'Right then. Over he goes!'

The seat tipped back and I somersaulted into the bath, by now distinctly murky from all the lathering and other questionable treatments dished out. The bears, stripped of their upper hairiness and looking like muscular Hawaiians in their grass skirts, grabbed me and thrust me under. They had had all morning to get their timing right because, just as I thought I was about to drown, they let me up to get one gulp of air before forcing me down again. Three times I was thrust under until finally I was allowed to surface coughing, spluttering and gasping, to be assisted out of the bath with a hearty heave and gales of laughter.

I lingered to see a couple of late captives being ducked although there were very few uninitiated left and by now the onlookers were getting restive. Like audiences at the Roman games, the novelty of throwing Christians to the bears was wearing thin; besides which it was nearly tot time. So the pageant came to an end with the fickle crowd turning on the providers of the morning's entertainment and, starting with King Neptune the whole court, mermaids, policemen and all were thrown into the water 'to demonstrate their aquatic prowess' as it was reported afterwards.

As for me, I went up to the bridge to continue my watch, still coughing and shaking my head to get the water out of my ears; and thinking over what I had just been through.

This wasn't the first time Neptune had communicated with me because in 1943, he had sent all of us who crossed the Arctic Circle in *Howe* a certificate conferring on us membership of the Ancient Order of Bluenoses. There had naturally been no initiation ceremonies chiefly because of operational conditions but also because with temperatures of minus forty degrees, duckings could be fatal.

But despite swallowing a good deal of soapy salt water and feeling sore both inside and out, I felt an odd kind of satisfaction in having been through this 'rite of passage' to become one of Neptune's approved subjects.

Now having gained the permission of King Neptune, we crossed the line and went on our way south, with the sun and the southern cross daily ascending higher into their respective skies.

During our travels in the Far East, there were a number of people who begged or were given passage to and from various destinations as they went about their wartime occupations and, in return for their free passage and victuals, they were cajoled into giving a talk over the ship's broadcasting system in an occasional series called 'Fares Please'.

On this trip the bulk of our 'tourists' consisted of the C-in-C's staff on their way to set up shop in Sydney and one of their number gave a very informative talk on Australia, its history and people and their life style. In a way we were being prepared for the culture shock of meeting people who were the same as us but with a difference. There was, we were told, little class distinction—a fact that seemed to vaguely worry the speaker but not his listeners—and in general their standard of living was better than ours. Given to calling a spade a bloody shovel, Australians were generous and from the speaker's experience hospitable.

How hospitable, warm and friendly we were about to learn and after a refuelling stop at Fremantle we arrived in Sydney.

There had been no public announcement of our visit which was supposed to be an official secret; but Australians had a notable disregard of officialdom and in particular its secrecy. Word had got around of the arrival in the Pacific of a British fleet and work had already been going ahead in setting up the C-in-C's headquarters. Due to wartime censorship nothing could be announced regarding the imminent arrival of the first modern British battleship to visit the city. Yet those in the know—which seemed to be everyone—were determined that we were to get a typically Australian welcome. Just before we arrived one of the Sydney papers, seemingly à propos of nothing in particular, published an article comparing the low pay of the British serviceman with that of their own. Sydneyites are not fools and were quick to grasp the meaning of this huge wink from the official eye.

On 18th December we entered Sydney Harbour, with the elements the only factor still trying to keep our arrival secret. But the bush telegraph still operated even in the urban environment.

'The heaviest dust fog in the harbour for years shrouded *Howe*'s arrival,' announced the *Sydney Daily Mirror*.

'She slid through the heads like a giant grey phantom, the tops of her masts hidden in the upper strata of the haze. *Howe* nosed her way slowly into the harbour, turned and then quickened her pace, her screws flogging the waters into foam as they bit faster. Her sleek, raked bow flung up a glistening bow wave that soon reached far back beyond her stern. The battleship was in faultless trim—the canvas capped 14 inch guns fore and aft, cork liferafts in even line around her enormous bridge, the multiple pom-poms pointing aggressively into the air, the long lines of white clad ratings along both sides of the main decks provided an inspiring sight.'

Despite being up on the bridge I could not see anything much of what was the biggest natural harbour in the world, owing to the fog. Even the famous bridge was hidden and yet whenever we came in sight of a promontory there were people by the hundreds waving to us as we passed. From seemingly nowhere came flotillas of launches, yachts, motor boats and even canoes to escort us in.

From the moment we went alongside the jetty at Woolloomooloo, the dock entrance was crowded with people and it was not long before we had the ship open to visitors. They had not come just to look at the ship for with overwhelming generosity, hundreds offered us the hospitality of their homes, putting their names down on a list to get someone to entertain.

The first and most striking thing about the people I helped to take around the ship was their eagerness for news from Britain. They called it 'Home', not because it was my home but because they thought in terms of it being from whence they came. They asked about the conditions and the bombing and food shortages and where was I from?

In much the same way that we really had no concept of the vast distances involved in their country so they were inclined to think that being a comparatively minute island everyone knew everyone else in Britain.

As I shook hands with one couple at the gangway, I was asked in a peculiar mixture of Australian accent and Welsh idiom 'Do you know Aberystwyth? That's where my mother's da came from, look.'

Almost on the first day I was introduced to Les and Red Tidmarsh. Red was so called because of her titian hair, which may have sounded obvious to our English ears but in Australia, as I learnt later red-heads are perversely called Blue or Bluey.

Like so many of our crew I was virtually adopted, feted and taken all around the city, staying with the Tidmarshes when I had all night leave. On the first day they picked me up at the dock gates and took me out for tea at Cahill's restaurant and then on to the cinema. Cahill's was a swish place where one queued for a table—like Lyon's Corner House only posher. Cinemas were run rather like our theatres and seats had to be booked in advance. They were also non-smoking which, despite being used to smoking, I found very agreeable as the picture was so much clearer. Before the films there was a stage turn which featured the tenor and bass Flotsam and Jetsam—or someone incredibly like them—who sang 'Is he an Aussie is he Lizzie?'.

The picture show was much on the same lines as in England with an A and a B film with the news in between. As in England the show was followed by the national anthem 'God save the King' but also what was then the New South Wales state anthem 'Advance Australia Fair'.

After the 'movies' I stayed with the Tidmarshes in their flat overlooking Elizabeth Bay. The style of living was a mixture of old tradition and new adaptation suited to the climate and seemingly influenced by America. Certainly the standard was very much higher than that obtaining in wartime—or even pre-war—Britain.

The Tidmarshes had no children, they were I supposed comfortably off and their flat seemed like something from a Hollywood film compared with what we had at home. Small things came as a surprise like starting breakfast with fresh sliced pineapple or fruit juice, chilled from a refrigerator. In Britain pineapple was a pre-war luxury unknown in wartime, whilst orange juice was available concentrated and rationed for children only. Few people had refrigerators in which to keep either.

Despite a desultory and possibly unnecessary sort of rationing, food was plentiful in Australia. Red looked on in surprise when, after bacon and two eggs, I automatically scraped an extremely thin layer of butter onto my toast.

'There's plenty more in the fridge!' she said

On Christmas Day I was taken along to Red's parent's home where the family gathered for dinner. December is of course mid-summer in the southern hemisphere and the 25th was a sweltering day even by Australian standards. There, with three generations of family, I sat down to roast turkey, roast pork with stuffing, roast potatoes and two other vegetables. The Christmas pudding that followed was doused with brandy and set alight but served with the only concession to the midday heat, Peter's Ice Cream—the Australian equivalent of Wall's.

Afterwards, as we all sat there with cups of tea, cigarettes appeared and Grandmother got out a tin of tobacco and cigarette papers.

'Would you like one of these?' I asked offering my packet of Senior Service.

'I don't get on with made cigarettes,' she replied 'Try one of these.' She passed her 'makings' over to me and watched approvingly as I rolled one.

'Good on you, I didn't know English people rolled their own!'

'Oh yes, we get tobacco at one and threepence a half pound on board.'

I had evidently made a friend because while many Australians traditionally rolled their own, the rest of the family had become sufficiently urbanised to smoke 'tailor-mades'. Not so Grandma, who was glad to have someone to keep her company.

Invitations continued to come from all sides and it was embarrassing to sometimes have to refuse people who were so eager to make us feel at home. It was not just the well-to-do that offered hospitality and in between visits to the Tidmarshes I went to other homes.

Another couple invited me out and their son met me at the ship in the afternoon to take me to their home near King's Cross.

As it was a bit early we went to a pub where, over quite a number of schooners we chatted. Fortunately I had just been paid and despite his protests I was glad to be able, as he put it 'to pay my shout'. He was about to go into the army and his older brother was already in.

Pubs shut at six in Australia and between five and six there comes the phenomenon of the 'five o'clock swill' when men come out from work straight into a pub to down a few beers before it closes. At quarter to six we left the now crowded bar, when I had had just enough beer to have to take a firm grip on myself in order to meet his parents.

Their flat was on the second floor of a tenement building that reminded me of film scenes I had seen of Brooklyn. As soon as I was in the door they made me welcome and throughout the meal they asked me about Home and where I had been and what I had been doing. There was a picture of their elder son on the sideboard in uniform, complete with Digger hat and the rising sun cap badge of the AIF. They told me he was in New Guinea in the Owen Stanley Mountains where the Japs were being steadily winkled out. Not being much of a letter writer they had not heard from him for a while.

There was not a great deal of room in the flat but they would not hear of me going back to the ship so they made me up a bed on the living room balcony overlooking the street where it was much cooler. Unfortunately there were also lots of mosquitoes that kept me awake most of the night.

After breakfast in the morning, I said goodbye and thanked them for their hospitality adding that I hoped they would hear from their son soon. Accompanying me down the stairs and out into the street the other son told me they were pretty worried about his brother. The unspoken thought was that he was a casualty and maybe missing.

As I boarded a tram to Woolloomooloo, the conductor ignoring the fare that I held out, it struck me how much these good people, with one son possibly missing and the other about to join the fighting, had gone out of their way to give a good time to someone else's son who was far away from his home.

In the middle of January whilst I was enjoying myself, the Hospital Ship *Oxfordshire* arrived and berthed not far from us. This was the signal for me to pack my kit put most of it in storage and have my hernia operation.

Oxfordshire was a converted liner but otherwise was run like an ordinary naval hospital. Most of the nurses were male sick berth attendants whilst the nursing sisters and the matron were QARANCs. The wards were down each side of the various decks central to which were lifts to the operating theatres. In port the beds were rigidly held by clips but could be released at sea to swing with the roll of the ship.

My hernia was successfully dealt with, the most painful part of the operation being when they marked the spot to cut with a cross using a very sharp indelible pencil. This was the first operation I had ever had and I naturally felt a bit frightened particularly when they made sure they had the correct details of next of kin and so forth. Nursing and care in naval hospitals is not the sympathetic sort that one gets in civilian establishments. Geared up to dealing with casualties of war the naval machine goes into action efficiently and well with very fine surgeons, whether dealing with five hundred cases a day or one. Sometimes it may have seemed almost off-hand but I found that this attitude more comforting than any mollycoddling. I had the feeling that they knew exactly what they were doing with such a run of the mill operation as mine.

The ward at that time seemed to consist of nothing but appendix and hernia cases from around the Dominions. Canada, Australia and New Zealand were represented and all seemed to be great jokers. The problem, as we all found out was that with stitches in the stomach, you could not laugh or cough without hurting. The New Zealander, naturally nicknamed Kiwi and who looked like Lou Costello, could somehow manage to make any situation funny which was extraordinarily painful with each of us literally holding our sides and trying not to laugh. Digger or Dig, the Australian had the usual brand of disrespect for authority, greeting the daily round of rather stuffy surgeons, doctors, matron and others with 'What-ho, Doc. How's yer luck?'.

Being regarded by the officers as a 'Colonial' who knew no better he got away with saying what were to us Pommies marvellously outrageous things.

The food was adequate and seemed no better or worse than that on the *Howe* but a lot of it was tainted with the smell of cockroach. The *Oxfordshire* specimens were huge, about one and a half inches long, a different breed from those I was used to. At night they flew up and down the ward purposefully like bombers on a mission. I never knew where they were going nor, despite diligent searching when I was allowed up, where they hid during the day. All they left behind as proof that they existed was their peculiar musty smell in the sugar, tea, cornflakes or any food or cupboard that they could get into.

On the whole a hernia operation is more about discomfort than pain and, apart from being marked by the indelible pencil, the most painful process was the removal of the band of sticking plaster when it came to having my stitches out. About eight inches broad, it stretched from the left of my navel right across to half way round my back on the right. If it is peeled off gently it takes hours of pulling carefully inch by inch and, as if laid down in the Seamanship Manual (Surgical), the drill for removing plaster was to get a firm grip on one end and tear it off with one heave. There was no haul away handsomely about it at all. Our Sick Bay 'Tiffy' was good at this and with an expectant hush from all the others he almost lifted me off the bed as he ripped the plaster from my stomach, now stubbly with the regrowth of hair.

The plaster came off with a ripping noise, accompanied by a loud, blasphemous yelp from me and hoots of laughter from my fellow patients, some of whom had all ready suffered this treatment.

Tiffy and I examined the results. The area where the plaster had been looked and felt as if scalding water had been poured on it.

'You must be allergic to plaster!'

I looked at him in amazement.

'It's not the plaster I'm allergic to, it's you pulling it off!'

Not long after the first batch of surgical cases had been dealt with, the new base naval hospital was opened ashore and as 'walking wounded' we were transferred by lorry.

At first there were only about eight of us in the whole hospital and we were attended by all female nurses. There was the full range of hospital functions in being and with so few patients at the time we got their undivided attention.

Christianity was represented by four ministers who came looking for their particular brands of sheep. They each appeared at different times and advanced down the ward whilst everyone suddenly became incredibly busy as with lowered heads they wrote letters, read or dived off to the heads, anxious to avoid eye contact. Following the lead given by Kiwi and Dig, no-one admitted to being a member of that particular padre's church. When the Methodist came around we were RCs and Anglicans. With the Anglican we were Baptists and RCs and so on.

It was Digger being ever more outrageous who let us down in the end. The RC padre was the last to turn up and after the usual ignored entrance he asked

'Anyone here Roman Catholic?'

There was a general murmuring of Noes as we got stuck into our occupations.

'How about you ? What religion are you then?'

'I'm C of E.'

'And you?'

'Yes, me too.

He went round everyone individually asking their religions until he came to Digger who was sitting on his bed in the corner.

'And I suppose you're C of E too!'

'No not me, Vicar. I'm a Buddhist'

'So you're a follower of the Gautama are you?'

Digger looked up indignantly, 'No, I told you, I'm a Buddhist!'

He stared at Dig for a moment and then walked out of the ward.

Behind the scenes there must have followed a quite remarkable ecumenical spirit of co-operation for those days because, when next the individual padres came. around they were armed with our details from the sister's office showing our names, ranks, next of kin and religions.

The library trolley came around daily for a while until they realised that we just could not physically get through one book a day each, particularly in view of the energies and enthusiasm of the Occupational Therapist. Great importance was attached to not just sitting in your bed idly and it became compulsory for us to have something to do. Almost on our first morning the OT lady came around with materials for baskets, dolls and embroidery, announcing that she had 'all sorts of useful things to make and keep your mind occupied and do you good!'

Promptly named Mrs Do-You-Good by the colonial contingent, there was no dodging the column with this persistent lady, particularly as there were so few of us in the hospital for her to concentrate on.

Laying out her wares like some itinerant tinker she called us up one by reluctant one to choose something from her stall. We had to pay for the materials so I chose a dutch doll made from felt as the cheapest. From then on Mrs Do-You-Good appeared every day to check on our progress, tut-tutting, chivvying, demonstrating and making sure we were hard at work on our various artifacts. So persistent was she that one man had a nightmare about her trying to catch us in huge baskets and we all began to fervently hope for a major epidemic in the fleet, or even a battle with hundreds of casualties to dilute her attentions a bit.

One of the in-mates who chose basketmaking decided the best thing to do was get it over with quickly, so he worked hard and completed a passable wicker container in two days. Mrs Do-You-Good was delighted with this example of industry and whilst he looked on smugly held him up as an example to us all. His self satisfaction disappeared the next minute when she told him to choose something else to make. As a result of this we all carefully paced our effort so that we never actually finished our artifacts.

Kiwi also chose basketmaking and each evening made a complete mess of it, twisting the wicker round the wrong way, breaking or missing out turns around the upright bits. The next day Mrs Do-You-Good would come in and clucking with dismay, unwind his efforts and remake the whole thing by way of demonstration, with Kiwi looking on earnestly saying 'Oh, I see!' and 'So that's how it's done!' Gradually, whilst the rest of us toiled away at our useful things, Kiwi's basket came on apace looking far better than any of ours, having been entirely crafted by the OT lady. Just as his basket was nearing completion Kiwi was due to go to on convalescent leave. So the night before with incredible deftness he tucked in the tops and finished his basket off and with great ceremony in the morning presented it to Mrs Do-You-Good saying that perhaps as it was so useful she could use it.

Subsequently I took my doll back to the ship where some time later she won a prize in a handicrafts exhibition. Having travelled a few thousand more miles around the Pacific she came home with me to be given to my small sister.

The food was very good with a lot of fruit and fresh vegetables. There were also salads which, typically of sailors, the rest regarded as insubstantial rabbit food not fit to be eaten. As I liked any raw vegetables, I would eat all the lettuce, cucumber and tomatoes issued for the whole ward which was up to fourteen strong when I left.

I was glad to get out of hospital when the time came. We had been allowed ashore for limited periods but it was getting claustrophobic. The original eight from *Oxfordshire* were being dispersed to various places and it had been arranged that I would go to a convalescent home.

The home was a large house on the outskirts of Sydney. As I went by train on the North Shore Line over the Harbour Bridge I felt a surge of excitement as if I was really going into the outback after having been in the town for so long. Even the stations changed from such prosaic names as St Leonards to Killara, Turramurra, Warrawee and finally Wahroonga my destination. It seemed like the real Australia.

Wahroonga was a well to do suburb with large houses set in big gardens, so spaced out that you were not aware of another dwelling within miles. The convalescent home stood in about two acres of garden where there were lawns, shrubs and trees with walks now slightly overgrown which made the whole seem more intriguing. Apricot trees stood outside the house—the ripe apricots full of maggots as I discovered later.

The temporary inhabitants were all Australian and it was a delight to be with them in the relaxed atmosphere so different from any British establishment. Like the British, many of them were volunteers or conscripts and they came from all walks of life. Unlike the British, the better educated or better off did not feel they necessarily had to be officers nor did they feel or act in any way superior to those not so fortunate. Amongst the small sample of Australian soldiery at Wahroonga, I learnt that there was a film director from Sydney, a graduate from Melbourne, two stockmen from Western Australia, a sugarcane worker from Queensland and a swagman or 'swaggie' from everywhere.

As a stray from the other side of the world, I was made welcome and as usual, asked about Home, even by the Queenslander who was of Italian extraction; and they told me about themselves and their homes. These men were like their country, open and big, not physically but in outlook. Quite loud when they spoke but also good listeners. They did not mince words and were not afraid to voice their opinions, yet they were not boastful as Americans can be. Most of them were casualties from the operations in New Guinea, where the AIF were engaged in a huge mopping up operation.

They were all reluctant to talk of their own experiences, usually preferring to tell me about somebody else. One such was a Victorian who had been wounded in the stomach and had stitched lines across his front like a railway map. Someone else told me he had been blown up by a mortar bomb. He told me about a small patrol under a new officer that came across some Japs who had just camped and were preparing their evening meal. The officer wanted to attack immediately but the others prevailed on him to wait awhile. When the Japs had finished their cooking the Australians attacked, killed the Japs and ate the hot meals.[1]

Whilst I was enjoying my convalescence in Australia, *Howe* as flagship and the British Pacific fleet—consisting, at that time of three destroyers—paid a visit to New Zealand. The New Zealanders were about as much in the dark about this 'secret' showing the flag as were the Australians on our arrival at Sydney.

Tongue in cheek, the New Zealand Post reported: 'After years of Security prohibition of news of naval happenings in these waters, people will read with astonishment—rather than surprise, in view of many rumours—that H.M.S. *Howe* has been in New Zealand.'

The Post Special Reporter went on to say: 'This naval visitation gave Auckland occasion for demonstration and receptions, and for an outpouring of hospitality about which, it seems, the ship's officers and men will talk for years.' He added that wartime conditions were observed '—to the extent that the public could not go aboard and were officially supposed to look at the *Howe*'s vast bulk with a blind eye and regard her as another of those things you mustn't talk about.'

The New Zealanders' blind eye was something to be experienced according to the euphoric reports I had from Whacker Payne and all my messmates when I finally rejoined the ship.

Being a tiny place in comparison with Australia, news of the hush-hush visit must have travelled fast. Despite the visit being very short, a trip to Rotorua was arranged; a matter of some 250 miles round trip from Auckland. Among the people in on it were the Ministry of Inland Affairs, numerous town councils, the naval authorities and ex-servicemen's associations. Despite a coal shortage, a special train was laid on together with a stop for tea and sandwiches; at which time crates of apples and beer also appeared on the train. All along the line the people of villages, hamlets and farmhouses (all presumably having signed the Official Secrets Act) were waiting to wave as the train went past. At Rotorua just about every motor car in the neighbourhood had been organised to take everyone to the various attractions of the neighbourhood.

Apart from the remarkable sights of the geysers, hot springs, boiling mud and the reception by the Maoris of Whakarewarewar, the biggest impression their hosts made on those that went was the amount of food pressed on everyone at the least provocation. Like the Australians, New Zealanders had heard of the food shortages at home and seemed determined to make up the deficiency in this one visit.

At first I was sorry to have missed the trip but on reflection I was amply compensated by my stay in Sydney. I had spent over two months there and had got to know more people and places than I would have done otherwise.

On Saturday evenings at Wahroonga we sometimes went to another convalescent home for servicewomen nearby for dances and socialising and it was there on my first visit I got talking to a very attractive VAD called Roseanne.

At seventeen and a half, Roseanne was four months older than me, and although she may not have realised it, I was very shy about asking her out. She was after all not the same as the Milton Park girls and since then I had not had a great deal of practice in the art of chatting girls up. Her parents, no doubt anxious for the welfare of their young daughter came hurriedly down from Moree, some 300 miles north of Sydney, to see what she had got herself entangled with. They were a charming couple who took us out for a meal and, deciding that Roseanne would come to no harm they gave me their approval and returned reassured to their home.

Neither of us had a great deal of money but there were a lot of places to see and with Roseanne to go around with, Sydney was much more fun. Together we went to Manley and Bondi, Taronga Park Zoo and Coney Island Fun Fair.

Once in a rash moment I took her to Cahill's for a meal. As we sat down at our table I saw the menu—and the prices; and my heart sank into my boots. Even though I had recently been paid I could probably just about pay for the cheapest of meals—for one!

'I'm not really very hungry, Robin.' With a maturity well in advance of her age Roseanne had guessed the situation.

'No, neither am I!' I replied, my stomach rumbling. 'I tell you what, let's just have some salad.'

So we ate our salad and departed for the pictures where we had an ice cream. Later, not far from the war memorial in Martin Square we found a milk bar where we had a snack and a milk shake more suited to our means. Chastened by the Cahill experience, the Martin Square milk bar became our normal rendezvous when we wanted something to eat.

By the middle of February after a holiday spent either in the companionship of Roseanne, with the Tidmarshes or countless other people who invited me to their homes, I returned to the hospital from my convalescent leave to be pronounced fit.

In the meantime the rest of the British Pacific Fleet had arrived in Sydney from Trincomalee by way of airstrikes against the Japanese held oilfields of Palembang in Sumatra and a fuelling stop at Fremantle. When I rejoined *Howe* she was anchored out in the harbour, our berth at Woolloomooloo having been usurped by *King George V.* The harbour was now crowded with aircraft carriers, cruisers and destroyers as well as a considerable number of tankers, merchant and supply ships that were to be our fleet supply train.

The people of Sydney still welcomed them all but it could be that they might start to wonder when we were actually going to do something for our keep. For us in *Howe* it did feel as if it were time we moved on.

Close Rangers at practice.—2-pounder pom-poms firing (*Auckland Herald*)

CHAPTER 16

Task Force 57

On 28 February 1945 the British Pacific Fleet sailed for Manus in the Admiralty Islands. Our C-in-C, Admiral Fraser was to stay in Sydney so *Howe* was bereft of her flagship status and Vice Admiral Sir Bernard Rawlings, as second in command hoisted his flag in *King George V.*

We had all had a great time in Australia and although we were sorry to say goodbye to all our new friends, albeit temporarily, there was no doubt that morale was particularly high as we left Sydney Harbour, amid the usual Antipodean official secrecy of small boat escorts, crowded headlands and sirens.

Since leaving Devonport, a very long and sweaty year before we had practised and exercised more or less continuously. Quite apart from the bombardments of Padang and Sigli we had fired over 250 14 inch shells, over 4,000 of 5.25, as well as numerous rounds of sub-calibre. With something in excess of 116,000 rounds the Close Range gunners had shot down countless towed targets and so effective had they become that it was rare for a drogue to survive unscathed a single run over the ship. We looked and felt a fighting force about to go into action and there was a feeling that we had a job to do which would be the culmination of all the training and exercise.

As we steamed north into the Pacific we continued with gunnery and communications exercises to perfect our translation to American procedures. Overhead aeroplanes from the carriers practised on us, each other and any other suitable object. Using a new vocabulary they flew missions as Ramrods or Caps whilst Fido (Fighter Direction Officer) vectored the fighters in on Bogies.

Aboard *Howe* we exercised taking on stores and personnel from ship to ship. Apart from the steady helmsmanship needed to keep two ships on a parallel course in close proximity, passing a cable over to the other ship proved a bit of a problem at first.

Manually heaving a line between ships is one way of establishing contact after which the main hawser is hauled across. But two ships at speed of about fifteen knots would not get close enough without some risk of collision. To go slower would mean an even greater risk of collision as well making a prime target for any lurking submarine. So the time-honoured method using rockets was tried, as laid down for life saving in the Seamanship Manual.[1]

Rockets are temperamental things and difficult to aim at the best of times.

With a line tied to the stick their course becomes even more erratic. There was also the difference between firing one from a stable cliff top as depicted in the manual and the deck of a rolling ship.

Our first attempt at this operation was pretty ragged. As the supply ship came up to about half a cable's length off our port beam the Chief Bosuns's Mate and his party stood by in the waist. Already rigged were the sheerlegs, block and tackle and the cables ready to pass over to the other side, whilst on a tripod with a cord fastened to its tail was a large Schermouli rocket.

Assuring himself that the reception party on the supply ship was ready, the Chief Bosun's Mate applied a smouldering bit of rope, which he called a 'portfire', to the fuse and retired a respectful distance. After a short pause, the rocket hissed off with a noise reminiscent of its manufacturer's name, broke free of its line and disappeared over the supply ship somewhere in the direction of the main fleet. The cord had burnt through because it had not been wetted for the first six feet as advocated.

On the second attempt the line got caught up in the launching tripod and the rocket, after darting around in the air like a captive bird on a string dived huffily into the sea. The third took off with the ship on a downward roll and instead of going over the top of the reception party, flew straight at them. Very wisely they scattered and took refuge whilst the rocket tried to bore its way through the superstructure before falling back exhausted into the sea.

Faced with a rapidly diminishing stock of Schermoulis, the Chief Bosun's Mate informed the supply ship via a megaphone that we would use a Costing Gun. This weapon fires a bolt to which the line is attached and is far more accurate at shorter ranges. After persuading the supply ship's captain to come a little nearer and a few words of re-assurance to the reception party, the distance was decreased and with a matter of only 50 yards between a line was shot across, followed by the main cable

Once rigged, the set-up worked quite well, the only problem being to keep the hawser taut between ships. To this end block and tackle were used as a sort of spring, with men hauling in or letting out as necessary. Once or twice the hawser slackened off too rapidly and the load was dipped into the sea. However as time went on the 'spring' became adept at maintaining the right tension. Particularly when it came to transferring the first man who, as it happened was a war correspondent. He came aboard white of face but nevertheless dry despite at one time coming within inches of the water.

In high spirits and anticipation we arrived at Manus in the Admiralties where we anchored and waited while arguments went on at high level about where—and if—we were to be used.

Having worked up to such a pitch our morale began to sag with the uncertainty. Manus, or Seeadler Harbour, is a huge anchorage and had the powers-that-be searched the whole Pacific, they could not have found a worse 'Scapa Flow' to inflict on us. Just about on the equator, it was hot and humid, which meant in the steel ships, pretty well unbearable. *Howe* with her wooden upper deck was hot enough but the armoured flight decks of the carriers were giant heat absorbers on which eggs could be fried if one were so minded. Nor were conditions made any easier by an acute shortage of water. Many of the ships of the supply train had been delayed by dockyard strikes in Sydney and amongst the non-arrivals were our water distillation tankers. The fleet, including the fleet train, was short of some 200,000 gallons of fresh water a day and use of it was severely restricted. In *Howe* we had to rely on our condensing plants for fresh water and they were just not adequate. For toilet and washing purposes salt water soap was issued which was supposed to lather but was not very successful. Salt water showers left one feeling sticky and merely added to the salts sweated out in the heat. It was not surprising that we felt let down for it seemed the same old story of working up to a high state of efficiency only to end up swinging round our anchor doing nothing.

The hard truth was that, despite agreeing to our help, the Americans did not need us as they were managing the Pacific war very well on their own with their huge military and industrial resources geared to all-out war. The battles of the Coral Sea[2] and Midway in 1942 had seen the seemingly inexorable advance of the Japanese halted and the elimination of their main carrier strike force. Between that time and 1944 the Americans had 'island hopped' in fierce and bloody battles against fanatical opposition. Tiny hitherto anonymous dots on the Pacific map became names enshrined in American history. Pulau, Eniwetok, Kwajalein, Tarawa, Iwo Jima.

In the south west Pacific, General Douglas MacArthur who had dramatically vowed 'I shall return!' when evacuating the Philippines in 1942 had duly done so with his usual flair for publicity, by wading ashore on Leyte complete with batteries of press cameras and a Philippino general's hat.

Backing these operations was the industrial power of the United States now geared up to all-out war production. By 1943 modern ships including the new Essex and Independence class carriers, battleships like the *Missouri* and *South Dakota* and numerous cruisers named after American cities were being added to the fleet. When the Japanese sank an American ship, another of the same name soon appeared on the scene, with a couple of new sister ships to boot.

The mobilisation of American shipbuilding was epitomised by the industrialist Henry Kaiser. Employing new techniques and prefabrication he built cargo boats—called Liberty Ships—in a matter of seventeen days from keel to completion. He took an area of swampland in Oregon and built shipyards and slips and a city in which to house the workers. Here he turned out escort aircraft carriers, completing them at first in 214 days, finally knocking that time down to 70 days. Vanport, the city, was to become the second largest in Oregon.

The Americans were justly proud of their achievements since Pearl Harbour and saw no reason to share their glory, a view firmly held by Admiral

Ernest J. King, the man in charge of the US navy and to whom we were offering our services.

Otherwise known as the Bald Eagle he has been described in polite terms as 'an officer of austere rigidity and quarterdeck style'. He was reputed by his navy to shave every morning with a blowtorch and his own daughter later described him as 'the most even tempered man in the Navy—he was always in a rage.'

Admiral King also disliked the British.

He and many other Americans saw British involvement in the Pacific as a purely political move and there were grave doubts on their part as to our ability to maintain and supply ourselves. As to the first, it may well have been partly true. In September 1944 Churchill had told the House of Commons: 'We owe it to Australia and New Zealand to help them remove forever the Japanese menace to their homeland, and as they have helped us on every front in the fight against Germany we will not be behindhand in giving them effective aid.'

I for one was not aware of his words and for our part they did not need to be uttered. No one that I knew ever questioned that the Japs were as much our enemies to be defeated by us as were the Germans.

In Washington there was talk of relegating us to minor roles in the South-West Pacific under General MacArthur where he was running an almost private war of his own. The American navy had adopted the more direct island hopping approach, capturing bases from which to strike direct at the Japanese mainland. Both strategies were likely to involve heavy casualties due to the fanaticism of the Japanese but the navy plan seemed to promise the greater success. This consideration among others had determined that priority was given to the Central Pacific area. And so, even at this late stage Admiral Fraser and the Chiefs of Staff in London were trying to persuade Admiral King that the Central Pacific was where we should be used and not in side shows elsewhere.

The Admiralty Islands were British possessions but having been recently recaptured from the Japs by the Americans, they were now under their control. Incredibly we could not use these British sovereign territories without Washington's permission. We were allowed to anchor in Seeadler Harbour and had access to the US navy's bulk fuel supply but everything else had to come from our own resources.

Such was Admiral King's determination that we should get nothing from him, we were even barred from going ashore where facilities included a 7,000-seat open-air cinema. The only people who managed to get ashore were some enterprising pilots from the *Illustrious* who organised a swimming party on a remote beach, far from prying American eyes. Their enjoyment was marred by an overpowering smell of putrid decay, which on investigation was found to emanate from a deep crevice in the rocks that was filled with Japanese bodies.

Luckily the Commander Pacific Ocean Area Forces, Admiral Chester Nimitz and others such as Admiral 'Bull' Halsey—who liked British wardroom hospitality and Scotch whisky—did not share King's anglophobia and subsequently a great deal of help was given us as long as Washington didn't have to be told and the Bald Eagle didn't find out.

For entertainment we had our cinema which was rigged amidships and, as we ourselves only had a limited supply of films, I believe some of those that we enjoyed were sneaked to us from the many sympathisers ashore.

The well organised and professional American Forces Radio was a source of comfort that we could hardly be denied. Every night as we waited for the air to cool so that we could lay out our bedding on the upper deck, we listened as 'The Voice of the Admiralties—and the Jungle Network' brought us news, music, Jack Benny and Bob Hope shows. For the first time we experienced the patter of disc jockeys as they played records of Bing Crosby, Lucky Mellender, the Andrew Sisters and others, singing songs about partings, longings and not sitting under the apple tree with anyone else. Curiously there was comfort in being reminded of a different life half a world away.

But still we sweated it out, the days passed and morale sank lower. Tempers flared and some insubordination broke out; together with an epidemic of boils and prickly heat.

Then one day, for the sake of morale and at least to give us a breath of fresher air, Admiral Rawlings took us all to sea for exercises. The idea was not exactly greeted with the greatest of enthusiasm as it seemed we were destined to spend all our war just practising for it; but on the other hand anything was better than the sweltering, sticky atmosphere of Manus. Once at sea, we had hardly started fleet manoeuvres and gunnery exercises when the outing was cancelled and we returned forthwith to Manus.

Back in harbour the Fleet Train was getting ready to move out and we hurriedly refuelled and replenished what stores we could before it got up steam and sailed out of harbour.

High morale returned to the ship as if pumped aboard with the oil. There was a hum of anticipation on the quarterdeck, on the bridge and in the messdecks. We had not been told what was happening and despite my efforts to get the buzz from Nippy nothing had been forthcoming apart from immediate notice for steam. But we did not have to wait long.

On the following day (17 March) at noon with the *King George V* leading the way, the Royal Marine band gaily playing on her quarterdeck, the 26 warships of the British Pacific Fleet steamed thankfully out of Manus. As soon as we were out of harbour there came the usual pipe: 'Special Sea Dutymen and Cable Party fall out. Hands secure ship for sea!' followed almost immediately by 'D'ye here there! This is the Captain speaking!'

At that moment I was half way between the bridge, where I had been for leaving harbour, and the messdeck. I raced down the six ladders—hands sliding down siderails, feet barely touching the steps—to the nearest SRE loudspeaker on the main deck. Everyone else had stopped work and listened with rapt attention while Captain McCall told us that the Americans were about to invade Okinawa and we were to work with them under the US 5th Fleet.

He went on to tell us about the reasons for the invasion. Okinawa was the main island of the Ryukyus archipelago to the south west of Japan proper and was important as the final step towards the invasion of the Japanese homelands. In between the Ryukyus and Formosa there was a group of islands called Sakishima Gunto that the Japanese could use as staging posts to bring up replenishments from Formosa. It was to be our task to ensure that the airstrips and other facilities on these islands remained unusable by continuous bombing and when necessary bombardment. He ended by telling us that we were now on our way to join part of the invasion force at Ulithi.

Most of us had never heard of any of these names before except Formosa (now Taiwan). But Sakishima and its three islands of Ishigaki, Myako and Iriomote were to be implanted in the minds of almost everyone in the fleet for the rest of their lives.

Meanwhile as we steamed north to our allotted task, the opening moves in the Okinawa battle were being made. On 18th and 19th aircraft from Task Force 58 had begun hitting airfields on the Japanese home islands and shipping in the Inland Sea to isolate Okinawa from the mainland. In the process the carriers *Enterprise, Wasp, Franklin* and *Yorktown* (the second of that name) were hit by suiciders. The *Franklin* was very badly damaged and nearly eight hundred of her ship's company were killed.

Ulithi, where we arrived on 20 March, was a vast atoll in the Marianas group. By definition an atoll must have the usual ring of coral islands around the perimeter but as I looked around I did not notice any land because my eye was taken by the huge concourse of ships within the lagoon. Our fleet had seemed impressively big when steaming along by ourselves in the open ocean. But now as we occupied a small corner of the harbour we realised how insignificant we really were and the size of the operation we were about to join. Our powerful British fleet was dwarfed by the 385 American warships which included 10 battleships, 18 carriers, 12 cruisers and 136 destroyers that were to take part. There were also 828 assault ships, one of them our Mediterranean friend the headquarters ship *Ancon*. Like Gulliver in Brobdingnag we had arrived in a land of giants.

The following day the atoll all but emptied as the Americans moved out, whilst we fuelled from US tankers. Once again, around the back door and out of sight of Washington, help was given by various American services. At 0630 on 22 March we sailed from Ulithi, changing as we went our meaningless title of Task Force 113 for Task Force 57; that is, Task Force No. 7 of Admiral Raymond Spruance's 5th Fleet. We assumed the rest of the American nomenclature calling our various groups Task Units. TU1 was *King George V* and *Howe*, TU2 were the Carriers *Indomitable, Victorious, Illustrious* and

Indefatigable TU5 were the Cruisers, *Swiftsure, Gambia, Black Prince, Argonaut* and *Euryalis* and TU8 consisted of the destroyers *Grenville, Ulster, Undine, Urania, Undaunted Quickmatch, Quiberon, Queenborough, Quality, Whelp* and *Wager.*

Although by American standards we were only the size of one of their task groups, we could collectively boast a proud war record. Nearly all the ships had been in action before. From the *King George V* which took part in the *Bismarck* hunt, the *Illustrious* at Taranto and elsewhere in the Mediterranean, where the *Victorious* and *Indomitable* also served with distinction. Even our newest carrier *Indefatigable* had cut her teeth on strikes against the *Tirpitz.*

As for personnel, we were a Commonwealth fleet with representatives from all the dominions. New Zealand supplied HMNZS *Gambia* and later *Achilles,* as well as a host of Fleet Air Arm pilots. HMCS Uganda was also to join us. Among the many Australians scattered around the fleet, in *Howe* we had six midshipmen serving on their first ship, whilst down below a group of tough Canadians sweated away among the stokers in the engine room.

We were headed by Admiral Bruce Fraser who sank the *Scharnhorst,* Admiral Vian was captain of *Cossack* in the *Altmark* incident and there was our own Captain who had distinguished himself during the battles off Crete, as well his earlier role at the River Plate. Others were names to be known in the future. Our Gunnery Officer, in fact two of them, were to become First Sea Lords and the destroyer *Whelp's* First Lieutenant was a certain Philip Mountbatten.

But although the fleet consisted of tried and trusted ships and people the Task Force was a new concept as far as the British navy was concerned. With Radar as early warning, fighter protection from the carriers covered the fleet against massed air attack of the kind that sank *Prince of Wales* and *Repulse.* Waiting for those planes that got through were the AA guns of the battleships and cruisers.

For strike power our four carriers had a total of 218 aircraft consisting of Supermarine Seafires—a carrier version of the Spitfire—Fairy Fireflies, Grumman Avenger Torpedo-bombers, Grumman Hellcats and Vought-Chance Corsairs.

CHAPTER 17

'Against a More Outlandish Enemy'

Now we knew where we were going we were more than interested in the sort of war we were going into and the people we were up against.

We had already seen newsreels of the fighting on Iwo Jima, Tarawa and Corregidor; glimpses of shattered palm trees, dead Japs and wrecked landing barges which seemed far removed from our normal concepts of war but we had on board an Australian War Correspondent, recently returned from the landings on the Philippines, who was persuaded to give us a talk in the 'Fares Please!' series.

John Loughlin of the Melbourne Argus gave us a graphic description of his sometimes horrific experiences of the landing on Leyte. His calm Australian voice recounting what he actually saw and what the American Marines were about to face on Okinawa painted, a vivid picture of the reality and bloodiness of the 'Pacific' war, in direct contrast to my notions.

'You men of the Royal Navy,' he said 'many of you with long and distinguished service in other theatres, have come out to join a fight across the wider waters of the Pacific against a more outlandish enemy, and the Australian people, I can assure you have been looking forward with great eagerness to welcome you.'

After a brief resume of the strategic situation in the Pacific and the background to the Philippines campaign, and the build up of the vast concourse of 'Troopships, battleships, cruisers, destroyers, LSTs, LSIs and the rest of that strange brood of craft designed for amphibious warfare' of which his LST was part he continued:

'The twenty four year old skipper once more went over the plans for the landing with us—they will give you some idea of how island assaults are made in the Pacific. They have actually been developed into a drill or routine. After the devastating bombing comes prolonged bombardment by the Navy. The troopships send off their crowded barges, which line up in waves a few hundred yards from shore. Then as the bombardment lifts, in go the assault waves under cover of a storm of rockets from LCIs. Bulldozers, with armoured driving cabins go up from the shore in the face of fire and clear away any obstacles for the tanks and amphibious Buffaloes that churn through the shallow water from LSMs and LSTs to the shore.

'Against this powerful combination of war machines, the Japanese usually have only small arms, automatic weapons, 75s, sometimes tanks; and always their fanatical courage.

'We have learnt in these landings that troops strongly entrenched in bunkers built with coconut logs covered with feet of coral sand can survive the heaviest bombardments and still give us a dangerous fight. We learnt this lesson first in the Gilberts, where US Marines went confidently ashore after a tremendous bombardment that should have obliterated everything. The coconut groves were laid waste, but as the marines waded through the shallows they were swept by a murderous fire and suffered terrible losses. We have learnt most of their tricks—their habit of leaving snipers all over the place, their night counterattacks and infiltrations, their weird howls and cat-calls which aim at our morale, their trick of imitating our commands to make us reveal our positions.

'From the bridge of the LST we watched the most terrific bombardment that had yet been laid down in the Pacific war. The old *Australia,* the *Shropshire* (cruisers) and the two destroyers *Arunta* and *Warramunga* which comprised the squadron of the Royal Australian Navy were not far away from us taking a full share in the pasting of Japanese positions behind the beach and back in the hills. Dive bombers from our carrier escorts were hammering away at some enemy concentrations farther down the coast.

'There were four selected landing places on this part of the east coast of Leyte, and ours was designated in the plans Red Beach. General Macarthur was going ashore at White Beach, a couple of miles to the north of us. At about 10.30 am the bombardment ceased, and we could see the rockets from the LCIs shooting over the assault craft as they sped into the palm-fringed beach. Our line of LSTs was moving in slowly to keep strictly to its schedule. Then we learnt an old lesson once more. In spite of the heavy bombardment, the Japanese opened up with 75s and mortars as the American troops moved into the shore and laid down a screen of shells through which we had to pass. Several of the landing craft were blown out of the water ahead of us. As the LSTs drifted in I saw the two ahead of us take a number of direct hits and the bridge of one went up in flames. Then we took our first hit, and almost simultaneously we ran aground. We remained fast for an hour while the Nip plastered us and we shot back with Bofors. And we thought a lot about a load of ammunition beneath us as we sweated out that hour, as we have sweated out no hour in HMS *Howe!* When finally we pulled off the sandbar, we were driven out into the bay with several other LSTs, and actually didn't get ashore until next morning.

'The troops ashore had had a pretty torrid time from snipers during the night and they were still being hotly engaged some distance in from the beach-head when we got ashore. The three other beach-heads, we learnt, had been taken with little opposition.

'A detailed picture of the land fighting would take too long, but a few incidents illustrate the Japanese style. Choosing to make a stand on the western side of the island, they fought rearguard actions, and left suicide squads to fight to the death in our path. These parties fight from pillboxes, dig themselves in under the roots of trees, or burrow out foxholes; and they die in them. When in danger of capture they almost invariably blow out their stomachs with hand grenades. I saw one American soldier poke his head inside a pillbox that had had to be blasted open by a 105mm gun. A wounded Jap seized him around the neck, dragged him in and blew both of them up with a grenade. At dawn one morning, a company of Japanese came down from the hills, formed up on the road, and marched straight into our machine gun fire, with an officer at the head of them waving his sword and shouting 'Banzai'. There were many examples of such fanatical but stupid bravery.

'Although after three days of the Philippines campaign official communiques were saying that the campaign was all over bar the mopping up, it took two months of hard fighting by four divisions to break the last stand made by the Japanese on the western coast of Leyte Island.'

John Loughlin's talk gave me pause to think about my own ideas of war. As a schoolboy I had played at war with my friends and so far in the real thing, I had taken part on the periphery of great events, whilst others had been in the thick of it. American films, starring Errol Flynn et al, had fed my imagination on dashing exploits in a Hollywood concocted Far East war but now after listening to John Loughlin things did not seem quite so dashing.

In order to get some understanding of the Japanese eagerness to sacrifice their lives so prodigally it is necessary to look back to the feudal system under which they lived in ancient times. In Japan the system carried a code of behaviour which developed into what was known as 'Bushido' or the Way of the Warrior. This emphasised the duties owed by the warriors or Samurai, the most important of which was to fight in battle for their overlords and if necessary, sacrifice their lives without question.

For the warrior death in battle expiates any faults and his spirit immediately returns to the Yakasuni Shrine near the Imperial Palace where the souls of all warriors gather in eternal friendship. The most dreadful breach of this duty was to surrender to the enemy. Such an act was regarded with utter contempt and the individual who did so would be unworthy of consideration as a human being.

These were the traditions with which the Japanese entered the second world war and is why they recklessly threw away their lives rather than attempt to save themselves, particularly when they might fall into enemy hands.

A prime example of this was their defence of Tarawa in the Gilbert Islands, mentioned by John Loughlin, where only seventeen Japanese surrendered out of a garrison of 4,500.

Whilst the American land forces were once again about to face this fanaticism on land, at sea we were to experience another aspect that owed much to Bushido and Japanese history as well as stemming from incidents prior to the American landings on Leyte five months beforehand.

The Japanese had suffered severe losses in the air due chiefly to the superb performance of the Grumman Hellcat fighter and the American's new proximity AA fuse, and they were now relying on pilots with barely enough training to fly their aircraft properly, let alone get to their targets intact and successfully dispose of their bombs and torpedoes. Such was their lack of experience that after flying a mission and in the rare event of their returning, carrier-based pilots were often diverted to airstrips ashore because they were unable to land back on a carrier. This latter problem resolved itself when most of the Jap carriers were sunk and the navy's air force took to the land.

The solution to the problem of unskilled pilots was demonstrated when, on 15 October 1944, Rear-Admiral Masafumi Arima got into an aeroplane and joined the attack on the American Third Fleet. Like so many Japanese pilots before him, his mission ended when he was shot down without coming within miles of a target'[1]. What was different about this flight, apart from the pilot being an admiral, was that he had taken off with the avowed intention of crashing his plane, together with its bomb, on one of the American carriers.

Such an attack was nothing new, Japanese pilots had crashed their planes on targets before, usually when they had been so shot up that they were about to die anyway. The first occurred during the attack on Pearl Harbour on 7th December 1941. Lieutenant Fusata Iida celebrated Japan's first day of the war by deliberately diving with his damaged Zero into an aircraft hangar.

But until October 1944 suicide attacks had been individual affairs and not official policy, although many Japanese commanders favoured the idea as an effective remedy for their air arm's lack of success. It needed only Admiral Arima's remarkable, not to say drastic, act of leadership from the front to move the idea along. He was said to have 'lit the fuse of the ardent wishes of his men' and only two days after his attempt a more practical, if less dashing admiral[2] organised the first Special Attack Group whose volunteer members, on a promise of instant translation to the warrior's heaven, would give their lives by crashing their planes into enemy ships.

These suicide pilots took their name from an incident in Japanese history when, in the summer of 1281, the Mongol Emperor Kublai Khan attacked Japan. Landing on Kyushu with 150,000 men, for fifty-three days a continuous struggle took place as, true to their tradition, the defenders fought with desperate courage to the death, without thought of surrender. The invaders however gradually began to get the upper hand, until one factor that they had not taken into account intervened. During the summer severe storms occur in Japan and on 15th and 16th August a typhoon struck the Mongol fleet, decimating it with terrible loss of life. Many vessels went down and others were wrecked on the coast of Kyushu. Cut off from their supplies, the Mongol warriors on shore were slaughtered by the thousand and the threat to Japan was averted for good. The Japanese regarded the typhoon as the direct intervention of the Gods and for this reason called it the 'Divine Wind'.

As the modern saviours of Japan, the Special Attack Groups adopted this name and, in the untranslated version gave the English language a new word—'Kamikaze'.

CHAPTER 18

The Divine Wind

Having left Ulithi on 22 March, as usual practising gunnery and communications all the way, we rendezvoused at 0630 on 25th with our Fleet Train to top up with fuel. Then before daylight on the following day we arrived 100 miles south of Sakishima and went to action stations.

Standing in the cool pre-dawn, I heard the sound of aero engines warming up from the as yet unseen carriers' flight decks. Then as the first signs of day lightened the eastern sky, the fleet turned into the wind and increased speed. With their engines revving to a crescendo, the aircraft took off one by one and after forming up into their squadrons, flew off on their first sorties against the Ishigaki and Miyako Shimas.

In our adopted American jargon these first flights were designated CAPs and ASPs, in other words Combat Air Patrols consisting of fighters to cover the fleet and operations over the islands and Anti-Submarine Patrols.

Half an hour later, as the rising sun turned the sea from a dark grey to deep blue, a strong fighter force took off. Called Ramrods, they were to carry out aggressive sweeps over enemy territory attacking with rocket and cannon fire aerodromes, shipping, harbours and anything else that presented a suitable target.

As they formed up and disappeared towards the north we stood down from action stations to second degree of readiness. This meant that we could go to 'breakfast and clean' in dribs and drabs whilst the remainder stayed by their stations. Turret hatches were opened and the guns crews came out on deck, whilst by the Pom-poms, Bofors and Oerlikons the close range gunners relaxed. As I went down below, opening and closing watertight doors as I went, the magazine and casemate crews were sitting around reading, all instantly ready to close up again.

'What's happening, Sticks?' one of the marines asked me.

'Nothing much. We've just flown off a lot of fighters who've disappeared. That's when we speeded up just now. Otherwise no excitement.'

I realised that I was lucky in a way to be up topsides in the fresh air where I could see everything going on. The only contact these chaps had was through orders coming to them via the phones or voicepipes.

Having had a wash, shave, a huge 'corned dog' sandwich and a mug of tea I made my way up to the after funnel again. Not long after we once again turned into the wind to land on the Ramrods and change over the CAPs. Then came the turn of the Avengers to be ranged on the flight decks ready for their bombing missions.

Things started on a low key for the fleet and much of the day was spent turning into the wind for the aircraft to land on or take off, whilst occasionally there was an alarm and we closed up as a 'bogey' was reported. At one time there was firing from the ships on the screen but nothing else developed. It seemed that the Japs on Sakishima were not yet awake to our presence. In between alarms food was brought around to everyone at their quarters, generally in the shape of sandwiches and tea. From the funnel we climbed down to the boatdeck to have ours and chat to the Pom-pom's crew just below us.

As sunset approached we closed up at dusk action stations and waited to see if there would be any final reaction from our days activities. It was a time to be extremely careful because CAPs and Ramrods were landing on and it was not unknown for Jap aircraft to follow them in, hopefully undetected. But nothing developed and thankfully we changed to defence stations, with half the armament only manned in watches whilst the other half secured and retired to our night cruising station.

Down below cooks of messes were drawing the evening meal which the galley staff had been preparing. The rum issue had also been delayed until the evening and was now being gratefully downed by those entitled to it.

Later in the evening the captain came over on the SRE, as he did henceforth on most nights, and told us of the day's events. The first Ramrods had swept over Ishigaki and Myako, the two main islands each with three aerodromes and claimed 23 aircraft destroyed on the ground[1]. They had met with little opposition but one Corsair had to ditch in the sea somewhere between the two islands. The pilot had been rescued by a Walrus, the old Pussers Spitfire of which there were two on *Victorious* for air/sea rescue duties.

Two squadrons of Avengers had made strikes in the forenoon and afternoon against the airfields, by which time the Japs had woken up to greet them with heavy AA fire. One Avenger was shot down over Ishigaki and the three crewmen lost. Another Corsair failed to return.

Over the fleet, during the morning a USAAF Liberator had flown into range and was fired on by the screen, which accounted for the firing I had heard. What he was doing in our area nobody ever found out. Earlier on a Japanese plane had been detected and chased away from the fleet.

In the early hours of the next day an aircraft showed up on radar which was shadowing the fleet which meant that the previous day's intruder had almost certainly reported our presence. The cruiser *Euryalus* opened out from the screen and fired at the shadower who then retired to a safer distance to monitor our progress.

Dawn found us once again at action stations in the same flying off position and carrying out virtually the same routine as the previous day. A Ramrod was sent off to Ishigaki and during the morning and afternoon two Avenger Squadrons together with Fireflies and fighter escort were sent off to bomb and strafe the shipping and harbour installations as well as Hirara and Sukama airfields on Miyako.

During the forenoon strike an Avenger was hit by flak over Hirara and splashed into the sea killing the observer and air gunner. The pilot himself bailed out and was spotted in his dinghy by an Avenger from the *Indomitable*. The American submarine *Kingfish* which was on air/sea rescue duties in the area was asked to look out for ditched British crews but, aware of the Bald Eagle's attitude towards the British, replied that she would have to ask her boss first. Admiral Vian, fiercely protective of his pilots, immediately appealed to Admiral Spruance in 5th Fleet with the result that *Kingfish* picked up the pilot after a search with the assistance of a wing of Corsairs from *Illustrious* lasting for three hours. As if to exemplify what allied co-operation is about the destroyer *Undine,* whilst rescuing another Avenger crew, also picked up an American Corsair pilot who had been drifting in his dinghy for forty-eight hours, after being shot down in the Okinawa area. One other Corsair was shot down over Ishigaki during the day.

All day I watched the aircraft taking off and landing on. The carriers' flight decks did not look long enough for such activities, particularly when a flight of some twenty or more aircraft were 'spotted' ready for take-off on the after part of the deck. The Avengers, with their deep bellies full of bombs looked pregnant as they roared along the flight decks, dipping heavily as they staggered over the carriers' bows.

When the aircraft returned from their sorties there was an awful fascination in watching them land. On the flight deck the lone figure of the batman guided each aircraft down, signalling with his outsize table tennis bats. Most landed well but some dropped heavily onto the deck as the pitching ship came up to meet them. The Avengers, Corsairs and Hellcats seemed robust enough to take this sort of treatment although there were one or two that bounced over the first arrester wires to be caught at last by the final one—known by the pilots as the 'Jesus Christ!'. It was heart-stopping enough to watch and what it must hake been like for the pilots I could not guess. The Seafires were not so tough, or lucky. On *Indomitable,* one whose landing gear collapsed, carry straight on through the arrester wires and crash barrier, over the carrier's bows to be overrun by the ship. Another Seafire also crashed on landing killing her pilot[2].

As darkness fell we retired to the replenishment area to meet the fleet train. We could have stayed for another day but it was considered better to replenish so that we could cover the crucial three days around 1 April when the Americans landed on Okinawa.

Retiring to the replenishment areas was not exactly a time of rest for the fleet. Although the Fleet train's carriers took over the CAPs and the ASPs, there was the refuelling of all the ships and ammunition, aviation spirit and other stores to be transferred. There was also the transfer of personnel as required including casualties to the Hospital Ship *Oxfordshire*. In accordance with the Geneva Convention she always lay some miles away from the other ships, painted white, marked with red crosses and fully illuminated at night.

Whilst the fleet train supplied us there was also a shuttle group that supported the train, bringing up supplies and personnel from Manus. Most welcome of all it brought the mail which was distributed around the fleet by a destroyer.

Meanwhile with all the stocking up going on a full training programme was carried out with close range drogue target firing, communications and bombardment exercises. The one difference to us in *Howe* and presumably the rest of the fleet was that we got regular meals during the day instead of snatched sandwiches and drinks.

This was the routine that was to continue all the time we stayed at sea, carrying out operations for about three days at a time before retiring to replenish from the fleet train.

There were at least two air strikes a day by the Avengers, as well as Ramrod sorties by fighters and the routine CAPs, ASPs and radar patrols.

As with any ship or fleet in hostile waters, we stayed at second degree of readiness during daylight hours and routinely went to action stations or, in this case, repel aircraft stations at dawn and dusk, the most likely times for an attack.

We returned to the battle zone at dawn on 31st March, flying off our usual CAPs, Ramrods and Avenger missions over Ishigaki and Miyako.

During the course of these sorties, one Avenger crashed on Ishigaki airfield whilst another was forced to ditch in the sea. For the pilot it was his second experience of being rescued, when together with his crew he was picked up by the *Kingfish* who was by now co-operating with full permission from above.

Around Okinawa, Task Force 58 had been operating for some time in preparation for the assault. The softening up bombardment of Okinawa had started on 25th but not without casualties. On the following day the US destroyers *Gilmer* and *Kimberly* were hit by Kamikazes as was Admiral Spruance's flagship, the cruiser *Indianapolis*. With the Japanese concentrating their efforts on the Americans, we had another quiet day with not even a threat from a bogey and in the evening we withdrew to our night stations.

On 1st April, as we in the British fleet went to our dawn action stations, the Americans started the final bombardment of the Okinawa beaches. At 0830, as the first assault wave landed, the battleship *West Virginia,* three transports and a Landing Ship Tank were hit by suiciders. Meanwhile the Japs woke up to our activities around Sakishima and what might have been a settling down to daily routine was shattered.

At 0650, after we had flown off the morning ramrods, a group of twenty aircraft were detected about seventy-five miles to the west. Forty miles out they split up into smaller groups and were engaged by our fighters. But despite the efforts of FIDO and the fleet CAP, the first enemy got through to us.

We were just standing down from dawn action stations and, as I passed P4 turret with its crew newly emerged in the morning sun, the armoured door flew open and like a cuckoo clock, a head encased in anti-flash hood and earphones appeared.

'Stand to! Stand to!'

The gun crews piled back through the hatch, slamming the door behind them as I turned and raced back up to the old boat deck and the funnel ladder.

Covers were coming off the guns again, ready-use ammunition lockers opened, and ammunition served to the Pom-poms, Bofors and Oerlikons. Some of the after 5.25 directors crews who, like me had been going down below, were also climbing back up into their perches.

The ship settled to action stations again and the various quarters reported 'Closed up and cleared away!'. Guns lifted from their housed positions, turned outwards and up to point at the sky.

I re-donned my anti-flash hood, mask, gloves and steel helmet. I tucked my trousers into my socks and examined my bugle. There was a dent where it had hit the iron ladder on the funnel—in time I was to give up worrying about them there were so many. A boatswains call piped over the SRE, 'D'you hear there!' and the gunnery officer's voice told us that a number of aircraft were approaching the fleet and were being engaged by the fighters.

I felt the usual tense excitement that the expectation of possible action brought on. Just below me the Pom-pom's and Bofors' crews, anonymous figures in their flash gear and steel helmets, were laying and training their guns on imaginary targets. The 5.25s of Blue Group (the two starboard after turrets) were also going through various drills as they waited. The right hand gun of S3 tested firing circuits, the crack of the detonator echoing hollowly in the gun barrel. Looking aft between the mainmast tripod and the 5.25 directors, I caught glimpses of the marines in the Oerlikon baths strapped into their guns. Like a giant the ship was limbering up and flexing individual muscles.

Otherwise, the scene was peaceful with the sounds of the sea and the vibrations of the engines. The newly risen sun lit up what promised to be a fine day as the fleet sailed along over the blue water.

Then came the sound of gunfire to starboard and, as I looked a plane came hurtling from the clouds. All the AA and close range guns from ships within range opened fire, sending converging streamers of coloured tracers towards the plane. Blue Group opened up with a crash, obscuring my view momentarily with yellow-brown cordite smoke. Surrounded by bursting shells, the Jap plane selected *Indefatigable* as his target and dived. Everything seemed to be in slow motion as I watched the plane's descent through a storm of anti-aircraft fire. It was impossible that the plane could not be hit. Yet undeflected it continued its dive. Then with an explosion of orange flame the kamikaze hit the carrier just in front of the island.

A column of black smoke rose into the air and almost immediately I saw the tiny figures of the fire parties running out hoses to dowse the fire.

As my ears were getting over the last battering from the guns, a plane appeared out of the clouds and decided to take on *King George V* and the *Indomitable* with his cannons. After two strafing runs he came to the conclusion that the odds were heavily against him and made off.

Almost at the same time a Kamikaze came out of the clouds, this time just astern of *Howe* where another of the carriers was stationed. Once again the close range weapons and 5.25s opened up, pounding the air with noise and sending streams of tracer and puffs of black cotton wool into the air around the plane.

Unlike his colleague's successful attack on *Indefatigable,* the dive was either badly timed, deflected by gunfire or else the carrier's evasive turn fooled the pilot. Whichever it was the aircraft dived with a resounding splash into the sea somewhere off the carrier's starboard bow.[3]

Further away on the outskirts of the fleet, another Jap plane arrived on the scene chased by a Seafire—a dangerous act by the latter. Finding he was hampered by his bomb, the Jap released it as he went over the destroyer *Ulster.* Although he narrowly missed, a large hole was blown in the ship's side.

All that day we were at action stations on and off as the fleet was threatened by the enemy.

In the evening four aircraft managed to escape the fighters and headed towards us. The Close Range loudhailer below me clicked on.

'Keep a sharp lookout, there is at least one bogey overhead now!'

All eyes turned to search the sky above and we waited tensely in the deceptive serenity of the Pacific evening.

Somewhere overhead where radar could not easily detect him the Jap waited in the fluffy white clouds, biding his time until a favourable target was offered.

The fleet had started a routine turn to port when out came the Jap.

'Alarm Port—' the rest of the call was drowned as all guns opened up at the plane diving straight down on to *Victorious*. The carrier took evasive action and tightened her turn. The trick worked and, despite attempting to correct his dive, the kamikaze glanced off the edge of the carrier's flight deck and blew up in the sea close alongside, scattering aeroplane fragments and water on the flight deck.

That was the last action of the day and the end of our first taste of Pacific warfare. As it grew dark we stood down from our action stations to have some well earned food and for those that were entitled, their rum ration.

Despite the fact that the Commander gave the odd running commentary over the SRE throughout the day, Whacker Payne and I had to give a resume of what had gone on because, being in the turrets and below decks, our messmates had no real idea what had been going on up top.

A miss—a kamikaze explodes off the starboard quarter of HMS *Victorious* (*IWM*)

It must have been harder for them while they worked the guns in the turrets at an unseen enemy, not knowing whether death was coming straight at them or passing by a thousand yards away. All they could hear were the muffled sounds of their own and other guns firing. As they ate their food, I noticed the hands of one or two of the younger Marines shook a little.

I talked about the near miss on the Victorious, which had been the nearest incident to us. I wondered jokingly whether the pilot's soul went straight to heaven, or whether there would be an enquiry at the portals over his ineptitude. One of the marines who had been quiet until then looked up and, stabbing at me with his fork, said, 'I don't give a fuck where he's fucking gone, as long as he don't fucking come back!'

With nerves still jangling, perhaps it was not the time to be flippant.

A few of our more exuberant fighter pilots had a taste of the unexpected when the fleet fired on them. It was nobody's fault really because up in the sky and in the heat of the moment our pilots would chase the enemy planes right over the fleet and straight into the firing line. To the gunners down below an enemy plane would appear closely followed by what appeared to be another. There were many similarities between some Jap planes and our own which made instant recognition impossible and to shoot first had to be the order of the day. One could not wait for aircraft to turn and show their profile or plan view as illustrated in the identification manuals before firing. Sometimes our planes were fired on without the benefit of a Jap ahead of them to take some of the flak. Whilst looking for a friendly flight deck to land on, they had appeared suddenly out of a cloud to the surprise of both the gunners and the pilot. Instant close range identification always remained a problem. Various remedies were suggested and tried including having our aircraft approach the fleet with undercarriage and flaps down in order to help identification. Even this did not always work. *Howe*'s 5.25s opened up on a flight of Corsairs coming in with wheels down, understandably to the annoyance of the pilots, even though we missed them by miles. However, other pilots were not to be so lucky.

The day and the fleet's first encounter with the Japs ended with one destroyer holed and being towed to Leyte by the cruiser *Gambia* and the carriers damaged but repaired.

As far as the latter were concerned there was a considerable difference in damage sustained compared with the American carriers which had wooden flight decks. The hit on *Indefatigable* had started fires and both flight deck barriers had been wrecked as well as the briefing room and sick bay. There was also a three inch dent in the armoured flight deck. Within fifty minutes her planes were landing on; the fires having been extinguished, the dent filled with quick setting cement and jury barriers rigged.

An impressed American liaison officer was heard to remark, 'When a kamikaze hits a US carrier it's six month's repair at Pearl. In a Limey carrier it's a case of "Sweepers man your brooms".'

But the Divine Wind had inflicted its first casualties on the fleet. *Indefatigable* fourteen killed sixteen wounded[4]; *Indomitable,* one killed, six wounded; *Ulster,* two killed, one seriously wounded.

Despite these and more casualties among the Americans the overall operation had gone well. On Okinawa a bridgehead had been established and 50,000 troops were on shore.

In contrast with the previous day, 2nd April was quiet for both the fleet and our air strikes. I spent most of the day sunning myself either on the funnel or on the close range gun deck, talking to the guns' crews as they waited. Reconnaissance and two Ramrods of Hellcats and Corsairs over the islands found only one aircraft on the ground and a 'Zeke' which was shot down over Ishigaki.

A Zeke was a Mitsubishi Type Zero single seater Navy aircraft, known to the Americans as the Zero and the best of the enemy's fighters. Japanese aircraft had strange names and long descriptions like Yokosuka Navy Twin-engined Bomber; veritable mouthfuls to spit out rapidly whilst being attacked. So codenames were used, bombers being given girl's names and fighters, boys. The Yokosuka already mentioned was the Frances whilst Judy was the same manufacturer's single engined Navy Dive Bomber. The names Kawasaki and Mitsubishi and their products were strange to us in 1945, so we called them Tony, Pete, Val, Tess, Sonia, Myrtle and so on.

That evening we retired once again to join the fleet train and refuel whilst a task group from TF58 took over. The weather was too bad for refuelling at the arranged rendezvous so we moved to another where better weather had been forecast. There was still a considerable swell running and refuelling was difficult. By 1930 on 5th, both battleships had only 50 per cent full capacity while the carriers had just enough aviation fuel for two days operations.

Nevertheless we arrived back on station early on 6th to start flying off. The programme began at 0450 with four Hellcats for a pre-dawn reconnaissance of Ishigaki and Miyako. Then followed the CAPs for the fleet and target areas. As usual the Japs had filled in all the craters in the runways and so the Avengers continued with what was becoming a Forth Bridge job. In spite of bad weather they succeeded in bombing all the airstrips and runways as well as Hirara town.

The day was a quiet one for the fleet until the evening when we were once again at dusk action stations. At about 1730 four bogeys were detected and one Judy was shot down by the CAP. A second got through and, diving straight through the clouds overhead aimed at the *Illustrious.* Although in sight and under fire for only about ten seconds, part of one wing and the tail were shot off. As it passed over the carrier it looked as if it might miss but the other wing hit the radar aerial, cartwheeling the plane into the sea close on the starboard side. In the explosion that followed a rubber dinghy was deposited on the main aerials and various pieces of the pilot were blown on board. Part of the skull and the eyeballs were picked up on the flight deck whilst the

Captain's Secretary commanding a Pom-pom crew was sickened to find what looked like a 'piece of bacon' sticking to the gunsight.

Immediately afterwards another plane came out of the same cloud. In company with the rest of the fleet our guns fired and at once came 'Check! Check! Check! Check!' over the loudhailers. But in the noise of the gunfire it was not heard until too late and the plane, a Seafire which had been chasing the Judy, crashed into the sea killing the pilot.

The planes that attacked us were part of the first massed attacks mounted against the US fleet. Called by the Japs *Kikusui* or Floating Chrysanthemum, on this occasion some 660 aircraft were involved including 350 kamikazes. Two destroyers and four supply ships were sunk and twenty-one other ships damaged, including the carrier *Hancock,* which had to retire from the scene.

Although a suicide attack on one of our carriers was nothing like as damaging due to the armoured flight decks it was spectacular—from a distance. I was fortunate to be an observer on a ship that had not so far been attacked. The action was short and violent and lasted a matter of seconds between the time the aircraft appeared out of the clouds above and selected its target, to when it hit the ship. Only very occasionally was there time for the Gunnery Officer to give fire orders over the loudhailer, generally the local directors or even the gun crews themselves would identify the target and open up without waiting. To wait for orders would have meant not a shot being fired.

The plane's attacking run would be accompanied by the ear-pounding noise of the anti-aircraft fire as first the 5.25s opened up and then, as the target closed the range the Bofors and Pom-poms, finally followed by the staccato of the Oerlikons. Hundreds of tracer and shellbursts streaked and blotched the sky, until the finale of the vast explosion as the Kamikaze hit. Then as a period to the piece the loudhailers would switch on, 'Check! Check! Check! Check!' In the sky, the blobs of smoke from the shellbursts marking the late passage of the plane dispersed in the wind whilst from the ship the suicider's pyre burned with licking orange flames and a column of black smoke.

On the evening of the 7th we again withdrew to one of the refuelling rendezvous whilst TF52 covered our patch. Having replenished on 8th and 9th we were rejoined by *Gambia* back from towing the holed *Ulster.* The Canadian cruiser *Uganda* also joined us making the fleet truly Commonwealth.

Our programme was to be more strikes on the 10 and 11 April after which we would go to Leyte for repairs and replenishment. But instead of going back to Sakishima Gunto we headed for Formosa to attack the airfields there.

The reason behind the change was because many of the aircraft used against the Americans were coming from Formosa, despite our efforts on the intervening islands. The South-West Pacific Air Force under General MacArthur was supposed to be responsible for neutralising the Formosan airfields; but with little love lost between Admiral Nimitz and MacArthur, the

A hit! HMS *Formidable*'s fire-fighters clear up the mess *(IWM)*

plight of the central Pacific forces was ignored by the General as he went about his separate war in the south-west.

So we were sent to carry out strikes at the Schinchiku and Matsuyama airfields on Formosa on an operation with a sort of sub-name, ICEBERG-OOLONG.

Arriving early on 11th the weather closed right down with extremely poor visibility so the operation was postponed for twenty-four hours when conditions improved. The strike on Schinchiku was successful despite heavy flak. Matsuyama was obscured by cloud so alternative targets were attacked. One Corsair failed to return from this flight.

The fighter pilots had on the whole a successful day, shooting down four Sonias and damaging a fifth, whilst elsewhere in various engagements two Zekes and a Dinah were shot down.

The enemy were stung into action against the fleet and in the evening came out in force. As dusk settled, we were told that enemy aircraft were searching for us and once again they were engaged by the CAPs. It was a tense time as we waited at action stations whilst out of gunshot range our fighters did their job. One group of three Hellcats shot down four Oscars and a Tony whilst Corsairs shot down a Val and another Oscar. One of the Hellcats was badly damaged and crashed when landing on *Indomitable* killing the pilot. Meanwhile the light faded and the enemy failed to reach the ships.

Dawn found the Japs back again when four aircraft approached the fleet. One dived bombed the *Indomitable* but missed whilst another was shot down by fleet gunfire. Once again tragedy intervened. A flight of four Hellcats had been launched but at the time of the attack on the fleet they were told to stay clear. Three obeyed but the other flew in low across the fleet and was shot down in the darkness.

Another group of bogeys was later detected twenty-five miles north-west of the fleet. The CAP intercepted and shot down two Zekes but if there were any more they must have dispersed because we waited in vain to greet them.

The Avenger strikes flew off at 0645 and hit the same targets as the day before. Runways, installations, petrol dumps, a barracks were all bombed whilst Ramrods dealt with other targets. Fireflies that were flying a CAP for an air/sea rescue plane took time off to destroy a radar station with rocket fire. In the evening we retired from Formosa to the refuelling area without any further interference from the Japs.

On the 14th April in the refuelling area, we were joined by HMS *Formidable* which replaced the *Illustrious*, the latter being the veteran of our force. Apart from needing a refit, her crew and particularly the aviators needed a rest from combat. *Formidable* was a sister ship to *Illustrious* and counted among her battle honours Cape Matapan, the battle of Crete and Operation Torch.

We were still not destined for Leyte after refuelling. During our Oolong activities the Americans had been having a hard time off Okinawa dealing with another Kikusui and in an effort to take some of the pressure off our allies, we returned to Sakishima for three more days of operations with a pause for refuelling. Fortunately we were not subject to any full scale attack as we were at the time short of fighter cover. There was however one interesting episode when radar picked up a number of fast moving bogeys which disappeared before interception. They were another Japanese suicide weapon in the shape of manned flying bombs. With their usual flare for equating their deathwish syndrome with beauty they called them Okha or Flowering Cherry. Launched too far from their target they had run out of fuel and splashed into the sea; hence their sudden disappearance from the radar screens.

On the same day, one of *Formidable's* Avengers was shot down into the sea within yards of Hirara town. The pilot and air gunner were killed but the observer was picked up by a Walrus from *Victorious,* whilst actually under small arms fire from the shore. The old Pussers Spitfire that we used to deride in the early days when we had two of them on *Howe,* proved its worth when it came to air-sea rescue; and doubtless, downed airmen were very pleased to see one bumbling into sight.

Once again we were due to go to Leyte but the Americans were under attack from a third Kikusui. Admiral Rawlings offered the hard pressed Admiral Spruance another day's operation which he gratefully accepted. And so after refuelling on 18th and 19th we were back again.

This time every airfield on the Gunto was given a thorough going over by four strikes of Avengers and rocket firing Fireflies. One Avenger ditched into the sea off Ishigaki and the crew were picked up the next day by an American air/sea rescue plane (which planes were given the extraordinary codename of 'Dumbo')

As it grew dark on this last day, we turned and set course for Leyte.

CHAPTER 19

'Dear John'

The San Pedro anchorage in Leyte Gulf was a large harbour like Manus but not quite so prone to weather from the open sea and the climate was a little better; or perhaps we were by then used to sweat and humidity.

As in Manus, there was an acute shortage of boats in the fleet to service the ships and there was also the usual shortage of water. The latter was not helped by a curious situation involving the distilling ship *Stagpool*. She was a coal burner and had to have her own attendant collier to supply her. In her turn the collier—an ageing Panamanian with the imposing name of *Atlas*—took most of *Stagpool's* output of water for her leaky engines and plant, leaving a minuscule amount for the fleet.

Having been at sea for some time there was a great deal to be done in the way of maintenance. Our floating docks had not arrived but being now in General MacArthur's domain docking facilities were made available and *Indefatigable's* damage was repaired in a matter of six days. One consequence of our having extended our operations was that all the perishable goods waiting for us had gone off, so we were stuck with our tins and dehydrated food.

There was no shore leave, the reason given being the shortage of boats but I would suspect also that those in command did not want any possibility of trouble between us and the Americans troops. However one luxury that did come aboard, as compensation for lack of shore leave, was beer. A ration of one can per man per day was allowed at 1s. 3d. per can. Not a bad price considering they were schooner size cans, about a third more than a pint. It was Australian beer and very warm but even if it had been freezing, it could not have been more welcome.

It was good to be able to sleep on the upper deck again after having been cooped up down below every night whilst at sea. At first, it was quite uncanny not to have the vibrations from the main engines all the time and, without the movement of the ship at sea, it was very peaceful.

The Americans had their local radio station going so we listened to 'The Voice of the Philippines and (inevitably) the Jungle Network'

One evening we had a live show on board sent to us by courtesy of the American equivalent of ENSA. Although it was not one of their topline shows with famous stars who used to entertain their troops, it was nevertheless very well done and certainly more professional than anything I had seen ENSA produce. The humour was American, but we had listened to enough on the radio to enjoy the jokes. The show ended with a group rendering 'You'll Never Know Just How Much I Miss You'. As the most popular song of that time and in that theatre of war, it brought the house down.

Another broadcast we enjoyed was Tokyo Rose on the Japanese radio. Like Lord Haw-Haw the renegade Englishman broadcasting from Germany, her main purpose was psychological propaganda aimed at spreading alarm and despondency. Also like her German counterpart she had no conception of the workings of the British mind and with the same perversity as the people at home in following the nightly broadcasts of Lord Haw-Haw, her words were relayed throughout the ship for our entertainment.

In the first broadcast we heard, she started with her usual opening of ''Allo Boys!' and in her intimate, sexy voice welcomed the British Fleet to the Pacific. In between records, she sorrowfully remarked on the shame of our having come all this way to be slaughtered by the Imperial Japanese forces, whilst at home our lonely wives and sweethearts were living it up with the men who stayed behind. Nightly she told us of heavy American casualties on Okinawa and of American and British ships being sunk or damaged beyond repair. She probably never realised what a following she had.

For most of us Tokyo Rose was good entertainment but having now been away from home for a year or so her remarks about wives and sweethearts had become only too true for a few of us, because at about this time what came to be known as 'Dear John' letters started to arrive. Fortunately rare, for the recipient they nevertheless arrived with all the devastation and subtlety of a kamikaze. One of the saddest things about these letters was that they were nearly always received by the person who had never so much as looked at another female and had written regularly several times a week, pouring out their hearts and writing of the future dreams of being together again.

One unlucky recipient was a Marine on my mess. 'Mike' was an HO and in civil life a draughtsman from Oxford. Despite the fact that he was in a reserved occupation he had volunteered at the age of twenty leaving behind his parental home and the girl he was going to marry. Doreen and he had been 'going out' for some eighteen months and had been looking forward to a future with a secure job for him in the firm he left temporarily. His commitment was such that he sent about ten shillings a week of his pay home to be put in their joint Post Office savings. On the remaining few shillings a week he could hardly have lived it up even if he had wanted to and he was also one of those rare birds with a T for temperance after his name on the ship's books, denoting that he drew threepence a day extra instead of his tot. He was a happy man, his cheerfulness founded on the knowledge of his future happiness when the war finally ended.

His bombshell arrived with the first mail we received at Leyte. Typically starting off ominously with 'Dear Mike,' rather than the hitherto usual opening of Darling or Dearest or My own True Beloved, the letter went on to say that life had been so dull stuck at home 'whilst you are away seeing the world' and that she happened to go to a dance with a girlfriend where they met these two fellows and she danced with one. 'Ever so nice, you'd really like him' The development of the relationship was then outlined with comparisons being made and the blame fixed firmly on Mike for being away '—after all I am only human'. Where before she had signed off 'Ever your true Beloved' or some other phrase of enduring devotion, there was the bare name Doreen, followed by the post scripted instruction not to reply. There was no mention of the joint savings and Mike could only presume they had been dissipated in the pursuit of this 'ever so nice' fellow. The only thing that one could say about Doreen was that at least she herself had written. Often the news was relayed through a relative or friend 'I just thought you ought to know that—'

In time Mike recovered his spirits though others were never the same again. He realised that Doreen had shown her true colours and he was better off without her. But he would probably never forget the shattering effect of the letter coming out of the blue informing him that the one thing he thought rock solid in his uncertain world had disintegrated at a time when he was totally unable to do anything about it.

Eventually, after much comings and goings of boats, ammunition barges, oilers and other craft, we were fuelled, ammunitioned and victualled, ready for another dose of Sakishima Gunto; and on the 1st May we arrived in the Sakishima area to begin what was officially known as operation ICEBERG 2.

In order to ring the changes and give other ships a more direct role in the action, Admiral Rawlings decided that the big ships should be given a go at bombarding the airfields on Miyako. Twice before bombardments had been planned only to be cancelled due to bad weather and in Britain the BBC had anticipated them by giving out the news. Accordingly, on 4th May, in company with *King George V,* and the cruisers *Swiftsure, Black Prince, Euryalus, Gambia* and *Uganda* we broke away from the carriers and made for the islands.

The day was clear and calm when we arrived about eight miles off-shore. Away to port I could see the brown and green of land. There was nothing particularly special about it but, like other times when near to the enemy coast, I thought about the people among whom we were about to hurl tons of high explosives. Sumatra had been an occupied territory when we bombarded targets there and at least some thought was given to the innocent civilians involved. This time it was the same as Trapani. They were all enemies who would do and had done as much to us and ours as we were about to do to them. These people whilst despising any other culture but their own, had adapted Western ways for their own ends. In particular, they had taken readily to Western warfare and weapons but without regard to the codes of conduct that went with them. In order to improve their efficiency they used live Chinese prisoners with their hands tied behind their backs for target and bayonet practice. Even now in 1945 word was coming through how they starved and ill-treated their prisoners of war and watched with indifference as, amidst if-not plenty at least sufficiency, they died of malnutrition and disease.[1] Along with all the rest of the ship's company and doubtless everyone in that theatre of war I looked on the Japanese as little yellow bastards for whom one could feel no pity. I was glad to be there.

As we glided silently into range on this peaceful morning, I felt the usual build up of tension, not only within myself but from all those at action stations around me. Generally big ship bombardments were pretty one-sided affairs with no reaction from the enemy. But there was always the possibility of air attack; and with the main armament closed up a good deal of our close range weapons were unmanned. Out of the corner of my eye I saw a huge battle ensign running up the foremast yard and glancing aft I saw the normal ensign had been replaced by a larger one and a third flying from an after yard. An age old tradition from the days of wooden ships and close action when it was as well to be recognised by one's own side and also to ensure there was always an ensign flying to show that you had not struck your colours.

As a sort of light introduction to the proceedings the cruisers opened up with their 5.25 and 6 inch guns. Then *King George V* erupted in a great belch of flame and smoke, sending a shock wave outwards, visible on the water as an expanding circle and reaching us with a noise that was felt rather than heard. Almost immediately after came the 'Ting-ting' from our directors followed by the vast explosion of our own guns, the effect of which inspired a New Zealand War Correspondent to write 'There's one way and one way only of knowing what they (battleship broadsides) are like and that is to be on board such a ship, when it silently trains its guns on a target, waits for men and instruments that are never seen to choose their moment, and then explodes with such a crashing of thunder, curtain of flame, upheaval of air, great clouds of dirty smoke and reek of cordite, that the very world seems to have come to an end.'

Having witnessed the main armament firing many times I had got used to the sight and sound of this minor end of the world. Nevertheless, as the guns depressed to the loading position, blasting a plume of steam from their muzzles to clear any residual burning cordite, I was still relieved to get the shock of the first broadside over so that in between the rest I could watch for any results on the shore.

As shell after shell poured into the island a pall of smoke and dust arose from the hinterland indicating that we must at least be hitting something. Amidst all the noise, smoke and flames I suddenly realised that I could actually see the shells as they left the gun. It was a very brief glimpse of a rapidly diminishing blob as the shell soared into its trajectory. Another phenomenon that I had never seen before was an enormous smoke ring blown into the still morning air by one of B turret's guns. It started as a thick yellow-brown doughnut that expanded to about forty feet in diameter as it past me, to be obliterated by the next salvo from Y turret aft. Closer inshore

Shelling Sakishima. The ships—*King George V, Howe* and the cruisers
Euryalus and *Black Prince* (*IWM*)

—and the target, AA installations near Hirara Airfield (*IWM*)

were the cruisers and I could see them pounding away with their 5.25 and 6 inch guns. There was no retaliation either from the shore or from the air and after about three quarters of an hour we ceased fire.

It seemed a fairly short bombardment but the reaction from the Japs was not what we had anticipated. Almost as soon as we opened fire we got word that the carriers were being attacked, so we broke off early and hurried back to the fleet[2].

Formidable was in trouble. A kamikaze had hit her and its bomb had pierced a hole in her deck and fracturing a steam pipe in one of her boiler rooms. She had been about to fly off aircraft and the suicider hit a crowded deck, killing eight and wounding forty seven, some very seriously burnt. One Corsair and ten Avengers were wrecked and fires were started in a number of places, including in the hangars below. Due to the damage in the boiler room, her speed was reduced to 18 knots for a time.

A further kamikaze, a Zeke, had hit *Indomitable* and bounced off to explode in the sea alongside the ship. Her radar, a superior American set, was put out of action, which caused some inconvenience to the fleet.

'The pilots right hand, some ornamental combs and other sentimental gewgaws were blown on board, with some documents describing the social life led by special attack pilots before their final flights.'[3]

Another Zeke attempted an attack on *Indomitable* shortly afterwards but had been shot down by gunfire from the carrier and the destroyer *Quality.*

By the time we returned *Formidable* had extinguished her fires and work was going on to rig jury barriers and repair the hole in the flight deck with quick setting cement.

All that day we were continually threatened by approaching bogeys which were shot down. Hellcats from *Indomitable* shot down a Jill, whilst two of *Indefatigable's* Seafires accounted for a Val. Later in an action lasting only six minutes, three seafires shot down three Zekes out of a group of four; and their controlling aircraft, a Judy, was shot down by Corsairs. Once again though tragedy struck when a Hellcat was shot down by *Formidable.*

The planes attacking the fleet that day had been more stray petals from another floating chrysanthemum. This was the fifth Kikusui against the allied fleet and involved 125 suicide planes.

Having watched the carriers being hit a number of times from my vantage point I had long ago got over my fear of the Kamikaze. It was a spectator sport as I went from side to side of the after funnel taking in the (literally) lurid details of each incident to see which one produced the greatest spectacle. I had become thoughtlessly indifferent to the fact that with each display of fire and explosion somebody was being killed or injured or at the very least being frightened out of their lives. My senses had become accustomed to the ferocious sight and sound of war, rather as if I were at the cinema.

So it was on the 9th May that I was standing on my catwalk, waiting events. At sometime around about 6 o'clock a Zeke dived out of the scattered cloud cover and, despite being hit by the fleet's fire, smashed on to *Victorious,* which was on our starboard beam. In what seemed no time at all, another attacked the same carrier in a low dive from astern. With everyone in range firing at it the plane was badly hit and set on fire before it skidded along the flight deck and in a vast tongue of flame bounced over the side. Obviously the Japs had decided to concentrate on one ship, for almost immediately another plane came at *Victorious.*

With the guns roaring away, I watched for the inevitable end of the plane crashing on the carrier's deck; but it did not happen. The Jap must have seen that he was going to miss, so he straightened out of his dive and chose another target, *Howe.* All our guns that would bear opened up with an urgency born of the fact that this one wanted to end his life in our ship. Engulfed in tracer and shellbursts the plane loomed bigger and bigger as it raced towards us. I stood unable to move, with my hands clenched tight on the guardrail. As it got to within 300 yards it was coming straight at the after superstructure and me. While 40mm shells tore holes in the plane's fabric I heard my own voice like somebody else's shouting above the noise of the guns, 'Get the bastard! Get the bastard!'.

Someone must have heard me. A heavier shell burst close to the plane deflecting it so that instead of hitting the superstructure it roared over the quarterdeck at a height of about 30 feet and blew up as it hit the sea on our port quarter. As it flashed over the ship about 100 feet from me and below my eye level I caught a glimpse of brown and green camouflage with the dull red rising sun roundel on the side. In the cockpit the figure of the pilot was hunched forward. He was probably already dead and on his way to the Yakasuni Shrine.

The Japs had not finished with us that night, for another kamikaze attacked *Formidable,* which once again had aircraft on deck. Coming in low from astern the kamikaze hit the flight deck right in the middle of the aircraft. The scene was again one of smoke and flame with the fire parties pushing burning aircraft over the side as fast as they could. This time the damage was more severe because burning petrol got into the hangar below and more aircraft were damaged by fire and water. *Formidable* was left with only very few operational aircraft and more or less became a spare landing field for other carriers' planes. She was however still operational; a far cry from the fate of the American carriers.

As we finally stood down from action stations that day, I was less exuberant than hitherto. When we had been attacked it seemed that the Divine Wind had blown for me personally. In the seconds before the plane had been deflected I realised that it was not a game and I was about to be blown up or burnt to death. I was much luckier than some.

As I gave my usual commentary on the day's happenings to the mess, I recalled the near miss and the way it seemed to come straight at me. I remembered too how it had been deflected by a lucky shot and the marine Oerlikon gunners on the quarterdeck still firing at the plane as it passed above them.

I also noticed that, as we talked and ate our food, my hands were shaking this time. I had grown up a lot in the last few hours.

Ironically at the same time in London people were drinking, dancing and singing in the streets to celebrate the end of the European war; a conflict on the other side of the world that had become as remote to us as ours was to many in Britain. For some time now the emphasis in the news had been the imminent defeat of the Germans and, freed from buzz-bombs, V2s and blackouts, the people at home had begun to feel that things were returning to peacetime normality. The Far East had taken on the aspect of those faraway trouble spots where, in Imperial days we sent troops and gunboats. The 14th Army fighting in Burma became known in the press as the Forgotten Army, whilst we in the British Pacific Fleet were seldom mentioned at all.

Meanwhile the Japanese showed every sign of fighting on to the very last man, woman and child. On Okinawa their defence tactics had put the US programme way behind schedule, their stubbornness bolstered by orders to every soldier to 'kill at least one American devil'. The Kikusuis continued over the American fleet which suffered a good deal of damage. Admiral Marc Mitscher's fast carrier task force had been reorganised from four to three task groups due to losses. Mitscher himself had had to transfer his flag twice as, like a cavalry commander charging the enemy, his ships were shot from under him.

In our area we continued with the routine of strikes and replenishment during May. Daily our Avengers flew off on their sorties over Ishigaki and Miyako, whilst nightly the Japanese filled the holes in on the runways. Despite the lack of any other activity on the airstrips, the AA gunners were still deadly and still claimed their victims.

Other factors as well as kamikazes were also beginning to take their toll. We were all getting stale and accidents in the fleet were becoming common. *Victorious* was temporarily put out of action, something the Japs had failed to do, when a Corsair crashed on landing. The aircraft tore away two arrester wires and both crash barriers, killing two, wounding four others and damaging two other Corsairs and an Avenger before going over the side in flames. Repairs were made but a further crash smashed the jury barriers.

A Corsair in *Formidable's* hangar accidentally fired a burst from its cannons into an Avenger which started a serious fire. The incident destroyed seven Avengers and twenty-three Corsairs. Together with the aircraft destroyed operationally and by kamikazes, this incident left her with virtually no operational aircraft.

Shortly afterwards the destroyer *Quilliam* collided with *Indomitable* causing no damage to the carrier but crushing the destroyers bows. *Quilliam* was towed away stern first to Manus.

But on the other hand we seemed to be having some effect on the airstrips on the islands. The Japanese appeared not to be using them and the bomb craters were not being filled in so assiduously.

Our job was coming to an end and after two more days operations in which *Formidable* was used as a spare flight deck, she left us for Sydney escorted by two destroyers which were due for refit. She did not miss much because on 25 May, after only two further days of operations during which time there was no enemy air activity, we turned away from Sakishima Gunto for the last time.

The British Pacific Fleet had done well not only with the job in hand but also in the eyes of the Americans. With a new respect for our capabilities came a congratulatory message from Admiral Spruance and a firm invitation to Operation OLYMPIC, the intended assault on Japan itself.

Fighting on Okinawa was not to end until 21 June when in a cave on Hill 89 the Japanese commander, Lieutenant General Mitsuru Ushijima and his Chief of Staff committed sepporo.

On the American side the 10th Army casualties were 7,304 killed or missing and 31,081 wounded. Their navy had 4,907 killed and missing with 4,824 wounded. They had also lost 36 ships with 368 damaged as well as 538 planes. Against this the Japs had lost the entire 32nd Army; mostly killed but for the first time in the Central Pacific, prisoners had been taken. Their air force had been decimated having lost 7,830 aircraft.

On our part operation ICEBERG had cost us 85 killed or missing and 83 wounded. We had lost 98 aircraft in total and two destroyers had been put out of action, one by the enemy and the other by collision. On the other hand our aircraft carriers were still operative, despite each one having taken punishment that would have meant a return to base for dockyard repairs had they been American.

We had been at sea for sixty-two days with an eight day break in Leyte; longer than any British fleet since Nelson's days. Our victuals were arguably better than that of Nelson's sailors, with dehydrated and tinned food compared to their rotten salt pork and biscuit, although we still shared the scourge of weevils in our bread. Now we all looked forward to proper meat, fresh vegetables and a return to civilised society.

The ships themselves were in need of repairs and refit—*Howe*'s bump with the old French battleship in Algiers was playing up and we needed some alterations to our close range weaponry to make it more effective.

Another problem to be dealt with was a rapidly increasing number of unwanted passengers, for we were infested with cockroaches and rats. So bad had it become that the cockroach smell I first came across on the hospital ship was apparent in the food. Rats were often to be seen and for some time now a huge specimen had run along a girder above my hammock each night just after Pipe Down.

At first he would pause before passing above the length of my reclining figure and look down uncertainly as I lay there. Then one night I waited for him, a piece of wood in my hand to put an end to his nightly excursions. But he stopped and stared at me from about eighteen inches above my head as if suspecting my intentions. My courage failed me as we eyeballed each other and I realised that in the restricted space I could not get a decent swipe to kill him outright. I certainly did not want an enraged rat falling into my hammock nor would my sleeping neighbours appreciate the visit if he happened to drop into theirs. So he went on his way having outstared me. Thenceforth, confident in his moral victory, he did not even spare a glance as he went about his business each night. Despite our uneasy relationship I would be glad to see him gone.

With this state of affairs we refuelled at Manus where we left the bulk of the fleet and went on our way to Sydney for a few days, where once again we were made welcome. Our stay was short however and we said goodbye to our friends—unbeknown to anyone, for the last time.

CHAPTER 20

South African Holiday

Our destination was South Africa and we set course along the Roaring Forties where the wind blows unhindered around the ocean above the Antarctic, building up the largest waves in the world. We were fortunate because there were no great gales and the sea was calm. The swell was nevertheless still high but being very long it was more like travelling over rolling downland.

One of our number was even more fortunate. As we were bowling along at our usual economical steaming speed of seventeen knots a shout came up from the quarterdeck 'Man Overboard!'.

Almost at the same time that he went over some quick-witted shipmate threw a lifebuoy to him. Even so he must have had nearly a hundred yards to swim in order to reach it. The news took only a very short time to reach the compass platform but the ship had travelled quite half a mile and, as she began a turn to starboard all eyes searched the water for what was becoming a rapidly diminishing scrap of white and red on the blue sea.

'Lifebuoy bearing green nine eight, angle of sight zero!' One of the aircraft lookouts, abandoning his fruitless search of the sky for non-existent enemies had picked him up. The Killick (Leading Seaman) in charge read off the bearings as the ship swung round. 'Bearing eight five degrees—bearing eight zero degrees—bearing seven five degrees—'

'Right,I have him!'

The Midshipman of the Watch had followed the bearings with the binoculars on the Sperry Gyroscope stand which kept the glasses steady against the roll. Automatically following the binoculars' direction was the forward 44 inch searchlight which gave a crack and sizzle as the brilliant carbon arc sent a beam over the water. No great help to the rescuers but to the tiny dot now over a mile away in the vast expanse of the Southern Indian Ocean a ray of hope that said we were coming to get him.

Howe completed her turn leaving a semi-circle of white wake as she sped towards the figure in the water. With a great show of seamanship Captain McCall brought the ship around beam on to windward of the sailor. A whaler's crew stood by but the chop was too high to launch a boat. Gradually the battleship's bulk drifted down on the wind until the lifebuoy and its occupant were right alongside the starboard crane. With a scrambling net on the hook and a man clinging to it the crane lowered away until both rescuer and rescued made contact. Then, as the net swung inboard the ship gathered speed and settled back on her course. The aircraft lookout resumed his scanning of the heavens where the only thing that flew was a solitary albatross.

The rescued man was lucky. Normally in wartime a battleship with over 1,600 men on board would not stop to pick up one man, thereby presenting a sitting target for any lurking U-boat. But at that time we were out of hostile waters.

As usual we were given a talk on our destination. It was a preparation for another culture shock as the South African situation needed some explanation to those of us who had not been there before. We were told that unlike any other country we had so far visited wide gulfs existed between the various ethnic populations varying from differences of opinion between the white settlers to laws forbidding contact between white and other races.

Most of the Afrikaners or Dutch settlers had still not forgiven us for the Boer wars forty-five years beforehand and were sufficiently anti-British to be pro-Nazi. It had actually been touch and go as to whether South Africa would join the rest of the Empire in the war. That they had was due paradoxically to the influence of a one-time Boer enemy turned world statesman, the then South African Prime Minister Field Marshal Jan Christiaan Smuts.

As far as white and coloured people were concerned, the word apartheid was not extant, or perhaps had not gained its notoriety. Nevertheless there was a definite legal partition albeit socially and not distinctly geographic between the whites on the one hand and the Cape Coloureds (those of mixed blood), the 'Kaffirs' or Africans and the Indian element on the other. We were warned, not only by the speaker but by the old hands on board, that the police were ever vigilant for any fraternisation between British service personnel and the coloured peoples. The talk was not given in the sense of approval or disapproval of the colour bar but to keep us out of trouble with the authorities. It was emphasised that the purpose of our visit was to refit the ship and get back into the war without leaving half the ship's company behind in South African jails.

On the face of it South Africa did not sound all that great as a place to visit. Generally speaking the only intercourse, social or otherwise, we had in most countries was to be found in shops, bars and bag-shanties run by the indigenous population where one was at least greeted civilly—as long as you had money. With the remarkable exceptions of Australia and New Zealand, most ex-patriate Britons regarded the ordinary serviceman as a somewhat distasteful prophylactic against the enemy—like quinine or condoms. Being forbidden contact with the coloured peoples, ostensibly left the lower deck precious little contact with any of the human race.

There were no great crowds to watch us as we docked in Durban but as I stood on the bridge a clear and beautiful soprano voice came floating up to us. I looked over the side and there amid the bustle of dockers making fast our moorings stood a woman with a megaphone singing arias from various operas. Wearing a white dress and a wide hat which she held in the breeze with her free hand she looked to have come straight from an English garden party.

'Who is that?'

'She's an opera singer and she has sung to every troopship or Navy ship that has come into Durban since the start of the war.'

The old hands all knew her and, although most had no understanding or liking for opera, had a great affection and respect for this lady who gave the one thing she could as her contribution to the war effort. Like the dolphin who led the ships in at Aden she had become an integral part of arriving in Durban harbour.

Almost as soon as we docked work on the refit started. Much of the manual work was carried out by Africans recruited from the surrounding rural areas, very few of whom spoke English or had ever seen a town before. In this instance the colour bar made sense and was as much for their protection as for whatever racial considerations then in force. They were as far removed from anything I had yet come across and I could understand that great difficulties would arise if we were to treat them in the same way as we treated our own dockyard maties in say, Plymouth. As far as I could see they were well treated. They were not slaves and worked in their own manner and probably in the only way they knew.

They operated in gangs under the overall charge of a white and a black ganger but the most important member of the group was the man who started and led the chanting that accompanied the effort. Whatever was to be done, whether lifting or heaving or humping sacks aboard a ship, would not start until the leader began. The men would be placed in position and wait. Then the leader would sing a phrase, all would chorus a response and the work would begin; heaving or lifting or whatever in unison accompanied by chant and response until a halt was called. The Africans had an innate ability to make any task into something of rhythm and harmony. They also worked very well and did not have the habit of starting card schools somewhere in the bowels of the ship.

This first contact with indigenous Africans set the standard of my attitude towards the rest but it was with as much curiosity about this situation as anything that I went ashore for the first time. All around there were signs saying Blankes (Whites) and Nie Blank Nie (No Whites) not only outside toilets but also on gates, doors, seats and buses. It seemed that separate entrances had to be built on every building for the two colours. Either that or separate buildings for the same purpose. There was another notice in particular areas that proclaimed Nie Root Nie which puzzled me at first, rooting being one of the many euphemisms for sex, until I found out that it meant No Smoking in Afrikaans.

I was wrong about the attitude of the British South Africans. Not only were they very friendly but they organised outings for groups and people from far and wide offered accommodation for holidays. We had hardly got alongside when we were told that we were to have leave and we had to choose where we wanted to go. There was a wide choice from all over Natal and many opted to stay in such places as Johannesburg. 'Jo'burg' was expensive so I chose the country and while the ship was sealed up and fumigated—and my midnight visitor the rat met his end—I stayed on a farm in Winterton, Natal.

Owned by Mr and Mrs Guested, the farm was large compared to those in England. It was a very pleasant change to get away from the overcrowded ship to the open air of the country. Our day would start early, having breakfast of mealie porridge, eggs and bacon in the kitchen after which I would wander off by myself and not see a soul for the rest of the day. The scenery was beautiful with the Drakensberg range making a backcloth to my wanderings. Very often I took a gun with me as there were plenty of pigeon or duck down by the river. There were also guinea fowl and I would spend a whole morning stalking them. They seldom flew off and mostly escaped by running unseen through the long grass so that it was difficult to get a shot at them.

When I was not going off on my own I watched the work on the farm; sometimes helping, like driving the cattle through the dip; big draught oxen as well as Friesian dairy animals. Manual labour was carried out by the 'kaffirs' who had their dwellings on the farm. I found it a relief to be away from the city restrictions of not having contact with them. Even though we had no common language we got on quite well with signs and occasional laughter, like the time when I was butted to one side by the leading cow as they came in to be milked. Mr Guested's right-hand man on the farm was called M'taga and was a mechanical genius with the tractors and did all the repairs. Nevertheless most of the blacks seemed fairly subdued, living as they did in constant fear of the local police who were nearly all Afrikaners. One of the small boys on the farm had been beaten by the police for some very trivial offence that all small boys of any colour commit. When Mr Guested lifted his leather loin cloth his bottom revealed some of the nastiest weals I have ever seen. I gave the boy a cigarette which I hoped would be some comfort. In the charming way of his people he accepted it in both cupped hands as if it were the rarest gift imaginable[2].

All too soon my leave ended and we were back together in the ship. There we found that the rats were gone but certainly not forgotten. Whilst many bodies had been collected up and removed, a lot of them had died quite inaccessibly in the fanshafts. For some time after in the messdecks we would be blasted with the smell of decaying corpses from the ventilators. Until the bodies mummified in the dry air, the alternative was to close the fans and keep all the deadlights and scuppers open in which case the messdecks soon became very stuffy.

While we were having our break in South Africa events in the Far East were progressing. The 5th Fleet had been released from Okinawa and under Vice-Admiral 'Bull' Halsey had undergone its periodic change to 3rd Fleet

On 16 July a depleted BPF, now Task Force 37, had joined with the Americans to keep up the pressure on the Japs. It had been decided that Japan could not be defeated quickly enough by blockade alone and landings were to be carried out starting with southern Kyushu on 1 November (operation OLYMPIC). The preliminary softening up had already started for the invasion of the Japanese home islands[3].

Then on 7 August came the news that a huge bomb had been dropped on a Japanese town called Hiroshima. At first it seemed of no great significance as far as the war was concerned. Our enemies had devastated enough cities in their time and we were now more proficient at it. Four days later another bomb was dropped on Nagasaki. This second bomb put the thought in our minds that the war might not last much longer although having had knowledge and experience of the Japanese preference for death rather than surrender we still had our doubts. Then three days later came the news that Japan had surrendered. It was evening and I had gone ashore with some of the marines from our messdeck to an amusement park where I had already spent most of my money.

Deciding that I would go back to the ship I put my last two tikkis (sixpences) in the nearest fruit machine.

Someone went running past us shouting away. He was so incoherent I could not understand a word he said.

I pulled the handle on the machine

'What's the matter with him?' I asked

But then everyone had started shouting and cheering.

'Didn't you hear? The war's over! Japan has surrendered!'

'Bloody Hell!' I yelled, startled as much by the news as by a cascade of tikkis falling all over the ground from the machine.

We did not get back to the ship until very late. With my jackpot we retired to the city centre and the bars. The streets were all crowded with singing and dancing people and sometime in the night I remember kissing a very pretty Cape Coloured girl under the unusually benign eye of an Afrikaner policeman.

CHAPTER 21

Last Post

Shortly after VJ-Day we were sent to Singapore to show the flag as the first battleship to do so since *Prince of Wales* and *Repulse* set out on their last sortie in 1941.

A very welcome visitor was Lord Louis Mountbatten who cleared lower deck and told us in his usual style that we could go back to Guzz with the knowledge that '—the Japs had been defeated not by a couple of bombs but by the guts and determination of you and all the allied fighting services engaged in the Far East'.

That was good to hear from an admiral for whom the lower deck had the greatest respect.

We did not go home immediately but stayed in the Indian Ocean for some time still nominally part of the British Pacific Fleet but with our place in the Pacific with *King George V* taken by *Duke of York*. It was not a very popular addition as far as the rest of the fleet was concerned because she arrived as the C in C's flagship and partook in all the glory of lying in Tokyo Bay as victor over the Japs without having fired a shot at them.[1]

After the immediate euphoria of VJ Day a state of uncertainty existed throughout the ship. The HOs, who made up the majority of the ship's company were now eager to quit themselves of their temporary war assignment and get back to their civilian life.

Demobilisation had already started after the end of the war in Europe with priority given to age, family commitments and length of service. Eager eyes scanned the notice boards and the question of the day became 'What's your Demob Number?'. The professional establishment also wanted to get back to their pre-war routine. Two days after VJ day the muzzles of the 14 inch guns almost magically appeared stripped of paint and with the steel burnished. As some wag put it they were now 'our Main Ornament'. Along with most other continuous service marines I was sorry to think of the HOs leaving us after our shared experiences.

Initially regulars had been instilled with the idea that they were somehow superior to these temporary soldiers, but we had found that there was no difference at all between us as far as soldiering, seamanship or comradeship were concerned. They had also brought a breath of fresh air on to the messdecks with their questioning of all manner of long standing and sometimes useless tradition. The regulars, without admitting they were wrong, had begun to look at themselves and re-examine some of their sacred cows. Now even some of the longer serving men regarded the transformed gun muzzles with misgiving as a portent of their future employment. The services were never to be quite the same again.

Admiral Mountbatten was wrong about going home to Guzz (Plymouth); we actually arrived in Pompey (Portsmouth our home port) early in January 1946, a long paying off pennant flying from the foremast, each foot representing a month of commission.

Christmas which we had spent in Aden was virtually a non-event with tinned turkey and, in view of our homecoming, a very half-hearted attempt at celebration.

But the most significant event for me occurred just before we left Trincomalee for the last time.

I was once again marched in front of the OCRM.

'Boy Bugler Rowe!' From the familiar doorway of the tiny RM office Sergeant Major Elsey shouted at me 'Quick March! Halt! Salute!

He turned to Major Ross 'PO/X 5136 Boy Bugler Rowe, requests to be rated Bugler, Sir!'

My service certificate lay on the desk and Major Ross carefully checked my date of birth, 11th November 1927. He then looked at the date on the wall calender, 11th November 1945.

'Well, er, congratulations on your eighteenth birthday, Rowe', he said, for once actually addressing me. 'Request granted!'

'Request granted!' the CSM shouted 'Well done, Drummer! Salute! About Turn! Quick March!'

On the mess at midday I was given 'sippers all round' to celebrate, although I would still be under age to draw rum until I was twenty-one. My pay was doubled and my service would from now on count towards my time.

After over four years service and over three on active service at sea, it had been officially acknowledged that I was now a man, no longer entitled to be called:

'Sticky-Blue'

Appendix

Chapter 2   1   I met one of the boys after a gap of fifty years recently and he said that the boys had been told they were being joined by a very young boy from an unhappy background—presumably because my brother had just been killed. This is the reason they all looked after me so well and for which I am eternally grateful.

Chapter 4   1   Having survived the sinking of the *Prince of Wales* the fifteen year old Boy Bugler then took part in the abortive defence of Singapore with his fellow survivors.

Chapter 5   1   3,000 tons over the maximum of 35,000 allowed by the Washington Agreement was nothing compared with the Japanese 18 inch gunned *Yamato* class ships of 64,000 tons standard displacement.

                        2   The 'Golden Rivet' was an apocryphal rivet invented by sailors and said to be the last one put in a ship, usually in the darkest recesses. On Navy Days around the world there have been not a few nubile girls whose tours of HM ships included being taken below for an introduction to the Golden Rivet.

                        3   Lieutenant Willasey-Wilsey became Major-General C.P. Willasey-Wilsey CB MBE MC, while Major Ross's son, Lieutenant-General R.J. Ross CB OBE is the Commandant General Royal Marines.

                        4   The Articles of War were the naval disciplinary code. Starting with the pre-amble 'It is the Navy whereon under the Good Providence of God that the Wealth, Strength and Safety of the Empire do chiefly depend.' It went on in minute detail about all the offences one could possibly commit and the appropriate punishments.

Chapter 6   1   As I stood on the bridge watching the proceedings all these terms were as much gobbledegook to me as they must have been to a lot of others; but I had the great advantage of having Wally alongside me to explain in landlubbers terms what was going on.

                            In words of one syllable he patiently told me that the anchor was tied (catted) to one side of the hole from which it normally protruded (the hawsepipe). The anchor chain (called a cable) was then released from the anchor and used to secure the ship to the buoy. The cutter was manned by oarsmen who in navy terms never rowed boats they pulled them.

                        2   There have been many accounts written of the *Royal Oak* sinking some of them flatly contradictory and others even denying that she was sunk by enemy action. Be that as it may, she remains to this day in her resting place marked by a Wreck Buoy and designated an Official War Grave

3 The Scranbag was a place where personal articles found sculling around the ship were impounded. The owner could reclaim the article on payment of one square inch of pusser's soap. Any person or thing regarded as untidy was 'done up like a scranbag' or 'a proper scranbag'

Chapter 7   1 The loch used for the Chariot exercise was Loch a' Chaim Bhain (Loch Cairnbawn) National Grid reference NC1934 or 58 deg.10′N, 5 deg 10′W.

Chapter 8   1 Being offered sippers was not to be taken lightly as the tot issue was one of the highlights of an otherwise boring and often frustrating existence on board a ship. In payment for a favour, a person could be invited round for sippers, gulpers or even a whole tot according to the gratitude deemed suitable. Anyone having a birthday was likely to get 'sippers all round' from his messmates.

Chapter 9   1 The 14 inch gun was of course not an anti-aircraft gun but as the trajectory reached a considerable height when at maximum range it was quite feasible to use it against aircraft at a greater range than they would expect to encounter AA fire. A shell weighing three quarters of a ton would be far more effective than say a shell of one hundredweight.

In the Mediterranean the battleship Nelson fired her sixteen inch guns at formations of torpedo bombers coming in low. By firing into the water there was not only the effect of the shells themselves but also the vast columns of water thrown up by the explosion. In the latter stages of the war the giant Japanese battleship *Yamato* in her last suicidal mission against the forces around Okinawa also fired 'splash barrages' at US aircraft with her eighteen inch armament.

Chapter 10   1 Lime juice was originally issued on board ships for the prevention of scurvy by reason of its vitamin C content. Because of this, American seamen called our sailors 'Limeys' which ever since has been their name for the British as a whole. Although meant derogatorily, it is without doubt a better nickname with which to be stuck than 'Bloodybacks' as they dubbed our soldiers from the British army custom of flogging defaulters.

Chapter 14   1 I forget what name he actually called the dolphin; it was the same sort of name as George or perhaps Rodney.

            2 Subsequently we learned from the locals that this fruit was 'very bad', bearing out what I was taught many years later in Malaya that, as a general rule, one should avoid anything red in the jungle as likely to be poisonous.

Chapter 15   1 More than anybody else the Australian soldier had exploded the myth of Japanese superiority in jungle warfare and was then arguably the best jungle fighter in the world. This story was a graphic illustration of the Australian army's new found confidence after the morale-shattering loss of the whole Australian 8th Division in Malaya in 1942.

Chapter 16 1 The correct methods for carrying out 99.9 per cent of the tasks performed in the Royal Navy were laid down in the Manual of Seamanship, Vols 1 and 2. One could look up anything from A 'Accumulators, charging' to Z 'Zone times'.

Replenishment at sea was too new a concept for the manual which was printed in 1934 and so one could only adapt from other operations, in this case the chapter on Life-saving Apparatus. Amongst other things this lays down how to erect a rocket launcher—called Machine, Rocket- as well as descriptions of 'Lines, Rocket' and 'Boxes, Rocket Line'; the last being a box full of pegs around which the line is 'snaked and faked'(sic) alternately. Even the Rocket was specified: the Boxer Life-saving Rocket; a fearsome two staged device of steel with a stick nine feet in length. By the 1940s it had been replaced by the Schermouli.

2 The Battle of the Coral Sea was claimed by the Japanese as a victory but although they had sunk the Fleet carrier *Lexington* and damaged the *Yorktown* against the loss of the light carrier *Shohu* and damage to two of their fleet carriers, the invasion of Port Moresby in New Guinea, for which these ships were supposed to provide cover, was called off. Thus the strategic advantage went to the Americans.

Chapter 17 1 The Japanese version naturally has Admiral Arima ending his life gloriously on the carrier *Franklin*.

2 In preparation for the forthcoming American assault on Leyte, Vice-Admiral Takijiro Onishi, commanding the First Air Fleet, formed the first Special Attack Group on 17 October 1944 based on Luzon and the following day another on Cebu Island.

Chapter 18 1 All but one of these were later thought to be dummies or non-operational aircraft.

2 Seafires were very prone to deck landing accidents. During Iceberg 1 and 2 there were twenty eight Seafires damaged or written off in this way out of a strength of 40. Compare this to the Corsair, which had 15 out of 73 and yet was deemed the most awkward aircraft to land on a carrier with poor visibility over its long nose. The American aircraft were designed as carrier planes and were far more rugged than the ours, although the British pilots at first viewed the Corsair with some trepidation. On seeing it for the first time with its Stuka-like wings and long nose, Lt.(later Lt. Cdr) Norman Hanson RNVR forthwith made out his will. But in time he and his fellows came to regard the 'Bent-winged Bastard' with some affection.

3 No other account or report mentions this Kamikaze, possibly because the other attacks were more effective. Memory can play tricks but this is a vivid recollection. I was struck by the contrast between the determined and spectacular attack on the *Indefatigable* and this quite useless dive into the sea.

4 One of *Indefatigable's* wounded was Ron Powell who has the dubious distinction of being the last Boy/Bugler casualty of the war and probably the last ever.

Chapter 19 1 Whilst some of the brutality committed by the Japanese was beginning to come to light in 1945, the full horror was not known until after the war. For an account of Japanese atrocities see *The Knights of Bushido* by Lord Russell of Liverpool (Cassell 1958).

2 Admiral Rawlings was criticised for his decision to bombard, thereby denuding the fleet of AA cover; but in view of what had happened in the past and the events of that day I feel that the criticism of Admiral Rawlings is unjust.

Whilst the battleships and cruisers were away, four groups of enemy aircraft were detected making a total of twenty six planes. These aircraft were part of the fifth Kikusui to be launched against allied shipping and not a rapid deployment to take advantage of TF57's lack of AA firepower.

Only three suiciders got through to the carriers, no more than had done so before. That more damage was inflicted on the carriers, particularly *Formidable,* during this attack than in any other could only be pure luck for the Japanese. There had been just as many hits at other times without causing so much damage.

As to the bombardment itself, it is significant that *Howe's* fourteen inch shells silenced the anti-aircraft guns on Miyako, something that had not been achieved by bombing. Had *King George V* been allowed more time to range properly the effect would have bean even greater. This leads to further conjecture that, if the big guns had been used against the Japanese AA positions earlier and more regularly in the operation, there may well have been a lot fewer of our aircraft shot down over the islands.

Chapter 20 1 Kaffir was a name used to denote all Africans of Bantu stock in those days. Strictly speaking it applied to us as well, being derived from the Arabic, Kafir meaning Infidel.

2 A habit that would have gone by the board chiefly because it came to be regarded by white and black as a sign of servility, whereas I am sure it was originally a gesture denoting very good manners.

3 One of *King George V's* first targets for bombardment is a now familiar name in Britain, the Hitachi Engineering works. Another target was The Japanese Musical Instrument Company which manufactured aircraft propellers!

Chapter 21 1 *Duke of York* was bombarded with insults and potatoes whenever she came within range of the Sakishima veterans, much to the annoyance of Admiral Fraser whose ship she was when together they sank the *Scharnhorst* in the last ever capital ship action of the Royal Navy.

Bibliography

Dugan, James: *Man Explores the Sea* (Hamish Hamilton 1956)

Gray, Edwyn: *Operation Pacific* (Leo Cooper 1990)

Hoyt, Edward P: *Carrier Wars* (Robert Hale 1990)

O'Neill Richard: *Suicide Squads* (Salamander Books)

Pack, S.W.C: *Operation Husky* (David and Charles 1977)

Roskill, S.W: *The War at Sea 1939-45,* Vols II&III (HMSO 1960/61)

Ruegg & Hague: *Convoys to Russia, 1941-1945* (World Ship Society 1992)

Smith, P: *Task Force 57* (William Kimber)

Stewart, Adrian: *The Battle of Leyte Gulf* (Robert Hale 1979)

Tarrant, V.E: *King George V Class Battleships* (Arms and Armour Press 1991)

Winton, John: *The Forgotten Fleet* (Michael Joseph 1969)

The Manual of Seamanship, (2 Vols) BR68 (HMSO 1932)

HMS *Howe*, 1944-1945: (Privately Printed in South Africa 1945)

The New Zealand Post (1945)

The Sydney Daily Mirror (1945)